TRADE AGREEMENTS FOR DEVELOPING COUNTRIES

TRADE AGREEMENTS FOR DEVELOPING COUNTRIES

GILBERT P. VERBIT

NEW YORK AND LONDON

COLUMBIA UNIVERSITY PRESS

1969

GILBERT P. VERBIT is

Assistant Director, Resources for Development

at the International Legal Center.

TO MY WIFE
MARTHA ANNE

PREFACE

This book is a direct outgrowth of my two years of service as Legal Adviser to the Ministry of External Affairs of the Republic of Tanzania. During that time I was called upon on several occasions to represent the Government of Tanzania in negotiating trade agreements. Like most lawyers, I knew little, if anything, about trade agreements; and so again, like most lawyers, I turned to the library for help. I found one book which proved invaluable— Henry Calvin Hawkins, *Commercial Treaties and Agreements, Principles and Practice* (New York, 1951). Nonetheless, as I grew more familiar with the area and the problems involved I felt the need for more material than was included in Professor Hawkins's slim volume. In particular, much had happened since it was published, and I found a need to cover issues more immediately relevant to the problems of a developing country. I decided therefore that upon my return to America I would attempt to write a book fulfilling this need. This book is the result of that attempt.

My book is designed to be a working tool for those officials in developing countries who have the responsibility of representing their governments in the negotiation of trade agreements and at meetings of the GATT (General Agreement on Tariffs and Trade) and the UNCTAD (United Nations Conference on Trade and Development). And although I am a lawyer, this book is intended to be useful to both lawyers and civil servants representing their ministries of foreign trade, commerce, and finance. My experience has shown that there is a definite communications barrier between these two groups, neither being particularly aware of what the other has to contribute to the solution of trade problems. It should be clear that no lawyer can participate in the negotiation of a trade agreement without a grounding in the economic issues involved. Nor can a civil servant negotiate without knowing what role the law and lawyers should play in such negotiations. This book is an attempt, therefore, to familiarize both civil servant and lawyer with the contributions each may make as negotiator.

I should like to give particular thanks to two people for enabling me to prepare this book. I am indebted first to Professor Carroll Wilson of the Sloan School of Management, Massachusetts Institute of Technology, for providing me with the opportunity to go to Africa and for further enabling me to collect my thoughts about these problems upon my return. The second person to whom I am greatly indebted is Professor Wolfgang Friedmann, Director of International Legal Studies at the Columbia University Law School, for his unswerving encouragement in my efforts to complete this project.

G. P. VERBIT

February, 1969

CONTENTS

I. Trade Agreements in Context

A trade agreement is a codification of the principles under which trade between the parties to the agreement will be conducted. Although it varies greatly in form and content, the basic aim of the agreement is the removal or amelioration of restrictions on trade so as to increase its volume and thereby enhance the economic well-being of the parties. Since the governments of developing countries have accepted the acceleration of economic growth as perhaps their most important function, it is not surprising that they have turned to trade agreements as one possible means of achieving this goal.

Although figures are difficult to obtain, a study by the Economic Commission for Africa gives some indication of the widespread use of trade agreements by developing countries.[1] According to that study Morocco entered into 29 separate trade agreements during the period 1957 to 1963. Senegal entered into 12 trade agreements during the years 1961 and 1962. And for the United Arab Republic, the figure was well over 40 agreements for the ten-year period between 1953 and 1963. These efforts to build a mutually acceptable framework for trade continued so that by 1964 over 60 separate trade agreements were in force between African states. Fifty more were added in 1965, of which seventeen were between African countries.[2] And while the figures have not been as large among the developing countries of Asia, the number

[1] See Economic Commission for Africa, Bilateral Trade and Payments in Africa, U. N. Doc. E/CN 14/STC/24 (1963).

[2] See Economic Commission for Africa, General Review of Activities in Trade and Customs, U. N. Doc. E/CN 14/W.P. 1/3, at 16 (1966).

of trade agreements between those countries is likely to increase under impetus from the Economic Commission for Asia and the Far East.[3]

But numbers do not tell the whole story. For some of the agreements entered into have been so general and vague as to amount to no more than statements of good intentions. Thus, while the number of agreements entered into annually may remain high—31 new agreements in 1966 by the author's count—any one agreement may outweigh in economic significance all the others combined. The purpose of this introductory chapter will be to indicate the kinds of trade agreements developing countries have been and are entering into and to give some indication of which agreements are likely to be of continuing significance. At the outset mention must be made of the most important trade agreement of all—the General Agreement on Tariffs and Trade.[4] Like all trade agreements, the General Agreement on Tariffs and Trade (or the GATT as it is generally known) aims at reducing the barriers to trade among nations. Unlike other trade agreements, however, the GATT was the first to successfully attack the barriers to trade on a general multilateral basis. From an original membership of 23, the General Agreement has grown to include in its roster of Contracting Parties a total of 76, many of whom are developing countries.

By acceding to the General Agreement a majority of developing countries have indicated that they agree to conduct their trade with each other and with the other Contracting Parties according to the provisions of the GATT. Nonetheless, developing countries continue, as the figures cited earlier indicate, to enter into new trade agreements. These trade trade agreements being created outside the framework of the General Agreement are of three kinds: (1) agreements whose existence is specifically provided for in the GATT; (2) agreements with countries which are not mem-

---

[3] See ECONOMIC COMMISSION FOR ASIA AND THE FAR EAST, THE ASIAN DEVELOPMENT BANK AND TRADE LIBERALIZATION, U. N. DOC. E/CN 11/707, at 86, 87 (1965).
[4] 55 U.N.T.S. 188 (1950).

bers of the GATT; and (3) agreements which are made in derogation of the GATT.

REGIONAL TRADING ARRANGEMENTS

The most significant agreements existing outside the GATT are the agreements which create regional trading areas. Article XXIV (5) of the GATT provides, in part, that ". . . the provisions of this Agreement shall not prevent, as between the territories of contracting parties, the formation of a customs union or a free-trade area or the adoption of an interim agreement necessary for the formation of a customs union or of a free-trade area." Customs unions and free-trade areas are partial economic unions and are similar in that they both aim at freeing trade between the parties. They differ in that the former establishes identical restrictions on trade emanating from the territory of third parties, whereas in the latter, the member states retain their different restrictions on external trade.[5] But the similarity is what is important. For in both cases, trade between the parties is subject to a different regime than is trade with the outside world. External trade continues to be conducted under the GATT. But the trade between the parties to a customs union or free-trade area is governed by the provisions of the agreement creating the union or area. Thus trade relations between members of the European Economic Community (EEC) are not governed by the GATT, but by the Treaty of Rome.[6] Similarly, trade between members of the European Free Trade Area (EFTA) is conducted within the framework of the Stockholm Convention[7] and not under the GATT.

Lest the case be overstated, it should be noted that the GATT does have some influence on the new agreements which govern the trade relations between the member states of a customs union or free-trade area. For the GATT requires that the new agree-

[5] In a free-trade area, trade between the parties is freed only on goods *originating in* the territory of one of the parties.

[6] 297 U.N.T.S. 2 (1958).

[7] U.N.T.S. 3 (1960).

ment must eliminate "duties and other restrictive regulations of commerce" on "substantially all the trade" between the parties (in the case of a free-trade area on "substantially all the trade . . . in products originating in" the territories of the parties). The word "substantially" has been the subject of much controversy among the Contracting Parties.[8] But it has not proved a barrier to the formation of any regional trading area. And once the test is met, the parties are free to begin operating under their new agreement in lieu of the previously applicable GATT rules.

Developing countries seek to join together in regional trading arrangements as the best means of promoting the growth of their manufacturing and processing industries. For the principal deterrent to the establishment and growth of industry in most developing countries is the small size of the market. And the developing countries have come to recognize that it is through regional cooperation and the establishment of regional trading areas that they can create a market of sufficient size to justify the establishment of most types of manufacturing enterprise. This recognition has resulted in a proliferation of proposals for the formation of new customs unions and free-trade areas.

LATIN AMERICA

After 35 attempts between the years 1840 and 1930—"all of them ended in dismal failure"—the five states of Central America joined together to form the Central American Common Market (CACM).[9] As of January 1968, 98 per cent of the items included in the tariff schedules of the member countries were freely traded between them and a common external tariff applied to 80 to 85 per cent of those items. Between 1960 and 1966, trade within the region increased 350 per cent and represented, in 1967, over 21 per cent of the area's total trade. Moreover, the annual rate of

---

[8] See Dam, *Regional Economic Arrangements and the GATT: The Legacy of a Misconception,* 30 U. CHI. L. REV. 615, 635 (1963).

[9] General Treaty on Central American Economic Integration, *done* at Managua, December 13, 1960, 1 UNITED NATIONS, MULTILATERAL ECONOMIC CO-OPERATION IN LATIN AMERICA 5, U. N. DOC. E/CN 12/621 (1962).

direct foreign investment trebled between 1960 and 1966. These figures are all the more remarkable when one considers that skeptics had dismissed the idea of a common market between countries which produced mainly coffee and bananas. Moreover, the CACM has produced, for the first time in Central American history, "a thin layer of entrepreneurial power in industry and services."

The Latin American Free Trade Area, created by the Treaty of Montevideo, is the other regional trading bloc in South America.[10] LAFTA has not, however, met with the same degree of success as the Central American Common Market. The LAFTA countries have experienced great difficulty in agreeing on the questions of internal tariff reduction, protection for less developed members of the region, and the allocation of industry within the region. In particular, unlike the CACM, the LAFTA countries have been reluctant to free trade on commodities produced in their respective countries under heavy protection. Moreover, unlike the EEC and EFTA agreements, the LAFTA agreement does not provide for automatic annual tariff cuts. Instead it provides that internal tariffs will be cut by a weighted average of 8 per cent annually (the Free Trade Area is to come into full operation within 12 years), but the composition of those annual reductions is subject to negotiations. Despite these limitations, however, trade among the LAFTA members has increased at an annual rate of 20 per cent since the entry into force of the Treaty of Montevideo. And the LAFTA has produced another benefit which may be more significant than all the direct economic benefits, "a growing sense of regional interdependence and solidarity." This spirit resulted in the commencement of discussions, in the summer of 1967, aimed at combining the Central American Common Market and the Latin American Free Trade Area.[11]

[10] Treaty Establishing a Free-Trade Area and Instituting the Latin American Free-Trade Association, *done* at Montevideo, Feb. 18, 1960, 1 MULTILATERAL ECONOMIC CO-OPERATION IN LATIN AMERICA, U. N. Doc. E/ECN 12/621, at 57 (1962).

[11] For another regional agreement in Latin America, see the Agreement Establishing the Caribbean Free Trade Association (CARIFTA), February, 1968 (British Commonwealth States in the Caribbean).

AFRICA

In West Africa, the states of Dahomey, Ivory Coast, Mali, Mauritania, Niger, Senegal, and Upper Volta have formed a customs union, the Customs Union of West African States, under a treaty which was signed in Abidjan on June 3, 1966, and which entered into force on December 15, 1966. The agreement provides for a common external tariff ranging from 5 to 75 per cent ad valorem. Trade between the members is to be freed and, as some third parties under special arrangements are also entitled to claim duty-free entry, there is an additional provision granting preferences to imports from member countries by a 50 per cent reduction in the fiscal burden, i.e., fiscal duties, surtaxes, and consumption tax, imposed on imported goods.

The trend towards regional trading areas in Africa has been encouraged by the Economic Commission for Africa. The Commission has proposed that the continent be economically restructured into four regional trading areas: Northern, Western, Central, and Eastern. The Western regional market envisaged by the ECA is wider than the customs union of West African states, which includes only Francophonic countries. Nonetheless, that development is a partial step in the right direction, facilitated by common legal and economic institutions. A further step was taken on May 4, 1967, when 12 states, meeting in Accra at a conference on economic cooperation in West Africa sponsored by the ECA, signed articles of association for an economic community of West Africa. The signatory states were Dahomey, Ghana, Ivory Coast, Liberia, Mali, Mauritania, Niger, Nigeria, Senegal, Sierra Leone, Togo, and Upper Volta.

Partial progress has also been made in the northern region of Africa. In September and November of 1964 the Maghreb states of North Africa, Algeria, Libya, Morocco, and Tunisia, met at Tunis and Tangier to begin laying the foundtaions for a Maghreb common market.

The approach in East and Central Africa has been to join both regions in one common trading community. The first steps in this direction were taken at a meeting in Lusaka in 1965. Thirteen nations of the region agreed at that session to form an Economic Community. They established an Interministerial Committee to draw up a treaty creating the Community. As of the time of this writing, the Agreement to establish the Community, *done* in Addis Ababa, May 4, 1966, had been ratified by seven of the signatory states.

In the interval before the Community is established, the Governments of Kenya, Uganda, and Tanzania have signed a treaty establishing the East African Economic Community and Common Market, which entered into force on December 1, 1967. The treaty provides that the three countries will maintain a common external tariff. And the volume of trade between the parties is to be regulated by a system of transfer taxes.

MIDDLE EAST

An Arab Common Market came into force between Iraq, Jordan, Kuwait, Syria, and the United Arab Republic on January 1, 1965. The Convention on the Establishment of an Arab Common Market provides for a free-trade area among its members that eventually will be transformed into a customs union. In pursuit of this end the agreement provides for the removal of quantitative restrictions between member countries in *five* stages for agricultural products and in *ten* stages for industrial goods.

ASIA

In Asia efforts aimed at the creation of a preferential trading area remain in the preliminary stages. Unlike the developing areas of Latin America and Africa, the developing states of Asia face the unique disadvantage of separation from each other by rather considerable bodies of water, which presents not only a physical but also a psychological handicap to efforts at unity. In addition, the trade relations within the region suffer from the legacy of the Second World War and the political upheavals and armed conflicts which continue to this day. Nonetheless, there is a distinct trend toward an eventual system of economic integration. As a first step it has been suggested that member states exchange attachés to explore trade possibilities. At the time of this writing, there was evidence that the pace of the trend toward regional cooperation was quickening, in part due to the feeling of frustration brought on by what the states in the area believe to be inadequate responses on the part of the developed countries to their pleas for more development assistance. Thus on August 8, 1967 Indonesia, Malaysia, the Philippines, Singapore, and Thailand established an Association of Southeast Asian Nations whose aims are, *inter alia,* to improve regional economic cooperation.

Paralleling the increased interest in regional trading blocs among developing countries has been the rise of preferential areas including both developed and developing countries. In particular, several developing countries have become "associated" with the European Economic Community with a view to freeing trade between the EEC and the respective developing countries. When the EEC was formed, France was a party to a system of preferential arrangements with what were then its overseas colonial territories. It was natural, therefore, that when France joined the EEC it should seek to preserve these preferences. At the same time, it was clear that French obligations within the EEC and the colonial preference system would involve conflicts. This situation was brought into sharper focus when the colonial territories became independent. The need to generalize within the EEC the preferences granted by France to its former colonies and the converse need for those former colonies to generalize to the other EEC members the preferences granted to France eventually resulted in the Convention of Association between the European Economic Community and Associated African States, *initialled* in Brussels, December 20, 1962, and which *entered into force* on June 1, 1964. The purpose of the agreement, according to its members, was to create "a free trade area" between the Six and each of the Associated States. Goods originating in the developing countries ("Associated States") were to be admitted into the Six ("Member States") duty-free. In turn, the Associated States promised to progressively abolish "duties and charges" on imports originating in Member States. This reduction is to take place at the annual rate of 15 per cent. There is, however, no obligation on the Associated States to reduce "customs duties and charges" where these are needed for "development" or "industrialization" or are "intended to contribute to . . . [the] budget." In addition, although there are general provisions providing for the abolition of quantitative restrictions, the Associated States may, if "customs duties and charges" are "insufficient to meet their development needs and their industrialization requirements, or in the event of difficulties in their balance of payments, or, where agricultural products are concerned . . . retain or introduce quantitative restrictions on imports of goods originating in Member States."

The immediate effect of the EEC-Associated States relationship was to give the Associated States preferential entry into the EEC market. As of December 1966, exports of cocoa from Associated States were admitted to the EEC free of import duty; cocoa exports of third countries faced a 5.4 per cent tariff wall. Coffee imports from Associated States are duty-free; those emanating from third countries are subject to a 9.6 per cent duty.

Although these preferences should have conferred a substantial benefit on the Associated States, they have not been pleased with the arrangement. At the midpoint of the period for which the Convention remains in force, the Associated States noted that they "were disappointed at the failure of their trade balance with the EEC to improve since association." The exports of the Associated States to the EEC have increased at a far slower rate than exports from nonassociated states, particularly those of Latin America. On the other hand, the EEC countries have been under some pressure to "extricate themselves from the appearance of favoring some African states over others and at the expense of others." Such mutual dissatisfaction could lead to a fundamental revision of the Convention when it expires on May 31, 1969. The groundwork for such a revision is already being laid by "association" agreements between other African states and the EEC.

On July 15, 1966, Nigeria signed an association agreement with the EEC. This agreement grants to Nigerian exports equal treatment with those of the Associated States, except for four products (cocoa, palm oil, groundnut oil, plywood) which are of particular importance to the Associated States. As to these latter goods, Nigeria was granted annually increasing quotas. In exchange Nigeria granted nominal preferences of 2-10 per cent to imports from the EEC.

In addition to those in Africa, the EEC has entered into Association Agreements with Greece and Turkey, and trade agreements with Iran, India, Israel and the East African States of Kenya, Tanzania, and Uganda. And, at the time of this writing, negotiations were pending for the association of Algeria, Morocco, and Tunisia.

Whether agreements between the EEC and developing countries will remain a significant category of non-GATT trade agreement is open to doubt. For there is pressure on the EEC from both nonassociated developing countries and from industrial states to do away with this type of agreement which is a divisive force within the developing world. The pressure is particularly intense on those EEC members who do not have close ties to the Associated States growing out of a post-colonial relationship. It seems likely that this pressure will result, as it has in the past, in a decrease in the preferential advantages conferred on the Associated States in exchange for increased commitments to assist their development efforts through various aid and investment devices.

Regional trade arrangements between developing countries, on the other hand, seem destined to continue as the most important category of extra-GATT trade agreements. For the developing countries recognize that they cannot develop industry on a viable basis if its products must be sold within their small home markets.

And the prospects for selling their manufactures in the markets of the developed countries are not good for several reasons. First, the developing countries do not have home markets on which to build production on a scale sufficient to permit marketing abroad at a low price. One of the lessons of the history of economic development is that nations tend to export those manufactures for which they have a large home market. Second, the tariffs in the developed countries on the manufactures the developing countries produce efficiently are high, so as to grant a large measure of protection to producers in the developed countries. Finally, even if the tariff barriers could be overcome, the developed countries might fall back on the use of quantitative import controls as they have in the case of cotton textiles. This is not to say that no developing country can hope to export manufactures to the developed world. The point is rather that the opportunities are limited, and are likely to be supplemented by joining together with other developing countries to form a regional trading area.

AGREEMENTS WITH NONMEMBERS OF GATT

The second important category of trade agreements which exist outside the GATT are those agreements in which one of the parties is not a GATT member. For the GATT is far from universal. Of the 122 nations invited to attend the first United Nations Conference on Trade and Development, only 76 are members of GATT.[12] Of the nonmembers, the following are developing countries: Afghanistan, Bolivia, Chile, China (Taiwan), Colombia, Costa Rica, Ecuador, El Salvador, Ethiopia, Guatemala, Guinea, Honduras, Iran, Iraq, Ireland, Jordan, Laos, Lebanon, Liberia, Libya, Mexico, Morocco, Nepal, Panama, Paraguay, Philippines, Saudi Arabia, Somalia, Sudan, Syria, Thailand, Vietnam (South), Venezuela, and Yemen. Few of these nations have ever articulated their reasons for not joining the GATT.[13] One

[12] There are, in addition, 11 states in some form of association with GATT.
[13] China (Taiwan), Lebanon, Liberia, and Syria were members but left for unspecified reasons.

can, however, speculate on those reasons. Several of the Latin American states which participated in the negotiations leading to the Havana Charter were either so embittered or so disappointed by the failure of the Charter to come into force that they refused to accede to the GATT, its offspring. In addition, several of the Latin American states have trade agreements with the United States which provide that trade concessions which the United States makes to its GATT partners will be passed on to the Latin Americans. And this has been United States practice even where there is no agreement presently requiring it. Since most Latin American trade is with the United States, the Latin Americans are able to profit from the tariff reductions resulting from GATT negotiations without participating in those negotiations. Other developing countries have probably viewed the GATT as an organization of Western Powers, and in pursuit of a policy of political nonalignment, declined to participate. For most, however, the costs of joining were probably thought to outweigh the benefits gained.[14] In this connection it is interesting to note that there are two routes for acceding to the Agreement. The usual route is via Article XXXIII which requires that a new member negotiate trade concessions with the Contracting Parties, in return for obtaining the benefits of the past concessions made by the Contracting Parties *inter se*. The new members' concessions are known as the "accession fee." Alternatively, former colonial territories to which the GATT was applied by the metropolitan power may accede "free" upon attainment of independence (Article XXVI (5) (c)). For they are considered to have participated in past trade negotiations during the period of their colonial status. This distinction may account for the large number of recently independent states which are GATT members and, on the other hand, the presence in the group of nonmembers of a

---

[14] This belief was articulated by the developing countries which attended the Havana Conference in 1947. After strenuous debate, these countries succeeded in adding an article to the Havana Charter (art. 15) which provided for new preferences "to ensure a market for a particular industry." This provision was not, however, incorporated in the GATT. The Charter is reprinted in C. WILCOX, A CHARTER FOR WORLD TRADE 231 (1949).

large number of older developing countries. Finally there are nonmember states "whose interest in world trade is practically non-existent," and those whose exports consist of only one product, in particular, the oil-exporting states.

Of more economic significance, and political significance as well, are the other group of countries which are not GATT members— the centrally planned countries, the socialist countries, or the Communist countries (depending on one's point of view). With the exception of Czechoslovakia, which joined prior to its becoming a centrally planned country and Poland, a recent member, those countries which have organized their economies along Marxist-Leninist lines have not joined the GATT.[15] In this they were following the lead of the Soviet Union. When the United States issued the invitations to join with it in the tariff negotiations which led to the creation of the GATT, an invitation was sent to the Soviet Union. No formal reply was received. At the time the parties who were to become the chief protagonists in the Cold War held different views on the reasons for Soviet nonparticipation. One of the American negotiators at Havana has written:

It was not to be expected that the Charter would commend itself strongly to the Soviet Union. It is a product of the philosophy of economic liberalism; this philosophy runs counter to communist ideology. It seeks to open markets and expand trade; the Russians have little interest in foreign markets; they are import minded; they sell only to pay for the things they buy; they see no advantage in the expansion of trade per se. The Charter would make for greater interdependence and a closer integration of the world economy; comprehensive planning makes for economic independence and national self-sufficiency. Under the Charter, trade would be freed increasingly from political control; in the monolithic state, trade is an instrument of national policy. The Charter will operate to restore an environment that is congenial to the preservation of private enterprise. This is not an objective that Communism shares.[16]

To a great extent, this is an accurate representation of the

---

[15] Hungary, Bulgaria, and Roumania enjoy observer status. Roumania has applied for full membership.
[16] C. WILCOX, *supra* note 14, at 164.

economic objections of the Soviet Union to the Charter. Their political objections, however, were of a more sweeping nature. The Soviet position was that, following the Second World War, the United States and the United Kingdom "spurned East-West collaboration and persecuted . . . [their] former allies." [17] The Soviet trade union journal, *Trud,* saw the Charter as evidence of an attempt by "the monopolies of the United States . . . to enslave, not only Europe, but the whole world." And in a series of articles in the periodical of the Soviet Ministry of Foreign Trade, it was charged that the Charter " 'deprives member countries of their sovereign rights and binds them to the will of the United States' . . ." [18] The draftsmen and promoters of the Charter were branded " 'professional crooks,' 'predatory Western capitalists,' and 'pretenders to world domination,' working toward 'economic expansion,' 'imperialist aggrandisement,' and 'American hegemony,' and brutally imposing 'the mandates of Wall Street on the other nations of the world.' " To the Soviet leaders of that day, institutions such as the International Monetary Fund, the International Bank for Reconstruction and Development, and the Havana Charter were all schemes to foster the spreading of the capitalist system.

Whether the Soviet Union was correct in its view of the Charter is not particularly significant. For there is no question that the Charter and the GATT rested on premises which were fundamentally different from those upon which the Soviet economy was organized. The Western economies are, more or less, organized along the principle of the allocation of goods by market demand. In international trade, their fundamental economic principle is comparative advantage. At the time the GATT was negotiated, the production and trade of the Soviet Union were based on neither of these principles. Production was grounded not in market demand, but on the goals established by the economic planners. That is to say, the leadership decided what goods they

[17] M. KASER, COMECON 9 (1965).
[18] Quoted in C. WILCOX, *supra* note 14, at 186.

would like to see produced in what quantities and then set about organizing their factors of production so as to achieve these goals. To illustrate, "the output of an industry—say, coal—is allocated to other users; these other users calculate the output of their product which is feasible with that coal (and other inputs similarly passed to them—in the case of steel, say, iron ore and limestone). By applying 'transformation coefficients' (the tons of coal, ore, and limestone needed per ton of steel), a planned output is calculated and this output, in turn, is allocated to other users. The users would include the coal industry, which then applies its own transformation coefficients to verify that it could produce the draft plan of coal. If an imbalance is shown (*e.g.* not enough steel to support the mine-sinking programme to extract the planned coal output), the procedure must be repeated . . . with variant figures." [19] The important point to note is that in this process prices as they are known in the market economy do not exist— goods and services are allocated in *physical quantity* ("material balances").

But without the uniform measuring rod of the price system, it is very difficult to calculate the comparative "costs" of producing different products. The relative economic desirability of producing automobiles as opposed to airplanes in such a system must be measured in physical quantities of inputs—an exceedingly difficult task. This is not, however, an insurmountable problem where the end products of the system of production are already determined by previously selected goals. The difficulties arise when there are certain goods which cannot under any circumstances be produced at home due to a lack of, for example, a particular raw material. The necessity for foreign trade then appears. But what to trade and at what price? The answer is that those goods are traded which are produced but which are not needed for domestic investment or consumption. Thus, there is little planning for export. Those goods are exported which are "surplus" in the domestic economy. And the export prices are determined not, as in the

[19] KASER, *supra* note 17, at 33–34.

market economy, by cost *and* demand factors, but solely by demand factors. Goods are thus exported on the basis of *world market prices*. Now it could be said that all goods which are exported, whether emanating from market or centrally planned economies, are sold at world market prices or they would not be sold at all. This is true enough. But the fundamental difference is that goods which are exported from market economies are normally produced at a cost less than the world market price, whereas in the centrally planned economy, little regard is paid to the "cost" of producing the goods exported. To state it another way, market economies export those goods which they produce relatively efficiently, (i.e. in which they enjoy a comparative advantage). In the centrally planned economy, those goods are exported which have been produced and are not needed—without regard to whether they have been produced efficiently in relative terms. With the formation of COMECON, in January 1949 this rather autarchic picture began to change. COMECON is premised on the idea that there should be a division of labor (specialization) among centrally planned countries along lines of relative efficiency (comparative advantage). It thus became necessary to find some basis for calculating such efficiency. In the end, the COMECON members "computed ingenious physical coefficients, as well as labor costs, to measure the rate of international transformation." [20] Nonetheless, most intra-COMECON trade continues to take place at prices established " 'on the basis of average world market prices on the principal market for the commodity in a clearly defined period.' . . ."

The theory underlying COMECON is a great step from the original system of trade obtaining in centrally planned economies —disposal of surplus goods. In substance, it puts the trading system of those countries on the same basis as that obtaining in

---

[20] M. Kaser, *supra* note 17, at 34. Cost calculations in the centrally planned economies have traditionally been subject to an ideological bias, "the devotion to the Marxist labor theory of value which ignores the productivity of capital and land." C. Kindleberger, Foreign Trade and the National Economy 159 (1962). Current reforms in several Marxist countries, however, have included instituting a "charge" for the use of capital.

market economies. Thus, the centrally planned economies are at present in a state of transition which should lay the groundwork for further integration of the market and centrally planned economies in the world trade pattern.

There is, however, another aspect of the commercial policy of centrally planned states which is antagonistic to the policies of the GATT. This is the practice of state trading. State trading will be discussed in detail further in this book, so that only a short treatment of the subject will be presented here. In a state trading system, all importing and exporting is done by state agencies. According to Soviet authorities, "under centralized planning, the only way to trade . . . [is] through a state monopoly." This is certainly true if by a centrally planned country one means a country in which virtually all enterprises—including those engaged in the import and export trade—are owned by the state. Not only is such a state-trading system necessary, but its proponents go further and argue that it is desirable, because the state can, for example, secure "the exact fulfillment of all commitments at the proper time." On the other hand, the opponents of state trading note that "state trading and all similar tools of commercial policy are in principle anathema to the Contracting Parties [of the GATT] because they make inevitable the preferential treatment of one country as against another for other than commercial reasons." The "other than commercial reasons" usually refer to political factors. That is to say, a system of foreign trading by government corporations is viewed as inherently discriminatory because those corporations will tend to divert their purchases towards political allies, despite the fact that other nations may be capable of producing the same goods more efficiently. In short, the criticism is based on the fact that governments are by definition patriotic, while private businessmen and traders are not.

There are thus two reasons why the foreign trade system of the centrally planned countries has been incompatible with the GATT —the making available for export of "surpluses" without regard to comparative advantage and the practice of state trading. As noted, the centrally planned economies are currently in a state of transition, and seem to be moving in a direction which would enable them to accept a pattern of world trade based upon comparative advantage and nondiscrimination. Nonetheless, the pace of the transition is slow and in the interim it is difficult to see how a centrally planned economy can operate under the GATT rules.

The developing countries have shown a great inteerst in trading with the centrally planned countries. This is the result of a natural desire to explore all markets for imports and exports. But there is another powerful reason behind the increased interest. Those developing countries which were colonies inherited, upon attaining independence, patterns of trade closely tied to the former metropole. Having decided to pursue a policy of political nonalignment, either from rather idealistic motives or as a means of exploiting Cold War competition between the great powers, the developing countries believe that a necessary corollary of this policy is one of economic nonalignment. In practice, given the patterns of preindependence trade, this has involved a conscious effort to divert a portion of their trade to the centrally planned economies. This effort has met with a ready response on the part of the latter group of countries, who have actively sought trade relations with the developing world as a source of needed imports, as a market for disposal of surpluses, and for the purpose of extending political influence. There is, however, one additional reason why trade with developing countries has a particular appeal for centrally planned economies. For the latter are, in many ways, also developing countries. And in their present stage of development they have been able to produce for export manufactured consumer and capital goods generally inferior in quality to similar goods produced under more efficient conditions prevailing in Western Europe and North America. If these manufactures are to be exported at all, they must be sold in the developing countries.

The trade between the centrally planned economies and the developing countries is carried on within the framework of individual trade agreements. This situation may change with the growing interest in the GATT on the part of the centrally planned economies. But this not necessarily so, for the latter seek primarily to increase their trade with the West. GATT is viewed as the major Western trading organization, i.e. the major *forum* for trade discussions. But whether the centrally planned economies wish to conduct their trade with the West in accordance with the GATT rules is another question. Czechoslavakia, a GATT member since its founding, has preferred to conduct its trade with developing countries which are also GATT members within the framework of individual trade agreements. Thus it is not so much formal GATT membership which will give rise to such trade being conducted according to the GATT code, but rather the evolution of the centrally planned economies to a point where they can validly accept the obligation of nondiscrimination and the organization of their national economies and international trade along the lines of comparative advantage. In the interim, the increasing volume of trade between the developing countries and the centrally planned economies—exports from the former to the latter rose from $610 million in 1950 to $1,630 million in 1962 and are projected to reach $3,000 million by 1970 and $5,000 million by 1980—will continue to take place within the framework of individually negotiated trade agreements and outside the scope of the General Agreement on Tariffs and Trade.

AGREEMENTS IN DEROGATION OF GATT

The third general category of trade agreements which exist outside the GATT are those made by developing countries which are Contracting Parties to the Agreement and yet agree among themselves to conduct their trade by a set of rules other than those laid down in the General Agreement. The clearest and most common example of such agreements are the preferential agreements made between two or more developing countries. Suppose, for example, that Country *A* and Country *B* each wishes to establish a manufacturing enterprise but neither has a sufficient home market to render manufacturing an economically viable proposition. If their relations are otherwise friendly, it is not unlikely that *A* and *B* will enter into an agreement whereby *A* agrees to freely admit into its territory products emanating from *B*'s new factory and vice versa. This simple arrangement for preferential treatment would run afoul of the GATT, which outlaws preferences unless they take the form of agreements aimed at freeing "substantially all the trade" between the parties, i.e., unless they aim at creating a free-trade area or customs union. Yet a developing country may believe that its present economic interests will best be served by a more limited agreement. This judgment can be supported by a brief examination of Article XXIV of the GATT as it applies to developed countries and developing countries. Article XXIV seems to have been incorporated in the Agreement specifically to provide for the establishment of a common market in Western Europe. Here were countries which had traded with each other for hundreds of years, between whom there existed a substantial volume of trade, and who were knowledgeable in what each could produce most efficiently. The gains from the formation of a customs union between them were calculable and the costs, in terms of the elimination of inefficient producers, apparent. This is not to say that the rationalization which the Treaty of Rome portended was or is easily brought about. But at the time the Treaty was negotiated, the parties had a fairly clear picture of what future trade patterns would be like. This is not the situation when developing countries propose to come together to form a regional trading area. More often than not those countries have had little experience in trading with each other, and even less in trading in manufactures or processed goods. Unlike the developed countries which come together to rationalize *existing* production, the developing countries come together to create a market for *new* production. In such circumstances the future patterns of trade within the market can only be matters of speculation. Aside from uncertainty caused by lack of data and the absence of trained personnel, development in a prospective regional trading area among developing countries will depend on the often fickle attitudes of foreign investors and aid donors. Thus it is not surprising to find that most developing countries will enter regional trading arrangements cautiously and will attempt to avoid as much as possible the opening of their borders to the goods, or prospective goods, of their neighbors.

The cautious attitude has been most apparent in the history of the Latin American Free Trade Area. During the 1930s most of the South American countries adopted trade and exchange controls in an attempt to isolate themselves from the Depression.[21] These controls were gradually refined and reoriented so as to grant preferential treatment to certain products of countries in the region. Those arrangements were later formalized in trade agreements between the parties. The system did not, however, lend itself to the type of overall regional cooperation which the parties desired and during the 1950s, with assistance from the Economic Commission for Latin America, the countries of the area sought a more "permanent" solution to their trade problems. LAFTA was the result. And while LAFTA continues to be handicapped by the cautious attitude of the countries which are party to the Treaty of Montevideo, it seems clear that the Treaty does represent an advance over the earlier systems of administrative trade preferences and individual preferential agreements.

The pattern leading to the formation of the Central American Common Market was much the same. In 1951 El Salvador negotiated preferential trade agreements with Nicaragua and Guatemala. Later, in 1953, El Salvador entered into a similar agreement with Costa Rica and, in 1954, an agreement with Honduras. After a certain amount of experience under these arrangements, the parties made their first attempt to establish a regional trading

[21] See Mikesell, *The Movement Toward Regional Trading Groups in Latin America*, A. HIRSCHMAN, LATIN AMERICAN ISSUES 125 (1961).

arrangement in 1958. Although this effort was not successful, it set in motion the train of events which finally culminated in the negotiation of the General Treaty in 1960.

The point is that rather than start with a scheme for a customs union or free-trade area, the parties' initial efforts at promoting regional trade consisted of limited preferential arrangements and individual trade agreements. This is the pattern which the Economic Commission for Asia seems to favor. The tendency in Africa and the Middle East, as summarized above, is to attempt to skip those steps and to go right from a position of limited trade to a customs union. If the political will is present, and there is sufficient outside encouragement and support, some of these programs will succeed. But it is more likely that most of them will result in nothing more than the creation of a system of limited preferences. For opening the barriers to competition where the effect may be the dislocation of one of a developing country's few manufacturing industries is a painful and risky act for the political leadership.

Limited preferential trade agreements in derogation of the GATT prohibition on such arrangements are likely to increase in number because they appear to be an essential prerequisite to the formation of a regional trading arrangement.[22] Although prohibited by the General Agreement, the Contracting Parties have taken an extremely sympathetic view of any efforts by the developing countries designed to encourage their economic growth. Moreover, even if such agreements were called into question by a Contracting Party, it is more than likely that the preferential arrangement could be recast in the *form* of a free-trade area or customs union and defended on the basis of those exceptions to the GATT. According to some authorities this has already occurred in the case of the LAFTA and the association agreements

[22] See, for example, the preferential agreement between India, the United Arab Republic, and Yugoslavia signed in New Delhi in December, 1967. The agreement provides for a 40 per cent reduction in tariffs on over 250 products to become effective in April, 1968, with an additional 10 per cent reduction the following year. The agreement is open to signature by any developing country.

concluded between developing countries and the EEC. Finally, if developing countries were really hard put to defend a preferential trading arrangement, they could request a waiver of their obligations under the GATT, for which there is ample precedent.

In concluding this brief discussion of trade agreements made in derogation of the General Agreement, mention should be made of those agreements which will be entered into by developing countries which are GATT members but who simply consider the GATT irrelevant to their trade relations. This may seem a contradictory statement since membership in the GATT should be conclusive evidence that a country considers the GATT a relevant framework for its international trade. But this is not the case. Many of the developing countries consider the GATT a "rich man's club." This conclusion is based on a number of factors. First, the GATT was originally a joint creation of the United States and the United Kingdom. Second, GATT-sponsored tariff negotiations have resulted in reductions of great benefit to the developed countries while tariffs on goods in which the developing countries would seem to have a comparative advantage have remained high. Third, while the Agreement prohibits new preferences, it makes specific exception for those which existed at the time it was negotiated, i.e., the preferential trading arrangements between the then colonial empires and metropolitan powers. And the Agreement generally prohibits the use of quantitative restrictions, yet permits their use to protect domestic agriculture, an exception principally benefiting the industrialized countries.

Disenchantment with the GATT led to a proposal at the United Nations Conference on Trade and Development for the creation of a new trade arrangement more in the interest of the developing countries. The proposal was partially successful in that it led to the creation of a Trade and Development Board, a continuing body designed principally as a forum where the developing countries could discuss their trade problems with the richer nations. That the GATT was not laid to rest at the UNCTAD is, however, a positive good. For in discussions of whether the GATT is

"good" or "bad" for the developing countries several issues tend
to become confused. It is well to remember first that the GATT is
no more than a reflection of the views of its member states. If the
GATT contains objectionable features, and does not, on the
other hand, contain certain provisions which the developing
countries would like to see incorporated in the Agreement, this
is not the fault of some abstract entity known as "the GATT,"
but rather of those Contracting Parties who speak with the loudest
voices in the organization. The developing countries are surely
ill-advised if they believe that through a change in form, a new
organization would be more amenable to altering the rules of international trade in accordance with their views. This lesson was
brought home at the first UNCTAD where resolution after resolution was passed by overwhelming majorities, but to little avail
where those few who opposed the resolutions were the countries
which would have to take action if the resolution were to be mean-
ingful. Moreover, in discussions about "the GATT" there is a
tendency to confuse the Agreement itself with the Institution.
The Agreement may contain features which the developing countries find undesirable. But there can be few who would fault the
efforts of the GATT Secretariat in assisting the developing countries to find their place in the pattern of world trade.

As early as the 1954 GATT Annual Report, the Secretariat took
note of the "relative decline in trade between the nonindustrial
and industrial areas, accounted for by the failure of the value of
exports from non-industrial areas to expand." Subsequent reports
continued to allude to this problem, and by 1957 the Secretariat
obtained the appointment of a Panel of Experts to look at current
and future problems in international trade and, in particular,
"the failure of the trade of less developed countries to develop
as rapidly as that of industrial countries." A direct outgrowth of
this report was the creation of GATT Committee III whose
terms of reference are "to consider and report to the Contracting
Parties regarding . . . measures for the expansion of trade, with
particular reference to the importance of the maintenance and

expansion of export earnings of the less developed countries to the development and diversification of their economies." In pursuit of it mandate Committee III has sought to: (1) identify the barriers to trade in products of particular export interest to the developing counries; (2) take steps leading to the removal of such barriers; (3) examine the development plans and export potential of developing countries; and (4) consider other measures which would aid in expanding the exports of developing countries. Under Committee III auspices, a study of the problems of trade in tropical products was undertaken, which produced concrete proposals for expansion of trade in that area vital to many developing countries. The export implications of the development plans of India and Pakistan have been examined and those of Chile, Kenya, Malaysia, Nigeria, Tunisia, Turkey, and Uganda are under study. More important, Committee III has provided a forum in which the trade policies of the developing countries could be discussed with the industrial nations. The idea of preferences to be granted by the industrialized countries to less-developed countries was first given wide currency in Committee III. And out of Committee III came the suggestion for what is now the GATT International Trade Center. The Center offers a variety of services to developing countries, including information on export opportunities in its regular publication *International Trade Forum* and through individual market studies. In addition, the Center has organized courses in export problems and techniques for officials of developing countries. And the Center has promoted study tours of various export markets for the officials of developing countries.[23] Thus insofar as the activities of the Secretariat have been concerned, the GATT has been a significant benefit to many developing countries.

Nonetheless, the view persists that there is a "GATT" which exists primarily to deal with the trade problems of the developed countries. And this view has been reinforced by the results of the

[23] With effect from January 1, 1968, the Center will be jointly operated by GATT and UNCTAD.

Kennedy Round of tariff negotiations which to all intents and purposes were between the United States and the EEC. Most commentators believe that the Kennedy Round was of little benefit to the developing countries. Perhaps the expectations of what they had hoped to gain from the Kennedy Round made disappointment on the part of the developing countries almost inevitable, but there is no gainsaying the fact that the Kennedy Round served only to reinforce the generally held view that the GATT is a rich man's club. It should not, therefore, be surprising that in establishing rules for the conduct of trade between developing countries, they sometimes overlook the fact that they are members of GATT and proceed instead to organize their trade relationships along lines of their own.

CONCLUSION

This brief introduction has been aimed at establishing the fact that despite the existence of a General Agreement on Tariffs and Trade, developing countries have been and will continue to negotiate trade agreements. The most significant of these agreements will be those regional trading arrangements which are permitted as exceptions to the GATT. A second broad category are those agreements between developing countries and those countries whose economies are centrally planned and which are unlikely, in the foreseeable future, to conduct their trade within the framework of the GATT. The third type of agreement will be that negotiated between a developing country which is a GATT member and a developing country which has not joined the Agreement. Finally, there are those trade agreements which will be entered into in derogation of the GATT by countries who believe the GATT has no role to play in their trade relations, or who wish to grant each other "special" treatment not provided for in the General Agreement.

The remainder of this book deals with the substantive provisions which may be found in the trade agreements of developing countries. In each case an attempt has been made to identify a problem which may arise in the trade relations of developing countries and to indicate the way in which that problem might be dealt with in a trade agreement. Needless to say, there are trade problems which cannot be dealt with in trade agreements. And even where a trade agreement takes note of a particular situation, there is not always a formulation adequate to meet all objections. Nonetheless, a trade agreement can be a means to broadening existing channels of trade and opening new ones and it is the hope of the author that this volume will prove a useful tool in fashioning such an agreement.

II. Most-Favored-Nation Treatment

In most poor countries economic development is equated with industrial development. Although the agricultural sector must not be overlooked—as is too often the case—in the developing world progress is thought of in terms of new manufacturing establishments. This desire to industrialize is the result of a combination of psychological, political, and economic factors. Almost one hundred years ago the German economist Friedrich List noted that: "In a country devoted to mere raw agriculture, dullness of mind, awkwardness of body, obstinate adherence to old notions, customs, methods, and processes, want of culture, of prosperity, and of liberty, prevail. . . . This condition of things is entirely changed . . . by establishing a manufacturing power . . . the mental, moral and physical stagnation of the population is broken up." [1] Although they may be unaware of List's existence, the political leadership in most of the developing nations share his views as to the relative merits of agriculture and industry. In part the position of the leadership is a response to the demands of the general population who, in an era of rapid communication, have been exposed to the patterns of consumption prevailing in the developed world. The "demonstration effect" of such exposure has aroused in them new wants and desires which the political leadership, if it wishes to remain in power, must seek to satisfy. Moreover, the colonial economy was characterized by the export of raw materials and the import of manufactured goods. With political independence has come the desire to shake off this colonial image, in part by reduc-

[1] F. List, The National System of Political Economy 197 (1888).

ing the level of imported manufactures and increasing the export of processed goods. In addition there are economic factors at work militating in favor of industrial development. For in practically all developing countries a market exists sufficient to support at least some manufacturing on an efficient scale. Finally, with the prospects of financing development out of increased exports of primary products not particularly bright, many developing countries seek to establish sales based in the home market as a first step in a program of exporting manufactures or processed goods.

The initial stage of the process of industrialization can be characterized as the import substitution stage. The domestic market of the developing country is examined to determine whether goods of a particular type are being imported in quantities sufficient to justify the establishment of a local industry on an economical scale.[2] In a few cases, e.g., cotton textiles, the answer will be positive. (It is interesting to note that the industrialization process in many of the developed countries started in just this way, the development of a textile industry to supply the home market.) Given a market of sufficient size to permit production on an economical scale, however, other problems remain. For there is a necessary time interval between the point at which the decision is made to go ahead with the production of a product and the point at which the product is produced at maximum efficiency. Workers and managers must be hired and trained, sources of raw materials located, a distribution system built. In addition, the establishment of a new factory may require bringing into being local trucking and warehousing facilities, as well as the supply of a host of minor services, legal, accounting, maintenance, protection. During the period these resources are being developed, the infant industry requires protection from well-established outside competition. If the industry is soundly based the need for protection will decline as the "learning process" is completed and the needed services are supplied.

[2] One writer has suggested that this traditional test (eventual economic scale) should be relegated to a minor role. He would ask initially whether an infant industry will result in foreign exchange savings. S. LINDER, TRADE AND TRADE POLICY FOR DEVELOPMENT 93 (1967).

History, of course, is replete with cases of infant industries which never grew up. But this history is that of the present day developed countries and it seems ironic that they should rely on it as the basis for their skepticism about the use of the infant industry argument for protection by many developing countries. Moreover, the history is one of *abuse* of the argument. The infant industry case remains economically sound where correctly applied. Finally, and perhaps most important, "[e]conomists who criticize excess emphasis on industrial development miss the point. Southern [hemisphere] leaders do not seek rising income alone, they want rising incomes in an industrializing society. If high-cost industry conflicts with maximizing the growth of income, most LDC governments are willing to pay the price." [3]

CUSTOMS DUTIES

The traditional means by which infant industries are protected is through the imposition of customs duties. Customs duties may be levied on either imports or exports. Import duties are like taxes in that they are a charge levied by a government, the effect of which is to increase the cost of imported articles to the consumer. By raising the cost of imported goods, domestically produced goods are made more attractive to the local consumer. In addition to their protective function, import duties provide the government with revenue. This is particularly important in many developing countries where the tax machinery is not well developed. Collecting duties at the point of importation and exportation is administratively easy and inexpensive. Thus, in the 1967 budget of Malagasy, 30 per cent of government revenue was produced by customs collections. For Dahomey the figure was 43 per cent and for Chad 55 per cent.[4] The particular goods upon which duties

---

[3] J. PINCUS, TRADE, AID AND DEVELOPMENT 170 (1967).

[4] For the portion of total government revenue supplied by customs collections in Southeast Asia, see *Trade Barriers in Countries of the ECAFE Region*, ECONOMIC COMMISSION FOR ASIA AND THE FAR EAST, THE ASIAN DEVELOPMENT BANK AND TRADE LIBERALIZATION, U. N. Doc. E/CN 11/707, at 110, 112 (1965).

are levied, and the rates of those duties will be determined by which effect—protective or revenue raising—the government wishes to emphasize. Duties aimed primarily at raising revenue will be levied on goods imported in substantial volume and at rates low enough so as not to encourage domestic production of the same or similar goods. A protective duty, on the other hand, will be set at a rate high enough to encourage consumers to purchase locally manufactured products. And, in fact, such duties may be set so high as to eliminate altogether the importation of similar goods from abroad.

Export duties, while more unusual than import duties, are found mainly in developing countries. They are imposed for the same reasons as import duties. That is to say, they are both revenue producing and protective. But both aspects of export duties operate a bit more indirectly than in the case of import duties. Export duties are rarely, if ever, imposed on semiprocessed or processed goods. Rather they are levied on primary product exports. This is so because primary product exports face a relatively inelastic demand. Thus the price of such goods can, in theory, be increased without a corresponding decline in demand. As far as revenue producing is concerned, this means that the foreign purchasers ostensibly pay the duty and fill the government coffers, instead of the local citizenry paying as is the case with import duties. In fact this is not the case, since the amounts equivalent to export duties would be flowing, in the absence of such duties, to the producers in the form of additional profits. In short, the export duty acts in much the same way as tax on producers of the exported commodity. It is, however, easier to collect than an income tax, particularly where the primary product exports are grown by many small producers.

The protective feature of export duties comes into play when the exports are used as raw materials in foreign processing industries. The export duty increases the cost of the raw materials to foreign processors. Other factors being equal, this will enable local processors, who do not have to include the export duty in their costs, to produce the processed goods more cheaply and thus be in a better competitive position in the world markets than foreign processors. To illustrate, take the case of Tanzania, the world's largest grower of sisal, which is processed into binder twine for use in harvesting. By imposing an export duty on sisal, Tanzania could encourage the local production of binder twine, since it could be marketed at an advantage compared with binder twine produced from Tanzanian sisal in other countries, the cost of which would include the export duty element not present in Tanzanian binder twine.

So long as a country levies equal duties on all products of a similar kind without respect to the country of origin or destination, it creates few problems in international relations. The problems arise, however, when an importing country discriminates between products of a similar nature depending on the country in which they are produced or for which they are destined. To illustrate, shoes produced in Country *A* might, upon importation, be subjected to a 10 per cent duty, while shoes manufactured in Country *B* might be subjected to a 30 per cent duty. Where a country maintains *one* rate of duty for each type of product imported, without regard to where the product was produced, it is said to maintain a *single-line tariff* (the total schedule of duties being referred to as a "tariff"). Discrimination begins where countries maintain a two-line tariff, generally known as a *maximum-and-minimum tariff*. In such cases the minimum rate is levied on goods from "favored" nations; goods of the same type originating in or destined for all other countries are subject to the higher rate of duty. The current ultimate in complexity is the *five-line-tariff*, such as the type maintained by New Zealand. The lowest rates of duty are levied on products originating in Australia, under the terms of a free-trade area agreement, the next column applies to Canada under the terms of a separate agreement, then a column of "British Preferential" rates, then most-favored-nation, and finally, general rates.

In order to minimize or eliminate the effects of multiline tariffs, countries have entered into agreements which provide that imports from one into the other should be treated the same, insofar as duties are concerned, as imports originating in any other country. This equality of treatment is formalized in the "most-favored-nation" clause.

At the outset it should be noted that the words "most-favored-nation" are somewhat misleading for the purpose of such provisions is not to render one nation more favored than all the others. Rather, the clause aims at placing all trading partners on an equal footing. So that when Country *A* promises to give Country *B* most-favored-nation treatment, what it is promising is that *B* will be treated as well as any other country with whom *A* trades, i.e., as well as the most-favored-nation.

The language into which the principle of most-favored-nation treatment has been cast has grown more precise through time. According to Hornbeck, the principle of most-favored-nation treatment was first incorporated in a treaty between Great Britain and Portugal, *done* on January 29, 1642, "whereby the subjects of Great Britain became entitled to enjoy all the immunities accorded to the 'subjects of any nation whatsoever in league with the Portugals.' " [5] Today the clause may be found in a variety of forms. The following are two versions in current use:

Each government shall accord to the commerce of the country of the other government treatment no less favorable than that accorded to the commerce of any third country.

Both contracting parties shall accord each other most-favored-nation treatment in respect of all matters related to their trade relations.

As statements of the general principle of most-favored-nation treatment, these provisions are quite acceptable. But they leave vague several important issues. For example, while few would doubt that the clauses cover customs duties, what of other types of charges which may be imposed at the time of importation? [6]

[5] Quoted in A. McNair, The Law of Treaties 273 (1961).

[6] Several European countries limit the application of the clause to tariffs, unless otherwise expressly stated. See Hazard, *Commercial Discrimination and International Law*, 52 Am. J. Int'l L. 495, 497 (1958).

Are the charges for the clearing goods through customs rather than the duties themselves covered by the most-favored-nation principle? The Syrian Arab Republic levies the following "taxes" on imports which are collected by the customs authorities at the time goods enter Syria: statistical tax, consumption tax, defense tax, school tax, and ocean tax. Are any or all of these "taxes" covered by the most-favored-nation clauses quoted above? Or suppose that regulations provide for the collection of duty on imports from certain countries at specified customs offices, and these offices are so located that the costs of importation are unduly increased by such a complication? Or regulations may provide, as some have, that duties must be collected at the frontier, and this provision is applied to some countries and not others? Moreover, could one party require that imports from the other be recorded, at the time of importation, on complicated forms in quadruplicate and admit imports of the same kind from a third country upon the completion of a short form of which only one copy might be required? While one could argue that the breadth of the clauses would cover these situations, it appears doubtful that the draftsmen even considered these possibilities. Yet all have occurred. And the issues are ones over which a bona fide dispute could arise.

A further question left unresolved by the general form of the clause is whether most-favored-nation treatment shall be conditional or unconditional. Although rarely used today, the conditional most-favored-nation clause was at one time widely employed as a means of limiting the effect of most-favored-nation treatment.[7] Its operation may be illustrated as follows. Assume that Country *A* and Country *B* have a trade agreement in which each promises to extend to products of the other most-favored-nation treatment.

[7] The conditional form of the most-favored-nation clause first appeared in the Commercial Treaty between the United States and France, February 6, 1778. Article II of that Treaty provided: " 'The Most Christian King and the United States engage mutually not to grant any particular favor to other nations, in respect of commerce and navigation, which shall not immediately become common to the other party, . . . who shall enjoy the same favor, freely, if the concession was freely made, or on allowing the same compensation, if the concession was conditional." Quoted in J. VINER, INTERNATIONAL ECONOMICS 17 (1951).

Further assume that the import duty on shoes from Country *B* imported into Country *A* is 20 per cent. *A* makes a trade agreement with Country *C* in which *A* promises that imports of shoes from Country *C* into *A* shall be subject to a duty of 10 per cent. In exchange for this concession, *C* agrees to admit rice from Country *A* into Country *C* duty-free, eliminating its previous duty of 10 per cent. Upon learning of this agreement, *B* demands that the tariff on its shoes entering Country *A* be reduced to 10 per cent. *B* claims that under the most-favored-nation provisions of its trade agreement with *A,* it is entitled to be treated as favorably as *A* treats any other country. Since the rate on shoes imported from *C* is now 10 per cent, the same rate should apply to shoes imported from *B*. *A* replies that it reduced the duty on shoes in its negotiations with *C* in exchange for *C*'s agreeing to admit Country *A*'s rice duty-free. The question is thus whether Country *B* is entitled to a reduction in the tariff on its shoes without making any concession itself or whether *B* must make a concession equivalent to that made by *C* to receive the same privilege from *A*. Where the most-favored-nation clause is "conditional," an equivalent concession must be made. Where the most-favored-nation clause is "unconditional," *B* is entitled to the tariff reduction granted to *C* without making any compensation to Country *A* whatsoever.

When it was in widespread use, the conditional form of the most-favored-nation clause frequently read as follows:

> In all that relates to duties of customs and navigation, the two high contracting parties promise, reciprocally, not to grant any favor, privilege or immunity to any other State which shall not instantly become common to the citizens and subjects of both parties respectively, gratuitously, if the concession or favor to such other state is gratuitous, and on allowing the same compensation, or its equivalent, if the concession is conditional.[8]

One problem with the conditional form of the clause is to decide when the compensation is "equivalent." Ordinarily in tariff

---

[8] Treaty of Commerce and Navigation between the United States and Belgium. 1875, art. 12, quoted in H. HAWKINS, COMMERCIAL TREATIES AND AGREEMENTS, PRINCIPLES AND PRACTICE 67 (1951).

negotiations numerous concessions are made on each side and only the sum of all these concessions may be regarded as equivalent. How, then, can one concession be isolated and a determination made of what compensation was given for it so that the third country can attempt to match that with an "equivalent" tariff concession? Moreover, to refer back to the example in the text, C reduced its duty on rice imported from A in exchange for A's concession on C's shoe exports. Suppose B is not a rice importer. Would a reduction of B's import duty on radios, for example, which A exports to B, be the equivalent of C's concession on rice? Furthermore, C admits A's rice duty-free. Must B admit A's radios duty-free for the concession to be equivalent? Fortunately, such problems as these need not often be resolved today because the conditional most-favored-nation clause has fallen into disuse. In fact, in the Anglo-American view of international law, it is generally assumed that most-favored-nation clauses are meant to be unconditional.[9] This, it should be emphasized, however, is only the Anglo-American view of international law. Other countries may have a different idea. It would therefore seem advisable when drafting a provision concerning most-favored-nation treatment that, if it is intended that the provision shall operate unconditionally, the word "unconditionally" be specifically mentioned in connection with the clause.

A comprehensive most-favored-nation clause dealing with the problems which have been raised would provide as follows:

1. Each Party shall accord to the other Party unconditional most-favored-nation treatment in all matters with respect to customs duties and charges of any kind imposed on or in connection with importation or exportation and with respect to the method of levying such duties and charges, and with respect to the rules and formalities connected with importation and exportation.

[9] See R. SNYDER, THE MOST-FAVORED-NATION CLAUSE 51 (1948). This represents, for the United States, a reversal of its earlier position, where it had maintained that a most-favored-nation clause appearing in unqualified form should be read as "if it implied the conditional limitation." J. VINER, *supra* note 6, at 18. For addtional problems involved in utilizing the conditional clause, see *id.* at 94, 103-8.

2. Accordingly, products of either Party imported into the territory of the other Party shall not be subject in regard to matters referred to in paragraph one of this article, to any duties or charges higher than those to which the like products of any third country are may hereafter be subject.

3. Similarly, products exported from the territory of either Party consigned to the territory of the other Party shall not be subjected in regard to matters referred to in paragraph one of this article, to any duties or charges higher than those to which the like products when consigned to the territory of any third country are or may hereafter be subject.

4. Any advantage, favor, privilege or immunity which has been or which may hereafter be granted by either Party in regard to the matters referred to in paragraph one of this article to any product originating in any third country or consigned to the territory of any third country shall be accorded immediately and unconditionally to the like product originating in or consigned to the territory of the other Party.[10]

Paragraph 1 of the above article states the general principle of most-favored-nation treatment. It provides for the application of that principle to "customs duties"—the traditional coverage—and also to "charges of any kind." This latter phrase was included to make clear the fact that the most-favored-nation obligation extends to such items as consular fees,[11] primage, import surtaxes and surcharges, clearance fees, and other "charges" for importation regardless of name.[12]

[10] This language is derived from Article I of the General Agreement on Tariffs and Trade. Similar language has been used in recent trade agreements. See, e.g., Agreement on Commerce between Japan and Peru, *done* at Tokyo, May 15, 1961, art. I, 451 U.N.T.S. 3, 30 (1963).

[11] But see Report of the Working Party, *Examination of the Montevideo Treaty*, in GATT, 9S BASIC INSTRUMENTS AND SELECTED DOCUMENTS, 90 (1961). ("Regarding consular taxes, it was stated that inasmuch as they represented services rendered they would not be considered as 'duties and charges' in the sense of Article III of the Treaty.")

[12] See also the formulation in Appendix A to ch. IX, pp. 209-10.

Method of Levying Duties

Paragraph 1 then goes on to apply the principle to the "method" of levying such duties and charges. Duties are generally levied in one of two ways. Ad valorem duties are calculated as a percentage of the value of the goods. Specific duties are computed in absolute sums of money per unit of goods (e,g., $10 per bushel, pound, yard, gallon).

Specific duties are detrimental to the interests of developing countries from two aspects. Insofar as their imports are concerned, protective and revenue-producing effects of a specific duty are gradually eroded by the inflation which usually accompanies development. From the point of view of developing country exports, specific duties "weigh heavily on lower-quality and cheaper products" which are the type of manufactures exported in the initial stages of development.[13] Thus where one country exports a product of high value and another exports a similar product of lower value, the imposition of the same specific duty on each product will result in discrimination in the economic, if not the legal, sense. Fortunately for the developing countries, the current trend is toward replacing specific duties with ad valorem duties.

In levying an ad valorem duty it is necessary to place a value upon the goods. Surprising as it must be to the uninitiated, this is an exercise which has been, and to some extent continues to be, surrounded by controversy. After a long history of rather shady practices, it was finally agreed at the Havana Charter negotiations that ad valorem tariffs should be calculated on "actual value." This formulation was aimed at stopping the practice of using "arbitrary or fictitious values" or values based, not on the product imported, but on the value of a similar domestically produced product. While the "actual value" rule was carried over into the GATT, the incorporation has not completely eliminated

---

[13] H. Johnson, Economic Policies Toward Less Developed Countries 104 (1967).

the abuses it was designed to correct.[14] Particularly obnoxious to the rule is the so-called American Selling Price system.

The American Selling Price system permits the calculation of ad valorem duties "as a percentage of . . . domestic wholesale price rather than . . . foreign, or export, price."[15] The system was designed to protect the infant American dyestuff industry in the 1920s. By the 1960s, when the American chemical industry was the most powerful in the world, it was still being applied to the extent that it afforded, in the case of some chemicals, tariff protection in excess of 100 per cent of the value of the imported goods. After hard bargaining in the Kennedy Round, the U.S. Government agreed to seek Congressional approval for abandonment of the system as it applied to Benezoid chemicals by January 1, 1969. But it continues to apply to knit gloves and rubber footwear, items of export interest to the developing countries.[16]

Aside from direct conflicts with the rule, however, the term "actual value" suffers from a considerable amount of imprecision. This was recognized at the Havana Conference, and there were

[14] See G. CURZON, MULTILATERAL COMMERCIAL DIPLOMACY 315 (1965). ("Though customs valuation and formalities with regard to importation and exportation are subject to Gatt ruling, Gatt control over these matters seems to have been negligible. There is evidence that differential customs administration make *de jure* tariff rates non-comparable. Though the Agreement states quite clearly that value for custom purposes 'should not be based on values of merchandise of national origin or on arbitrary or fictitious values,' this regulation frequently falls a victim to mandatory domestic legislation.") (Footnote omitted.)

[15] Anderson, *An American Views American Selling Price*, EUROPEAN COMMUNITY, February 1967, at 13.
> . . . [T]he American selling price of any article produced in the United States shall be the price, including the cost of all containers and coverings of whatever nature and all other expenses incidental to placing the article in condition packed ready for delivery, at which such article is freely sold or, in the absence of sales, offered for sale for domestic consumption in the principal market of the United States, in the ordinary course of trade and in the usual wholesale quantities, or the price that the manufacturer, producer, or owner would have received or was willing to receive for such article when sold for domestic consumption in the ordinary course of trade and in the usual wholesale quantities, at the time of exportation of the imported article.

Tariff Act of 1930, as amended, Title IV, § 402 (e), 19 U.S.C. 1401 a (1965).

[16] Under the provisions of § 336 of the Tariff Act of 1930, as amended 19 U.S.C. § 1336 (1965), rubber-soled fabric-upper footwear (designated by headnote 3(b), part iA, Schedule 7 of the Tariff Schedules) and wool knit gloves (designated by headnote 4, part 1C, Schedule 7 of the Tariff Schedules) are subject to the American Selling Price System.

several proposals defining the term. This is where the dispute reached its peak. One formulation was "to define actual value as the price established in the ordinary course of trade between an independent buyer and an independent seller." This definition was strongly supported by the United Kingdom and just as strongly opposed by the United States. The reason for the opposition was that the great majority of United States foreign trade is conducted through "associated houses"—where buyer or seller is a subsidiary of the other—and the formulation would exclude this trade for valuation purposes.

Another proposal, championed by Canada, provided that "customs value should be so assessed as to satisfy clearly defined and stable conditions which conform to commercial usage." Here again the United States objected, this time to the latter phrase— "conform to commercial usage." The issue here was that the Canadians wanted to recognize that when goods are imported in quantity, their price per unit is lower, and therefore the total tariff bill should be proportionately lower. This, the Canadians maintained, was the only possible content that could be given to the rule of "actual value." The United States, on the other hand, "objected to any definition which would result in generally lower duties per unit for large importers than those paid by small importers at the same time and place." [17]

Eventually a compromise formula was reached. Actual value was to be "the price at which, at a time and place determined by the legislation of the country of importation, such or like merchandise is sold or offered for sale in the ordinary course of trade under fully competitive conditions." It was also agreed that if "the price of such or like merchandise is governed by the quantity in a particular transaction, the price to be considered should uniformly be related to either (i) comparable quantities, or (ii) quantities not less favourable to importers than those in which

[17] W. Brown, The United States and the Restoration of World Trade 107 (1950).

the greater volume of the merchandise is sold in the trade between the countries of exportation and importation." [18] This formula met both controversial issues. On the question of imports by associated houses, the words "in the ordinary course of trade" and "under fully competitive conditions" were designed to protect the tariff revenues of the importing state from being eroded by having associated houses value goods imported from parent companies at a nominal rate. At the same time, the United States agreed to accept an interpretation which permitted imports by associated houses to be included in establishing customs values in all cases except where "price is not the sole consideration" in the transaction.[19] The second sentences relates to the quantity discount question and incorporates both the Canadian and U.S. positions. Under alternative (i) an importing state may take into account quantity discounts, while under (ii) small importers are protected against having to pay more than the "usual" amount of duty.[20]

The key point that the formula leaves open is the "time and place" that the price should be fixed. This is left to the legislation of the importing state. There are two schools of thought on this issue. One practice, with the United States as its principal proponent, determines value as the price at the *time of exportation*

---

[18] Article VII, 2(b), GATT, 55 U.N.T.S. 188, 216 (1950). This language is virtually identical with art. 35, 3(b) of the Havana Charter. See C. WILCOX, A CHARTER FOR WORLD TRADE 270-71 (1949).

[19] Havana Charter *Ad* art. 35, para. 3, note 3, C. WILCOX, *supra* at 325; *Ad* art. VII, para. 2 (2), GATT, 55 U.N.T.S. 188, 298 (1950).

[20] Countries which take into account quantity discounts in calculating customs value may make it difficult for developing countries to break into their markets, as initial quantities of goods from a new source are apt to be smaller than the volume of imports from established suppliers. See Annex II, Addendum to art. I, note 3 of the Brussels Convention, 171 U.N.T.S. 305, 322 (1953), "Where the normal price would depend upon the quantity in the sale, it shall be determined on the assumption that the sale is a sale of the quantity to be valued"; Customs Tariff of Canada, § 36(1), CAN. REV. STAT. c. 58, as amended, ". . . value for duty shall . . . be the fair market value, at the time when and place from which the goods were shipped directly to Canada, of like goods when sold . . . in the same or substantially the same quantities for home consumption in the ordinary course of trade under competitive conditions."

in the *place of exportation*.[21] The other view, which might be termed the Brussels position, is incorporated in the Convention on the Valuation of Goods for Customs Purposes, *done* at Brussels, December 15, 1950,[22] and carried over into the domestic legislation of the signatories to that Convention, mainly the United Kingdom and the countries of Continental Europe. The Brussels approach fixes value at the *time when the duty becomes payable in the importing country*.[23] The principal difference between the two approaches is whether the cost of freight will be included in the value of the goods for customs purposes. Freight is included in the Brussels definition; it is not in the American. What this means in practical terms is that distant exporters, already handicapped by having to absorb greater freight charges than their competitors who are located closer to the markets, are doubly handicapped because their large freight charges form the basis for their having to pay larger customs duties. Thus the Brussels approach seems designed to penalize the United States and Japan as against exporters on the Continent. It also works a discrimination between developing countries which are closer to Europe and those which are farther away. On the other hand, from the point of view of ease of customs administration, the Brussels system is clearly preferable. For it is easier for an importer to establish the value of an imported commodity in his own country

---

[21] ". . . [T]he export value of imported merchandise shall be the price, at the time of exportation to the United States of the merchandise undergoing appraisement, at which such or similar merchandise is freely sold or, in the absence of sales, offered for sale in the principal markets of the country of exportation, in the usual wholesale quantities and in the ordinary course of trade, for exportation to the United States, plus, when not included in such price, the cost of all containers and coverings of whatever nature and all other expenses incidental to placing the merchandise in condition, packed ready for shipment to the United States." Tariff Act of 1930, § 402, as amended, 19 U.S.C. § 1401 a (b) (1965). If such value cannot be determined, then the "United States value" or the "constructed value" (in that order) are to be used. *Id* at § 402 (a).

[22] 171 U.N.T.S. 305 (1953).

[23] "For the purposes of levying duties of customs, the value of any goods imported for home consumption shall be taken to be the normal price, that is to say, the price which they would fetch at the time when the duty becomes payable on a sale in the open market between buyer and seller independent of each other." Annex I, art I(1), 171 U.N.T.S. 305, 320 (1953).

than it is for him to establish the price in the "principal markets" of the exporting state. As a corollary, it is easier for customs officials to verify the figures produced by the importer if they relate to the value in the importing state.

PRODUCTS OF EITHER PARTY

Paragraphs 2 and 3 of the above-quoted most-favored-nation provision define the meaning of most-favored-nation treatment with respect to imports and exports. Note that Paragraph 2 limits the operation of the most-favored-nation principle to the "products of either Party." The reason for this limitation may be illustrated by the following example. Assume Country A has a two-line tariff according to which it levies a 10 per cent ad valorem duty on radios imported from countries with which it has a most-favored-nation agreement and a 25 per cent ad valorem duty on radios imported from all other countries. Countries B and C both export radios. A and B are parties to a trade agreement providing for most-favored-nation treatment. There is no agreement between A and C, so that radios exported from C and A would be subject to the 25 per cent rate. In an effort to circumvent this high duty, could C ship radios to B, and B then reexport these radios to A and have them admitted to A after paying only a 10 per cent duty (the rate which radios exported from B to A are charged?) Without reference to the trade agreement, one's initial reaction must be negative. If A had intended that radios produced in Country C should enter its territory at the 10 per cent rate, it would have entered into an agreement to that effect with C. To allow such round about transactions would undermine the whole purpose of a two-line tariff, which is to discriminate between countries with whom A has most-favored-nation arrangements and those with whom she does not.[24] Yet in the past, bona fide disputes have

[24] Problems concerning country of origin are particularly important in a free-trade area, where preferential tariff treatment is limited to goods originating in the member states. For an explanation and insight into the complexities of the origin rules in the European Free Trade Area, see *How to Claim EFTA Tariff Benefits,* SUPPLEMENT TO 192 BRD. OF TRADE J. 20 (1967).

arisen between parties to trade agreements over problems of this type, although they have not been so clear cut as the one used for illustration. For example, Mauritania exports to the EEC fish caught by its nationals off the Canary Islands. If those fish are the products of Mauritania, they are entitled to favorable tariff treatment since Mauritania is an Associated State; if, on the other hand, they are the product of the Canary Islands they are subject to import duty.[25]

To meet these problems, Paragraph 2 of the most-favored-nation clause covers only "products of either party." This phrase raises the question of just what is a "product of a party." One approach to resolving this issue would be to tighten up the language of Paragraph 2 by adding after the word "products" in line 1, the words "originating in the territory." This is sometimes done. The usual technique, however, is to include in the trade agreement a separate article defining "products." Such articles are of three types.

First, there is what may be termed the "national" approach to defining "products" which is illustrated by the following provision:

In this agreement, "products," when referring to Country *A* means products which are eligible under the customs law of Country *B* to be imported into Country *B* as the produce or manufacture of Country *A*.

"Products," when referring to Country *B,* means products which are

---

[25] See also Treaty of Commerce, Establishment and Navigation between the United Kingdom and Japan, *done* at London, November 14, 1962, art. 16, [1963] Gr. Brit. T.S. No. 53 (CMD. 2085) at 10. ". . . (2) For purposes of this Article . . : (a) fish, whales and other natural produce of the sea taken by vessels of either Contracting Party and (b) products produced or manufactured at sea in vessels of either Contracting Party from fish, whales and other natural produce of the sea . . . shall be deemed to be products originating in the territories of that Contracting Party;"; Protocol of Signature, *id.* at 23 ". . . [11] The provisions of paragraph (2) of Article 16 shall not preclude Japan from treating fish, whales, and other natural produce of the sea taken by vessels of the United Kingdom within the territory of any other foreign country, and products produced or manufactured at sea therefrom, as products originating in the territory of that foreign country."

eligible, under the customs law of Country *A* to be imported into Country *A* as the produce or manufacture of Country *B*.[26]

With this type of provision, it is up to the importing country to decide whether the goods are the product of the exporting country and thus entitled to most-favored-nation treatment. This approach represents the generally accepted international law on the subject, so that in the absence of any attempt at defining "products" in the trade agreement, each importing country may determine the country of origin of imported goods. This approach has the drawback of requiring that each of the parties have complete knowledge of the other's system or procedures for determining the country of origin of imports. Where such information is available and such procedures considered adequate to protect the exporting country, such a formulation is perfectly acceptable. Where the information is not available, however, or where exporting countries desire to have more of a voice in the determination of what goods will be considered as their products, the following provision may prove more acceptable:

1. For purpose of this agreement, goods originating in Country *A* shall be regarded as *A* products and goods originating in the Country *B* as *B* products.[27]
2. The country of origin shall be deemed to be the country where a product was produced and manufactured or underwent its last substantial processing, or in the case of non-processed agricultural products the country where the products were actually produced.

This article provides objective standards for the determination of what are the "products" of a particular country. And although these standards are not at all precise—"produced or manufactured," "last substantial processing," "actually produced"—they do

[26] See, e.g., Trade Agreement between New Zealand and Malaya, *done* at Wellington, February 3, 1961, art I, 447 U.N.T.S. 251, 252 (1962).

[27] See, e.g., art. 2 of the Trade Agreement between Turkey and Pakistan, *done* at Ankara, December 18, 1964, reprinted in TURK. OFF. GAZETTE, No. 12,005, May 24, 1965 (unofficial translation). "For the purpose of this Agreement, commodities produced or manufactured in and exported from Turkey shall be termed as Turkish commodities, while commodities produced or manufactured in and exported from Pakistan shall be termed Pakistani commodities."

represent a different approach to solving the problem than the one presented by clauses which refer to the legislation of the parties. For, in interpreting these standards, practice and usage under other international agreements containing similar language would be much more relevant than would each party's legislation. Thus an international law standard has been substituted for that of the domestic legislation of the parties.

For countries desiring a more precise solution, the following language may be substituted for paragraph 2 above:

2. Non-processed agricultural products shall be deemed to originate in the country where the products were grown or raised.
3. Semi-processed, processed, or manufactured goods shall be deemed to originate in a country when at least 50 percent of the value of the goods is composed of the value of raw materials originating in that country and/or labor expended on them in that country.[28]

Clauses such as these are usually drafted to reflect the domestic legislation of one or both of the parties and thus incorporate elements of the national clause discussed earlier. They have the advantage, however, of incorporating the local standards into the agreement, and thus limiting the ability of a party to change its laws in a way which might be detrimental to the other party.

In addition to incorporating in trade agreements a standard for determining the origin of goods, countries have on occasion sought to expedite the application of the standard to imported products by requiring certificates of origin. Certificates of origin are nothing more than statements that the goods are the product of Country *A* or Country *B*. Their value is that instead of this statement being made by the exporter and/or importer, as would normally be the case, the statement in the certificate of origin is made by a responsible body designated by the government of the exporting country. "Both parties reserve the right to subject the

---

[28] See, e.g., Final Protocol of the Treaty of Commerce and Navigation between Finland and Latvia, *done* at Helsingfors, August 23, 1924, 37 L.N.T.S. 383, 397 (1925), in H. HAWKINS *supra* note 7, at 220, note 2 to Chapter IV; Trade Agreement between the Union of South Africa and the Federation of Rhodesia and Nyasaland, *done* at Salisbury, May 16, 1960, art. 7, 376 U.N.T.S. 217, 221 (1960).

importation of goods to the submission of a certificate of origin issued by an organization authorized in this respect by the Government of the country of origin."

GOODS IN TRANSIT

Attaching a nationality to shipments of goods may raise problems in another way. Suppose there is a most-favored-nation agreement between Country *A* and Country *B* and products of Country *A* are first shipped to Country *C* and then transhipped to Country *B*. Are they entitled to most-favored-nation treatment or do they become products of Country *C* which do not qualify for most-favored-nation treatment?

At one time exports from the United States to Poland, between whom there was a most-favored-nation agreement, were shipped from the United States to Hamburg, Bremen, or Antwerp and then trans-shipped to Poland. Poland, however, desired to build up the port of Gdynia and also to increase the traffic on Polish shipping lines which ran directly from the United States to the port of Gdynia. The Poles, therefore, refused to grant most-favored-nation treatment to goods which originated in the United States but which were first shipped to Hamburg, Bremen, or Antwerp and then on to Poland. The outcome of the dispute turned on the manner in which the goods were handled in the three ports. Under general principles of international law, if the American goods were merely *stored* in Hamburg, Bremen, or Antwerp and then trans-shipped to Poland, they would be entitled to most-favored-nation treatment under the agreement. In order for Poland to legally deny most-favored-nation treatment to such goods, it would have been necessary to state in the agreement that such treatment would only apply to "products originating in *and coming directly from*" the United States.[29]

[29] This is not uncommon. The Canadian Government limits most-favored-nation treatment to goods imported directly from the country of origin. See Customs Tariff, CAN. REV. STAT. c. 60, § 3 (3) (1952); G. ELLIOT, TARIFF PROCEDURES AND TRADE BARRIERS 19 (1955). Australia maintains a similar requirement. See 191

Countries preferring not to rely on the vagaries of general international law may include in the trade agreement a provision stating that goods which arrive from a third country shall receive most-favored-nation treatment in the country of ultimate destination. This may be done in either of two ways. The most-favored-nation provision itself may be worded to apply to products of either party "from whatever place arriving." [30] More commonly, however, trade agreements provide that

1. The products of either Party after they have been in transit through the territories of one or more third countries shall not, upon their importation into the territory of the other Party, be subject to duties or charges higher than those to which they would be subject if they were imported directly from the territory of the other Party.

2. The provisions of the preceding paragraph shall also apply to goods and commodities which during their transportation through the territory of a third country underwent trans-shipment, repacking, or storing in warehouses.

LIKE PRODUCTS

Most-favored-nation clauses guarantee equal customs treatment with respect to "like products." This phrase has occasionally

---

BRD. OF TRADE J. 1547 (1966). However, the "Australian Department of Trade have advised that goods shipped from Britain via European ports or by any other indirect routes will be accepted as complying with the direct shipment provision if evidence is produced to the Collector of Customs at the port of importation to show that the intended destination of the goods, when originally shipped, was Australia." *Id* at 53.

Limiting most-favored-nation treatment to direct shipments was prohibited in the early drafts of the Havana Charter. See Meeting of the Preparatory Committee of the International Conference on Trade and Employment, October 30, 1946, U.N. Doc. E/PC/T/C 11/27, at 4. At Canadian insistence, however, an exception was created to allow members to "maintain . . . requirements of direct consignment existing on the date of the Charter . . ." W. BROWN, THE UNITED STATES AND THE RESTORATION OF WORLD TRADE 446 (1950) (art. XXXIII, 7).

[30] See, e.g., Treaty of Commerce and Navigation between Japan and Poland, *done* at Warsaw, December 7, 1922, art. 5, 32 L.N.T.S. 61, 66 (1925); Treaty of Commerce, Establishment and Navigation between the United Kingdom and Japan, *done* at London, November 14, 1962, art. 16, [1963] Gr. Brit. T.S. No. 53 (CMD. 2085) at 10.

caused problems. For example, at one time Germany made a special tariff concession to Portugal on sardines. At the time Norway had a trade agreement with Germany providing for most-favored-nation treatment. Norway, which exports herring to Germany, claimed the benefit of the concession on the ground that its herrings were prepared in a " 'like manner' " as Portuguese sardines and the herrings were, therefore, a " 'like product.' " [31]

To circumvent the requirement of equal tariff treatment for like products, countries have on occasion resorted to tariff reclassification.

Tariff Reclassification

Assume that there exists a most-favored-nation agreement between Country A and Country B. A exports bananas to B. B's rate of duty is 10 per cent. B makes an agreement with Country C providing that C may export bananas to B at a duty rate of 5 per cent. In the normal course of events the 5 per cent duty should now be applied to exports of bananas from A because A is entitled to most-favored-nation treatment. But suppose that B amends its tariff so that it now provides that green bananas shall be subject to an import duty of 5 per cent and yellow bananas to an import duty of 10 per cent. If C's bananas are of the green variety and A's of the yellow variety, the tariff concession made to C need not then be passed on to A. By virtue of the most-favored-nation principle, country A is entitled to be treated equally in regard to "like" commodities. B could maintain that yellow bananas and green bananas are different commodities, and therefore A is not being discriminated against.

This type of escape from the obligations of most-favored-nation treatment was not unusual prior to the Second World War. The classic case occurred in the German Conventional Tariff of 1902.

[31] For a brief discussion of this dispute, see I. KRAVIS, DOMESTIC INTERESTS AND INTERNATIOAL OBLIGATIONS 125-26 (1963).

Germany desired to grant Switzerland a preferential rate of duty on the importation of Swiss cattle, but did not wish to have this new low rate apply to Belgium, Denmark, France, Holland, and Russia with whom the Germans had most-favored-nation agreements. The solution was to amend the German tariff to provide for the importation, at a new low rate of duty, of "large dapple mountain cattle or brown cattle reared at a spot at least 300 meters above sea level and having at least one month's grazing each year at a spot at least 800 meters above sea level." Another example of such shenanigans is the tariff negotiation between Canada and France which resulted in the Canadian tariff being amended to create as a class of goods "mineral water from the springs of Vichy." Nor are these isolated examples. In a survey made in 1927 it was found that the Indian tariff classified cotton piece goods under 169 sections, and that the Italian tariff schedules contained 252 varieties of iron and steel chains.

To forestall discrimination by means of tariff reclassification, parties to a trade agreement may include an article such as the following: "In all matters relating to tariff classification, the Parties agree to adhere to the tariff categories set forth in the Convention on Nomenclature for the Classification of Goods in Customs Tariffs, *done* at Brussels, December 15, 1950."

The Brussels Nomenclature (BTN)—as it is usually referred to —is the result of studies begun in 1947 by the European Customs Union Study Group. It was early decided that one of the most pressing problems with which the group should concern itself was the matter of establishing a standard tariff classification system to prevent the type of discrimination illustrated above. When general agreement had been reached on the classification of different goods in international trade, the results were incorporated in an international agreement. The nomenclature has now been adopted in all the countries of Western Europe and many developing countries.

For countries which do not maintain customs traiffs based upon the Brussels Nomenclature, a provision such as the following included in the trade agreement will help to forestall injury by discriminatory tariff classification:

1. The Parties agree to consult together prior to putting into effect any reclassification of their customs tariffs which may materially affect a product in which either Party has a vital trade interest.
2. A Party shall be deemed to have a vital trade interest in a product if exports of that product constitute ...... per cent of that Party's total exports to the other Party.

LIMITED MOST-FAVORED-NATION TREATMENT

In the early stages of the growth of trade between two countries, one or both of them may be reluctant to grant to the other across-the-board most-favored-nation treatment. A country may be uncertain as to the extent to which the goods of the other party may find a market in its territory. This may lead to fear that the reduction of trade barriers will be followed by a flood of imports which would disrupt traditional trade and distribution patterns in the country. Moreover, an unexpected substantial increase in either export or import trade may have undesirable political repercussions. Trade may be shifted from friends and allies to less friendly though more "efficient" newcomers. A country may also wish to limit the granting of most-favored-nation treatment because it believes that the value of its concession may far outweigh the advantages to be derived from them. This would be true, for example, where one country is a low tariff country and the other maintains high rates of duty. Most-favored-nation treatment will prevent discrimination; it will not, however, aid in lowering the higher tariff barriers. For these reasons, among others, trade agreements are sometimes found in which the granting of most-favored-nation treatment is limited to one or a few products. In the 1926 Trade Convention between France and Greece, for example, most-favored-nation treatment applied only to the importation of Greek wines into France. To limit the grant of most-favored-nation treatment in this manner, countries may include a provision in their trade agreement as follows:

1. The products of either Party enumerated in the schedules annexed hereto on importation into or exportation from the territory of the other Party shall enjoy in all matters with respect to customs duties and charges of any kind imposed on or in connection with importation or exportation and with respect to the method of levying such duties and charges, and with respect to the rules and formalities connected with importation and exportation, treatment no less favorable than that accorded the like products of any third country.

2. Each Party undertakes to receive with good will and to give consideration to any request which may be made by the other Party for the grant of most-favored-nation treatment with respect to Products of that Party other than those enumerated in the schedules referred to in paragraphs 1 hereof.[32]

Most-favored-nation treatment has occasionally been limited by country. India, for example, at one time classified its trading partners according to "currency group." It granted most-favored-nation treatment to all countries within "the same currency group." Other countries have granted treatment as favorable as that accorded to member states of the Organization for Economic Cooperation and Development (OECD), or the "Hague Club" (a multilateral trade and payments arrangement in force between Brazil and Austria, the Benelux Countries, France, the Federal Republic of Germany, Italy, and the United Kingdom). And some members of the British Commonwealth grant "most-favored-country" treatment, i.e., treatment as favorable as that received by any other non-Commonwealth country. A more unusual limitation on most favored-nation is found in the Peace of Frankfort (1871) which provided that both France and Germany would grant the other as favorable treatment as that accorded by either to Austria, Belgium, England, Holland, Russia, and Switzerland.

Although limited grants of most-favored-nation treatment are

---

[32] See Exchange of Notes between New Zealand and Switzerland, *done* at Wellington, May 5, 1938, art. 1, 189 L.N.T.S. 167, 168 (1938). See also Exchange of Notes between the Bulgarian and Greek Governments constituting Commercial Agreements, *done* at Sofia, May 25, September 16, March 11, and March 15, 1938, 195 L.N.T.S. 27, 28 (1939).

more the exception than the rule, there is a possibility that this type of legal provision will again come into wide use if current proposals for preferences from the industrialized countries to the developing countries are put into force. At the first United Nations Conference on Trade and Development (UNCTAD), it was proposed that the developed countries eliminate their tariffs (and nontariff barriers) to imports of manufactured and semimanufactured products of the developing countries while maintaining their existing restrictions on imports of similar products from the industrial states. If such a proposal were adopted, its implementation might take several forms. Initially, a developed country might suspend its tariffs on certain specified products emanating from the developing world. This is what has been done by Australia. As this action is experimental, and on a very small scale, the total volume of goods involved is approximately $15 million, this unilateral format is probably the most desirable. But its unilateral nature is also its principle shortcoming. A developing country would hesitate to reorient its trade to take advantage of these preferences if they could be changed at will by the Australian Government. Instead, a developing country which saw an advantage in such a preferential system would most likely seek a trade agreement commitment from the Australian Government as to the extent and duration of the preferences. To generalize from these observations, it would appear that any scheme for preferences from the rich to the poor nations would, to be effective, have to contain a commitment that the preferences would last for a specified period of time. Moreover the proposal at the UNCTAD was that preferences would be open to all developing countries. Rather than have each developing country enter into an agreement with each industrial country granting preferences, a clear case is presented for including all such commitments in a multilateral agreement. Such an agreement would provide that all the industrialized nations which are parties to it would agree to suspend their tariffs on all manufactures and semimanufactures originating in developing countries. The legal terminology would be a suspension of duties on a most-favored-nation basis to all developing countries, i.e., a limited most-favored-nation clause.

Students of the preference proposal have pointed out that preferences open to all developing countries might benefit only the most developed, leaving poorer nations with little or no benefits from the scheme. In an effort to aid the less-developed, limited most-favored-nation treatment might be further refined by establishing categories of developing countries and granting varying levels of preference to each category. While refining the preference proposals, however, such a suggestion would compound the difficulties in administering the scheme. The simplest preference proposal involves adding another column to the tariff schedule to cover imports from developing countries. To further break down this classification into more developed developing countries, less developed developing countries, etc., would involve creating a new column for each separate category. The ensuing complication of customs administration in the developed countries might loom so large in terms of opposition from customs officials and added costs of customs collection that the refinements might well be counterproductive. Whatever form of preference arrangement is adopted, however, its reduction to a legal commitment will take some form of limited most-favored-nation treatment.

CONCLUSION

At the beginning of this chapter it was noted that customs duties are the traditional means of controlling imports. They are not, however, the most precise method for achieving this end. For it is extremely difficult to predict exactly what effect a given rate of duty will have on the quantity of goods imported. Economists may be able to plot curves showing how demand will vary the price, but the curves themselves must be based on the kind of data which is nonexistent in most developing countries, and only accurate in a very general way in the remainder. Moreover, to the extent that duties are imposed to protect local producers, they are liable to fail in their purpose for two reasons. As foreign producers become more efficient and the costs of their products decline, a given tariff becomes less effective as a means of protecting local production. With each decrease in the cost of an imported product, the rate of duty will have to be raised to provide an equivalent degree of protection. Since this cannot be done expeditiously in most governments, local interests tend to favor other forms of protection. Duties will also fail to protect local producers where the supply of the imported product is relatively inelastic, i.e., where it remains high despite a drop in price. Where this situation prevails, an increased import duty may be absorbed by the exporters and a large volume of goods continue to flow to the importing country. From the standpoint of the importing country's revenues, this may be an excellent result, but it will not aid domestic producers who seek reduction or elimination of the foreign supply from the local market.

These "shortcomings" of customs duties became readily apparent in the 1930s. During the Depression many countries witnessed a collapse of their export markets. In an effort to maintain a favorable balance of trade it was believed necessary to place substantial restrictions on imports. This could not have been done effectively by tariff increases for several reasons. First, many tariff rates were "bound" (fixed) in commercial treaties. Second, prices were falling so rapidly that tariffs could not be changed quickly enough to keep out imports. Finally, as noted above, the effect of any given tariff rate could not be measured in accurate enough terms. In addition to restricting total imports, many countries felt a need to reorient their trade towards their principal foreign creditors, yet were bound by most-favored-nation provisions to treat all trading partners equally insofar as tariffs were concerned. In those circumstances, countries resorted to other types of import controls, the most popular being quantitative import restrictions.

III. QUANTITATIVE RESTRICTIONS ON IMPORTS

Every country, developing and developed, maintains quantitative restrictions on some categories of imports.[1] And several commentators have taken the view that since the Kennedy Round, quantitative import restrictions have become more significant barriers to world trade than customs tariffs.

Quantitative import restrictions are almost totally prohibited by the General Agreement on Tariffs and Trade (Article XI). There are, however, two major exceptions to this rule. The first covers agricultural or fisheries products and is utilized primarily to protect producers of temperate zone foodstuffs in developed countries. Since the demand for such food products is relatively inelastic, tariff barriers do not offer desired protection. As most developing countries do not grow temperate-zone foods, they have not been directly affected by these quantitative restrictions.[2] Moreover, technological innovation has made the production of many temperate-zone foods a capital intensive process so that the comparative advantages in such foods would seem to lie with the capital rich industrial nations.

The second exception to the GATT prohibition permits the

[1] The extent of the use of quantitative import controls can be gathered generally by examining the recent editions of GATT, BASIC INSTRUMENTS AND SELECTED DOCUMENTS and INTERNATIONAL MONETARY FUND, ANNUAL REPORT ON EXCHANGE RESTRICTIONS. Details as to particular national import quotas are reprinted in THE BOARD OF TRADE JOURNAL.

[2] For an argument that these restrictions have an adverse indirect effect on developing country exports, see SECRETARY-GENERAL OF THE UNITED NATIONS CONFERENCE ON TRADE AND DEVELOPMENT, TOWARDS A NEW TRADE POLICY FOR DEVELOPMENT 13, U.N. Doc. E/CONF. 46/3 (1964).

use of quantitative restrictions for balance of payments purposes. This exception was originally designed to cover the postwar monetary arrangements in Europe. That purpose has largely been accomplished with the return to external convertibility in Western Europe. But GATT Article XVIII provides for the use of quantitative restrictions by a developing country to "safeguard its external financial position and to insure a level of reserves adequate for the implementation of its programme of economic development." This provision has been interpreted liberally—too liberally for some commentators who have characterized it as a "rubber clause"—and many developing countries have taken advantage of it to impose quantitative import restrictions. Moreover, as Article XVIII permits a developing country coming within its terms to choose the products on which it will impose the quantitative restrictions (Subsection 10), the provision has been used as a means of protecting infant industries from competing imports. Thus despite the GATT prohibition on quantitative restrictions the exceptions are sufficiently broad as to permit their continued use on a significant scale.

From the point of view of the developing countries the most important quantitative restrictions existing today are, however, totally outside the GATT and in open violation of the Agreement. These are the restrictions imposed by the developed countries on the world trade in cotton textiles which constituted between 20 and 25 per cent of developing country manufactured exports during the period from 1961 through 1965. The history of these restrictions goes back to the time that Japan sought full membership in the GATT. Many of the Contracting Parties feared that if Japan were accorded the full rights of nondiscrimination to which she would be entitled as a member of GATT, "cheap" Japanese goods would "flood" their markets. The fear that this would happen was grounded in the "low wages" paid to Japanese workers. It was believed that these low wages enabled the Japanese to cut prices on cotton textiles to such a point that the protective effects of the tariffs in the major Western nations could be completely negated. And this despite the fact that *nominal* ad valorem tariff rates were already high. On woven fabrics the rates ranged from 16 to 21 per cent in the EEC, 7.75 to 33 per cent in the United States and 17.5 per cent in the United Kingdom. Since tariffs were considered ineffective, the "injured" parties turned to the certainty of protection offered by quantitative restrictions. But quantitative restrictions are not permissible under the GATT rules apart from the two exceptions mentioned above, neither of which was applicable. The result was that Japan "voluntarily" agreed with several of the Contracting Parties to *restrict exports* of cotton textiles.[3] Although quantitative restrictions on imports and on exports differ in minor aspects to be discussed, the economic effect of either device in these circumstances is the same and there can be little room for doubt that the voluntary export quotas "violated the spirit of GATT." Nonetheless, they were effective in greatly reducing Japanese cotton textile exports, So effective, in fact, that similar arrangements were worked out by the United Kingdom with regard to cotton textile exports from Hong Kong, India, and Pakistan on an *ad hoc basis.* Rather than have this situation continue, with each importing state reaching a separate agreement with each exporting state, and because of its political interest in Japan, the United States proposed in 1959 that the GATT undertake a study of the problem of "sharp increases in imports, over a brief period of time and in a narrow range of commodities [which] can have serious economic, political and social repercussions in the importing countries." The GATT investigations led to the Contracting Parties adopting a definition of a new kind of economic evil, "market disruption." The Contracting Parties decided that market disruption occurs where the following elements are found in combination:

(i) a sharp and substantial increase or potential increase of imports of particular products from particular sources;

[3] For a detailed discussion of the tortuous path of these negotiations see G. PATTERSON, DISCRIMINATION IN INTERNATIONAL TRADE, THE POLICY ISSUES. 1945-1965, 272-302 (1966).

(ii) these products are offered at prices which are substantially below those prevailing for similar goods of comparable quality in the market of the importing country;

(iii) there is serious damage to domestic producers or threat thereof;

(iv) the price differentials referred to in paragraph (ii) above do not arise from governmental intervention in the fixing or formation of prices or from dumping practices.[4]

While the impetus for consideration of the "market disruption" problem came from the accession of Japan to the GATT, it is clear that Japan was not the only country on the minds of the Contracting Parties. In particular, officials of the European Economic Community were worried about future exports from the developing countries. They reasoned that by importing advanced capital equipment and by increasing labor productivity, while paying low wages, the developing countries could soon begin to "disrupt" their markets with a variety of products. This was already happening in the case of cotton textiles. So that at this time imports of cotton textiles from Hong Kong, India, Japan, and Pakistan were faced with "almost complete restriction" in France. The Federal Republic of Germany "applied restrictions on imports of several important items." And the Benelux countries, Italy, and the Scandinavian countries "restricted imports of most items from Japan."[5] The EEC was thus ready to support the United States proposal, made in 1961, that the GATT devote its attention to the trade in cotton textiles "with a view to reaching agreement on arrangements for the orderly development of the trade in such products, so as progressively to increase the export possibilities of the less-developed countries and territories and of Japan, while at the same time avoiding disruptive conditions in import markets."

The developing countries were willing to go along with the proposal for several reasons. They focused on the portion of the American proposal which provided for a progressive increase in

[4] GATT, 9S Basic Instruments and Selected Documents 26-28 (1961). On dumping, see pp. 162–66 infra.

[5] GATT, A Study on Cotton Textiles 82 (1966).

the export possibilities of the less-developed countries and hoped that this might be a breakthrough in their gaining access to a larger share of the European and American markets. Moreover, the Kennedy Administration was seeking new, liberal trade legislation which the developing countries supported. The price for passage of the new legislation, however, was increased protection for the American cotton textile industry. In addition, the developing countries favored a scheme which would bring the system of bilateral export restriction agreements under the GATT, hoping thereby to subject them to the GATT's periodic inspection and review procedures. Finally, the developing countries feared that if they did not agree to this new proposal, the alternative would be the increasing imposition of import quotas on their cotton textile exports.

The Long-Term Arrangement Regarding International Trade in Cotton Textiles entered into force on October 1, 1962.[6] As of July 1966 there were 29 parties, divided into three categories. Group I includes Australia, Austria, Canada, Denmark, the member states of the European Economic Community, Finland, Norway, Sweden, the United Kingdom, and the United States. Group II consists of Colombia, Hong Kong, India, Israel, Jamaica, Mexico, Pakistan, Portugal, the Republic of China, the Republic of Korea, Spain, Turkey, and the United Arab Republic. Japan occupies a separate category, being both an industrialized country and a major exporter. The Arrangement defines cotton textiles to include yarns, fabrics, made-up articles, garments, and other textile manufactured products, in which cotton represents more than 50 per cent (by weight) of the fiber content. The Arrangement incorporates the definition of market disruption mentioned above. It then goes on to provide that countries maintaining non-tariff import barriers (i.e. quantitative restrictions) will progressively

---

[6] The text is reprinted in GATT, 11S Basic Instruments and Selected Documents 25 (1963).

The initial period of validity of the Arrangement was 5 years. On April 3, 1967, the text of a protocol was agreed upon which extends the Arrangement for 3 years beginning October 10, 1967. See Int'l Trade F., June 1967, at 35.

relax them, and, in particular, specifies a percentage by which the quotas of certain countries will be increased between 1962 and 1967. In the case of an importing member not imposing non-tariff barriers, such a member may, after finding that its market is being disrupted or threatened with disruption, and after consultations, limit imports either by agreement with the exporting states [7] or, failing such agreement, by the imposition of quotas which limit total imports to "actual imports . . . of such products during the twelve-month period terminating three months preceding the month in which the request for consultation is made." In the latter case, such quotas must be increased by 5 per cent for each subsequent twelve-month period.

The Arrangement represents an improvement over the previous situation in two respects. It specifically recognizes the claim of the developing countries to increased shares of the markets of the developed countries. And the Arrangement provides for an annual review of the operations under GATT auspices. On the other hand, the Arrangement erodes a cardinal principle of international trade theory, that low labor costs are not a legitimate ground for restricting imports. They could not be if the theory of comparative advantage is to have any real meaning, for an excess of labor and the resulting low labor costs are a factor of production, which are crucial in determining comparative advantage. In addition to such a fundamental departure from the accepted basis for international trade, the Arrangement has several other shortcomings. The import quotas existing in the EEC at the time the Arrangement was made were so low that even the commitment to double them by 1967 was regarded by some exporters "as bordering on fraud." [8] Moreover, although the Arrangement provides for periodic review of its operation, the crucial question of whether "market disruption" is occurring within the meaning of the Ar-

---

[7] This provision has been invoked mainly by the United States. As of July 1966 "agreements were concluded between the United States and sixteen major exporting countries." GATT, A STUDY ON COTTON TEXTILES 83 (1966).

[8] G. PATTERSON, *supra* note 3, at 311 (footnote omitted).

rangement was left solely to the determination of the individual importing members.[9] Thus the Arrangement does not contain the elaborate consultation procedures required by Article XIX of the GATT.[10] Moreover, in making the determination of market disruption, the Arrangement permits a very narrow definition of "market," thus allowing "almost anything." In effect, the Arrangement amounts of an agreement that the developed countries will limit and even decrease their violations of the GATT, and, in exchange, the developing countries will "refrain from exercising their full rights under the GATT and from resorting to its complaint procedures." [11]

The real test of the Arrangement, however, is how it operates in practice. In particular, have the export opportunities of the developing countries been expanded and have the developed countries significantly relaxed their import restrictions on cotton textiles? "[T]he Arrangement has not worked in the trade-expansionary way intended . . ." [12] One reason, according to the

[9] "If imports from a participating country or countries into another participating country of certain cotton textile products not subject to import restrictions should cause or threaten to cause disruption in the market of the importing country, that country may request the participating country or countries whose exports of such products are, *in the judgment of the importing country,* causing or threatening to cause market disruption to consult with a view to removing or avoiding such disruption." Article 3(1), GATT, 11S BASIC INSTRUMENTS AND SELECTED DOCUMENTS 25, 27 (1963) (Emphasis added).

[10] The Arrangement also fails to provide for the "suspension" of "substantially equivalent concessions or other obligations," i.e. compensation, for parties "affected" by the imposition of import restrictions provided for under Article XIX. See W. HUNSBERGER, JAPAN AND THE UNITED STATES IN WORLD TRADE 357 (1964).

[11] *The Developing Countries in GATT,* V PROCEEDINGS OF THE UNITED NATIONS CONFERENCE ON TRADE AND DEVELOPMENT 430, 454 (1964). See, e.g. art. 2(2), GATT, *supra* note 9, at 26: "Without prejudice to the provisions of paragraphs 2 and 3 of Article 3 [the right to impose limitations in the event of market disruption], no participating country shall introduce new import restrictions, or intensify existing import restrictions, on cotton textiles, insofar as this would be inconsistent with its obligations under the GATT."

[12] H. JOHNSON, ECONOMIC POLICIES TOWARD LESS DEVELOPED COUNTRIES 22 (1967). Professor Johnson attributes this to "the strength of protectionist forces in the United States." See also PATTERSON, *supra* note 3 at 312; I. Frank, *New Perspectives on Trade and Development,* 45 FOR. AFF. 520, 534 (1967) (". . . [W]hat started out as an understandable accommodation to certain social and political realities in the advanced countries has in practice become the vehicle through which highly restrictive quotas have been imposed . . .").

developing countries, is that the definition of market disruption
has been misapplied. They charge that importing countries have
found market disruption whenever domestic production has declined, and have disregarded the definition's prerequisite of a
sharp and *substantial* increase in imports. On the other hand,
spokesmen for the developing countries find that some importing
states have disregarded the domestic production side altogether,
and have found that any increase in imports over the base year
was "disruptive." Finally, by narrowly defining the various categories of cotton textiles, and establishing a separate base period
figure for each category, the importing states have kept total imports below what the developing countries assumed they would be
when the Arrangement was signed. The figures provide some
support for these views. During the period 1960 to 1964, cotton
goods imports into the EEC rose from 5 to 8 per cent of total
consumption in member countries. For the United Kingdom, the
figures were 35 to 41 per cent. And for the United States the
figures were 5 and 6 per cent. While it is true that the participating developing countries increased their shares of the import
markets of the industrial countries from 21 to 26 per cent from
1961 to 1964, the total import market itself was not growing very
rapidly. Thus from 1961 to 1964 the developing countries participating in the Arrangement increased their total cotton textile
exports to the participating industrial countries by a figure of "a
little less than" $180 million.

The Cotton Textiles Arrangement is the "first formalized
market disruption agreement." [13] The developing countries fear,
however, that it will not be the last. For the Arrangement has
given "formal international respectability to trade restraints designed to avoid unusually severe competition based on low costs." [14]
A similar situation in trade in other lines of goods could call forth
a similar response. Although the Textile Arrangement specifically
provides that the measures contained therein " 'are not to be con-

[13] G. PATTERSON, *supra* note 3, at 307.
[14] *Id*. at 318.

sidered as lending themselves to application in other fields,' " [15] it has already been observed that in the discussions which led to the Arrangement, officials of the European Economic Community noted that their fears were not limited to Japanese competition, nor to trade in cotton textiles. The developing countries are afraid that the quota restrictions which now exist on their exports of floor coverings and jute bags will now be legitimized on the basis of market disruption. And they fear the extension of the concept and the measures it justifies to products in which they have the greatest comparative advantage.[16]

The possibility that quantitative import restrictions are likely to be applied to the manufactured exports of developing countries is reason enough for trade officials in those countries to acquire a background in just what quantitative restrictions are and how they work. In addition, many of the developing countries them-

[15] Despite disclaimers, the Arrangement lays the groundwork for restrictions on other than cotton textiles. Article 6(b), GATT, *supra* note 9, at 29, begins by noting that "It is not the intention of the participating countries to broaden the scope of this Arrangement beyond cotton textiles . . . ." The next word is "but." The "but" introduces the idea that market disruption caused by an abnormal increase in imports of fibers which directly compete with cotton and are substituted deliberately and solely to circumvent the Arrangement may also be prevented by limiting such imports. In an era of "wash and wear" and "no iron" fabrics, made of a combination of cotton and man-made fibers, this provision could have sweeping implications. Suppose Country A agrees to limit exports of 100% cotton men's shirts and subsequently begins to export 75% dacron and 25% cotton shirts. *A* argues that this does not circumvent its export limitation commitments, since there is a good market for dacron and cotton shirts. But the reason why there is a good market is that limitations on exports of 100% cotton shirts have forced the price of cotton shirts up to the price of dacron and cotton shirts. Absent a restriction on exports, cotton shirts would be cheaper, and dacron and cotton shirts more expensive and, therefore, less attractive to consumers. Thus a restriction on a directly competitive product, cotton shirts, will always affect the market for its competitor, dacron and cotton shirts. But if part of the market for the latter is determined by the restrictions, would not any attempt to satisfy that part of the market be a circumvention of the restrictions? For the restrictions are the basis for that portion of the market being in existence. It is thus difficult to see how increased exports of any directly competitive product could not be a deliberate attempt to circumvent the Arrangement. The opportunity to export them—the market—only exists because of the Arrangement. What this comes down to is that once a country agrees to limit cotton exports, it may also have to limit exports of competitive products if they tend to disrupt the market for domestic cottons.

[16] See, e.g., N. Kaldor, *Dual Exchange Rates and Economic Development*, IX ECONOMIC BULLETIN FOR LATIN AMERICA 215, 222 (1964).

selves resort to the use of quantitative restrictions as devices for protecting their infant industries and absolutely prohibiting the importation of luxury goods. Given this situation, these countries can profit by studying the experience of others, both in the use of quantitative restrictions as an import control device and the means by which the administration of such controls can be placed on an equitable basis.

QUANTITATIVE RESTRICTIONS IN GENERAL

Whenever a restriction is placed on the importation of a product, the price of that product will ordinarily rise in the markets of the importing country. Where the restriction is by imposition of a customs duty, the effect on the price is direct. The price in the importing country will be increased by a new cost element, the import duty, so that the price on an imported item will include both the landed cost and the customs duty. Quantitative restrictions on imports also raise the price of imported goods, but they do so indirectly. The price increases in this case because the supply has been decreased. The same number of buyers are now bidding for fewer goods, with the inevitable result that the price of those goods rises. The effect on the consumer of either type of import restriction is the same. But in the case of tariff restrictions the customs duty portion of the price goes into the coffers of the government of the importing country. This is not necessarily so, however, where imports are limited by quota. In this latter situation the price increase may go into the pocket of the private importer whom the government permits to import the goods. For where imports are controlled by customs duties the importer must pay the landed cost plus the customs duty, but where they are controlled by quantitative restriction he continues to pay only the landed cost. Thus the use of quantitative controls rather than tariffs as a means of limiting imports may result in a decrease in government revenues. This is a particularly important consideration in those developing countries where a large proportion of total government revenues are derived from import duties.

Several economists have advocated the auctioning of import licenses as a means of recovering the "quota profits" for the government. The auction prices in this situation would presumably reflect the margin of quota profit. Such a system, however, has not been widely used by countries imposing quantitative import controls. In part the reason is that it is generally opposed by the large commercial import houses who fear that the results of the ensuing "free for all" might destroy their established trade channels. A more powerful factor operating against the exchange auction system is the fact that "quota profits" are often "shared" between private importers and government civil servants. For the administration of a quantitative restriction system is a complex administrative task generally involving considerable grants of discretionary authority to the government bureau responsible for granting permission to import. This combination of discretion plus profit has lead to considerable corruption in many developing countries.

In some cases quota profits fall into the pockets of exporters. Where a government fears that its own import control system does not contain adequate safeguards against corruption, or where the imposition of quota restrictions may provoke an unfavorable political reaction in the home country, or where a government lacks statutory authority to impose quantitative restrictions, or where—as in the case of the Cotton Textile Arrangement—quantitative import restrictions would directly contravene international agreements, a government may arrange with its suppliers for the latter to limit exports. As well as these negative factors, there may be positive administrative reasons why export controls are to be favored over import quotas.

The export trade may be more concentrated than the import trade, with respect to either number of firms involved or location, or both. The application of quota restrictions can in such cases be more effectively policed against evasion and against the tendency, because of multiplicity of ports of entry, for imports to overrun the maximum quantities sanctioned by the prescribed quotas before the customs authorities can become aware of the fact, and shipments can be better adjusted to seasonal or other variations in market conditions, at the export stage than at the import stage. Control at the export stage is particularly convenient in trades where shipments are commonly made on a consignment basis at the exporter's risk, where storage facilities are superior at the export points than at the points of import, and where trade practices and the nature of the commodity are such that ascertainment of the country of origin of shipment on the part of the customs authorities of the importing country is necessary for proper allocation of quotas by countries but would be difficult without cooperation of the exporters.[17]

Export controls are not common, however, primarily because importers generally have enough influence in their respective governments to insure that quota profits are kept at home.

A B S O L U T E   Q U O T A S   A N D   T A R I F F   Q U O T A S

Quota restrictions on imports are generally of two types. *Absolute quotas* are those which impose a maximum limitation on the value or quantity of goods which may be imported in a specified period (usually one year). Quotas which limit goods by value, i.e., $5,000 of cotton textiles, are usually part of a system for conserving foreign exchange. Restrictions on quantity, i.e., 100 yards of cloth, have the particular characteristic of operating in favor of high-cost imports. Thus, an importer could import 100 yards of cloth at $10 a yard, giving him a total of $1,000 worth of cloth. Alternatively, he could import cloth worth $1 per yard, which would give him a total of $100 worth of cloth. If his profit margin were the same on $1 cloth and $10 cloth, the importer would undoubtedly prefer to import the more expensive cloth.[18]

Less common than absolute quotas are *tariff quotas* which estab-

---

[17] Viner, *Trade Relations Between Free-Market and Controlled Economies,* LEAGUE OF NATIONS, II.A. ECONOMIC AND FINANCIAL 56 (1943).

[18] The illustration is based upon one in 1. J. MEADE, ON THE THEORY OF INTERNATIONAL ECONOMIC POLICY 380 (1951).

lish no maximum on the total amount of imports but provide that a specified quantity of imports may enter free of duty or at a low rate of duty during a given period and that all imports in excess of that quantity will pay the usual, higher rate. For example, under the United States Tariff Act of 1934, coconut oil imported from the Philippines was subject to a tariff quota. Up to 200,000 long tons were admitted free of duty annually. Imports in excess of that quantity were subject to a duty of two cents per pound [19]

GLOBAL QUOTAS AND ALLOCATED QUOTAS

Quotas are also categorized according to whether they are allocated or unallocated. The unallocated quota, sometimes called the global quota, establishes a specific quantity of permitted imports for a given period of time without regard to the country of origin of those imports. This unallocated import quota system has not worked well. It has caused large quantities of goods of the type covered by the quota to appear on the domestic market early in the quota period, since each exporting country seeks to get as great a quantity of its goods as possible into the importing country before the quota is filled. Towards the end of the quota period, shortages of the product inevitably arise. This early surplus and subsequent scarcity causes sharp fluctuations in the price of the product on the local market. In addition, the global quota system discriminates between potential sources of supply because neighboring countries are able to move large quantities of their goods into the quota country before more distant countries can even begin to deliver to the quota market. Proximity to the market is particularly important where quota periods are short, i.e. less than one year.

To remedy these defects of the global quota system the allocated quota or country quota was devised. The country quota first provides for the total amount of goods which may be imported

---

[19] Many of the quotas which have been granted by the EEC to developing countries are tariff quotas.

and then allocates portions of that quota to various exporting countries. The usual basis for allocation is the percentage of that type of goods supplied by a particular country during a period prior to the establishment of the quota. This procedure cures many of the shortcomings of the global quota system. The primary disadvantage of the allocated quota, however, is that it tends to freeze the market position of the exporting countries. For it makes no provision for the new supplier or the supplier who may have increased his efficiency and may therefore be able, because of new lower prices, to find a market for larger quantities of goods than he previously sold. This effect is particularly important to developing countries which seek outlets for their newly established manufacturing and processing industries, since they are either new competitors, or competitors whose efficiency is rapidly increasing as their infant industries mature. The problem could be dealt with by a periodic reallocation of quotas among exporting countries. But the inertia which characterizes bureaucrats works to prevent this from happening. Moreover, if the importing country wishes to retain its total limitation on the amount of imports of the goods in question, reallocation of quotas will mean reducing the quota of one or more countries in order to increase the quota of the newly efficient producer. But reduction of a country's import quota may give offense to that country and put a "strain" on relations between the two states. Most countries will seek to avoid such a situation by retaining the status quo. Finally, a system of allocated quotas guarantees each recipient country a particular share of the market, freeing its exporters from competition with exporters from other countries. This situation makes it more likely that the profits resulting from the import restrictions, i.e., "quota profits," will go to the various exporters, than would be the case where importers were free to buy wherever they liked. Thus, both global and allocated import quotas confer advantages on some and penalties against others. Exporting states aware of this situation attempt in their trade agreements with countries maintaining such systems to ensure that the restrictions will work in their favor. If this cannot be accomplished, they hope to minimize the discriminatory effect of quantitative restrictions on their exports.

MOST-FAVORED-NATION TREATMENT AND QUANTITATIVE RESTRICTIONS

The simplest technique for preventing discrimination with regard to the imposition and administration of quantitative import restrictions would appear to be the application of the most-favored-nation rule: "No quantitative restriction shall be applied by either Party on the importation of any product of the other Party unless the importation of the like product of all third countries is equally restricted."

The crucial word in this provision is "equally." If a country imposes a global quota on imports of bicycles, that quota would apply to all exporters and it could be argued that they are thus "equally" treated. But it has been shown that global quotas discriminate in favor of exporters located near the importing country. On the other hand, the word "equally" suffers from ambiguity when applied to allocated quotas. Assume that a country imports 10,000 bicycles a year: 5,000 from Country A; 3,000 from Country B; 2,000 from Country C. The importing country wishes to limit bicycle imports to 3,000 per year, so it establishes a quota system which permits importation of 1,000 bicycles from A; 1,000 from B; and 1,000 from C. Has each country been "equally" treated? The answer is "yes" insofar as each has had its exports cut to 1,000. But the answer is "no" in terms of the percentage decrease in exports. For A has suffered an 80 per cent drop in its bicycle exports, while B and C have lost only 66⅔ per cent and 50 per cent respectively. At a minimum, therefore, a party to a trade agreement will desire more than "equal" treatment in regard to the imposition of quantitative import controls; what it will seek is "equitable" treatment.

In the event of one of the Parties applying a system of import quotas or similar restrictions affecting the exports of the other Party, the Party applying such restrictions shall accord to the other Party treatment as equitable and as favorable as possible for the products concerned, taking into account the figures of the normal trade therein between the two countries and the total amount of the quotas for each product.[20]

This provision represents an attempt to find a formula which provides that a quota system will not discriminate against the other party to the agreement. It is, however, designed to protect an existing supplier and comes very close to requiring a system of quota allocations. A new trading partner, i.e. a developing country, might prefer to use the formula only up to the word "concerned," since the phrase beginning "taking into account . . ." might be viewed as a limitation where the past level of trade between the parties was low.

Where a developing country is already a major supplier in a particular market, it might prefer to include in its trade agreement the following provision, which goes as far as possible to protect the market position of exporting states:

1. If either Party establishes or maintains any form of quantitative restriction or control on the importation of any product in which the other Party has an interest, or imposes a lower import duty or charge on the importation of a specified quantity of any such product than the import duty or charge imposed on importation in excess of that quantity (hereinafter referred to as a "tariff quota"), the government taking such action will:
   (a) prior to the entry into force of such quantitative restriction or control or tariff quota, give public notice of the total quantity, or any change therein, of any such product permitted to be imported and of the quantity permitted to be imported for such lower duty or charge, during a specified period;
   (b) allot to the other Party for such specified period a share of such total quantity, as originally established or subsequently changed in any manner based upon the proportion of the total

[20] See Commercial "Modus Vivendi" between Spain and Uruguay, *done* at Montevideo, January 2, 1935, art. 2, 164 L.N.T.S. 95, 107 (1935).

importation of such products that such other Party supplied during a previous representative period, account being taken insofar as practicable of any special factors which have affected or may be affecting the trade in that product so that the distribution of trade in such product shall approach as closely as possible the share of the market which the other Party might be expected to obtain in the absence of quantitative restrictions or controls; and

(c) give public notice of the allotments of such quantity among the several exporting countries, and at all times upon request, to advise the other Party of the quantity of any such product, which has been imported or for which licenses or permits for importation have been granted.[21]

2. In the event of any other exporting country renouncing or forfeiting in whole or in part its allotment, the Party establishing or maintaining a quantitative restriction or control or tariff quota shall increase the allotment of the other Party in a ratio no less favorable than that accorded to any other exporting country.

3. No Party establishing or maintaining a quantitative restriction or control or tariff quota shall impose conditions or formalities which would prevent the other Party from utilizing fully the share of the total quantity of any product permitted to be imported which has been allotted to it.

4. In those cases where a Party is a relatively large supplier of any product upon which a quantitative restriction or control or tariff quota has been imposed, the other Party shall consult with such Party, whenever practicable, before the share allotted to such Party has been determined.

5. The Parties agree not to impose quantitative restrictions or controls or tariff quotas in such a manner as to prevent unreasonably the importation of any description of goods in minimum commercial quantities the exclusion of which would impair regular channels of trade.

This provision deals with many of the problems discussed above. It applies both to quantitative restrictions and tariff quotas. Further, it requires that if quotas are established, they must be allocated between exporting countries (1(b)). And these allocations are to be based on a "previous *representative* period." This phrase,

---

[21] See Commercial Agreement between the United States and Honduras, *done* at Tegucigalpa, December 18, 1935, art. VI, 167 L.N.T.S. 313, 318 (1936).

derived from American treaty practice, has been defined by its proponents as "a series of years during which trade in the particular article under consideration was free from restrictive measures of a discriminatory character and was not affected by unusual circumstances such as, for example, a crop failure in the case of an agricultural product." [22] Of course the phrase is relatively vague and ambiguous. Nonetheless it has been noted that "it comes closer to a generally applicable formula which would prevent deliberate discriminatory treatment in the allotment of quotas by countries than any other formula which has so far been . . . suggested." [23] As far as a developing country is concerned the term should be no great handicap since for a new supplier there is no representative period. It must therefore be granted a quota *de novo*. And in an effort to prevent the representative period formula being used as a limitation, where a developing country is supplying some goods in the market and hopes to expand its sales as its infant export industries mature, this provision requires that in allocating quotas, the importing country must take into account "special factors . . . affecting trade in that product." This language is an attempt to avoid the "freezing" of market shares which occurs when quotas are allocated. The "special factors" which are to be considered are mainly changes in the efficiency of production of the goods in exporting countries.[24] Finally, the establishment and operation of a quota system must be opened to scrutiny by the exporting country (1(a) and (c)). This requirement will act to limit favoritism and corruption in the administration of the quota system. It will also enable exporters to inform themselves as to what goods may be exported to a particular country and to prepare to act accordingly.

Paragraph 5 is based upon Article XII 3(c) of the General

[22] Department of State, Policy of the United States Concerning Generalization of Tariff Concessions, April 1, 1935, quoted in J. Viner, *supra* note 17, at 65 n. 1.

[23] Viner, *supra* note 17, at 66.

[24] The phrase "special factors" 'is used in a similar context in Article XIII, GATT, 55 U.N.T.S. 188, 236 (1950), to mean "the existence of new or additional ability to export"; "changes in relative productive efficiency." See GATT, ANALYTICAL INDEX 72-73 (Rev. ed. 1966).

Agreement on Tariffs and Trade. The purpose of the provision "is to keep open the channels of trade, to make it just worthwhile for the exporter to keep his sales organization together in the overseas market." [25] Developing a market, including the establishment of a demand for a particular brand of goods and a distributing organization to supply them, requires a substantial investment on the part of the exporter. Once a market has been developed, it represents a valuable asset. The object of this provision is to protect an exporting country against loss of this asset. It requires that the country imposing controls allow in a sufficient quantity of goods of the type *previously sold in the market* to keep the brand name before the public and distributing organization intact. Such provisions also benefit importing countries by subjecting local producers to at least a modicum of competition. On the other hand, if a developing country plans the total prohibition of certain classes of luxury imports, it would be well advised to omit a provision of this type from its trade agreements.

Prohibiting the Use of Quantitative Restrictions

On occasion, where the exporting country has exercised superior bargaining power, agreements are sometimes found which totally prohibit the imposition and operation of quantitative import restrictions:

No prohibitions or restrictions other than duties, taxes or other charges, whether made effective through quotas, import or export licenses or other measures, shall be instituted or maintained by either Party on the importation of any product of the other Party or on the exportation of any product destined for the territory of the other Party.

This language is based on Article XI of the General Agreement on Tariffs and Trade. The theory of the General Agreement, as

[25] ANALYTICAL INDEX, *supra* at 64.

noted above, is that quantitative import restrictions are not legitimate trade barriers, primarily because they cannot be operated on
a nondiscriminatory basis. From the outset, however, even the
Contracting Parties found it necessary to incorporate in the General Agreement certain exceptions to the "no-quota" rule. For instance, import prohibitions or restrictions are permitted where
"necessary to the application of standards or regulations for the
classification, grading or marketing of commodities in international trade." Under such an exception a country would be permitted, for example, to restrict imports because it lacked the
storage facilities necessary for the orderly marketing of the
commodity.

Another GATT exception referred to earlier permits the imposition of quantitative restrictions on agricultural or fisheries
products where the importing country maintains a domestic price
scheme:

The provisions of paragraph ...... of this article shall not extend to:
import restrictions on any agricultural or fisheries products, imported
in any form, necessary to the enforcement of governmental measures
which operate:
(1) to restrict the quantities of the like domestic product permitted
    to be marketed or produced, or, if there is no substantial domestic
    production of the like product, of a domestic product for which
    the imported product can be directly substituted; or
(2) to remove a temporary surplus of the like domestic product or, if
    there is no domestic production of the like product, of a domestic
    product for which the imported product can be directly substi-
    tuted, by making the surplus available to certain groups of domes-
    tic consumers free of charge or at prices below the current market
    value; or
(3) restrict the quantities permitted to be produced of any animal
    product, the production of which is directly dependent, wholly
    or mainly, on the imported commodity or the domestic production
    of that commodity is relatively negligible.

A similar though considerably less detailed provision was incorporated in the Trade Agreement between the United States

of America and Mexico, *done* at Washington, December 23, 1942.[27] This provision covered all products, and not only those of fisheries or agriculture. "The foregoing provision shall not prevent the Government of either country from imposing quantitative regulations in whatever form on the importation or sale of any article in conjunction with governmental measures or measures under governmental authority operating to regulate or control the production, market supply, quality or prices of like domestic articles. . . ."

Finally, it is generally accepted that quantitative import controls may be established and maintained to enable a party to "safeguard its external financial position and balance of payments." [28]

LIMITING THE SCOPE OF QUANTITATIVE RESTRICTIONS

There remains to be discussed yet a third approach to quantitative restrictions. Where the parties cannot agree either on an across-the-board acceptance of import restrictions, or a blanket prohibition with limited generalized exceptions, they can provide that quantitative controls shall not be applied to a limited number of products specified in the trade agreement. "No prohibition or restriction or any form of quantitative regulation shall be imposed by Country *A* on the importation of any product of Country *B* enumerated and described in Schedule 1 to this agreement, or by Country *B* on the importation of any product of Country *A* enumerated and described in Schedule 2 to this Agreement."

Such a provision would be particularly appropriate where trade between the parties is in one or a few commodities. A variation on this theme, with particular appeal to a developing country, is

---

[27] Art. X (2), U.S. EXECUTIVE AGREEMENT SERIES No. 311, pp. 12-13 (1943), quoted in H. HAWKINS, COMMERCIAL TREATIES AND AGREEMENTS, PRINCIPLES AND PRACTICE 176 (1951).
[28] See art. XII (1), GATT, 55 U.N.T.S. 188, 228 (1950). And see pp. 94-96, *supra*.

the following from the Trade Agreement betwteen the United Kingdom and Estonia, *done* at London, July 11, 1934, in which the United Kingdom unilaterally agreed not to impose import restrictions on products of interest to Estonia.

ARTICLE 5

1. . . . Government of the United Kingdom undertake not to regulate the quantity of imports into the United Kingdom of butter and bacon and hams, the produce of Estonia, except in so far as such regulation may be necessary to secure the effective operation of a scheme or schemes for the regulation of the marketing of domestic supplies of these or related products. In the event of such regulation of imports being introduced, in the case of all or any of these products, paragraphs 2 to 7 of this Article shall have effect in so far as they may be applicable. [Paragraphs 2-7 provide for the allocation of quotas based on past market activity, consultations before the imposition of quotas, etc.]

. . .

6. Having regard to the fact that in recent years the imports of the following agricultural products, viz., eggs, potato flour, milk powder, condensed milk, meat and fish conserves, cheese and poultry, from Estonia into the United Kingdom have been insignificant in quantity, in comparison with imports from other countries, the Government of the United Kingdom will endeavor to arrange that in the event of any quantitative regulation being imposed on imports of these products, imports of such products produced in Estonia shall remain unregulated. If, however, imports from Estonia of any such products increase to such an extent that it is necessary to regulate them quantitatively, the Government of the United Kingdom undertake to enter into discussions with the Government of Estonia as to the quantity of such product to be allowed to be imported into the United Kingdom from Estonia.[29]

[29] Agreement between Estonia and the United Kingdom, Supplementary to the Treaty of Commerce and Navigation of January 18, 1926, with Protocol and Annexes, *done* at London, July 11, 1934, art. 5, 152 L.N.T.S. 131, 135, 137 (1934).

LICENSING

Licenses are the means by which quantitative import controls are administered. The importing country first establishes the quota for a given period, then issues licenses to commercial houses permitting them to import goods—from any country if the quota is unallocated, from a particular country if the quota is allocated—up to the amount stated in the license.

Import licensing may also be used without accompanying quotas. Authorities in a country may issue import licenses from time to time on an *ad hoc* basis or there may be rough quotas which the authorities utilize for making decisions on imports, but which are not made public. In either case the potential inequity of such a system is great. No trading nation knows what quantity of a product may be imported into the country. Exporters cannot plan what and how much they can sell. And the system, by leaving permission to import to the discretion of the administrative personnel in the licensing office, leaves the door wide open to corruption in the allocation of licenses. Most export-minded countries, when faced with a situation like this, seek to outlaw such licensing systems by providing in their trade agreements that:

No restriction of any kind shall be imposed by either Party on the importation from the territory of the other Party of any product, whether by means of import licenses or permits or otherwise, unless the total quantity or value of such product permitted to be imported during a specified period, or any changes in such quantity of value, shall have been established and made public.[30]

A less satisfactory alternative for an exporting country would be to provide in the agreement that licenses will be issued under the fairest possible conditions:

[30] See Trade Agreement between the United States and Argentina, *done* at Buenos Aires, October 14, 1941, art. III(2), U.S. EXECUTIVE AGREEMENT SERIES No. 277 (1943), quoted in H. HAWKINS, *supra* note 27, at 171.

The conditions under which licenses are given for products of one of the Parties imported into or exported from the territory of the other shall be fair and equitable and as favorable as the conditions under which licenses are given in the case of any third country.

The shortcoming of this provision is that in the absence of a publicly known quota it is very difficult to establish whether licenses are really being given on a fair and equitable basis.

Since the total quantity of imports that will be permitted is unknown, an exporting country can never determine what proportion of the market it is being permitted to obtain and thus whether it is receiving equitable treatment.

A third alternative, even less attractive, is the type of provision present in many current trade agreements which provides:

The Parties undertake, in conformity with their laws and regulations in force, to issue such export and import licenses as may be required, and, from the administrative point of view, to facilitate the exchange of goods in accordance with the provisions of this Agreement.[31]

There are two difficulties with this article. First, the two parties "undertake, in conformity with their laws and regulations in force, . . ." This phrase is frequently found in trade agreements of recent origin. While seemingly clear on its face, its implications are murky. Suppose that the regulations of one country provide that there shall be no import licenses for steel, shoes, radios, etc. The provision could then mean that licenses will be issued except where the laws and regulations provide that no licenses will be issued. Such a commitment is obviously worthless. On the other hand, it has been said that a phrase such as this when qualifying a promise in a trade agreement cannot be read to make completely valueless the principal obligation.[32] From this it is argued that

---

[31] See, e.g., Trade Agreement between Cuba and Czechoslovakia, *done* at Havana, June 10, 1960, art. 3, 447 U.N.T.S. 75, 84 (1962).

[32] ". . . [R]egulations are violative of the treaty if they in effect destroy the right or render it illusory. To allow . . . [parties] to enjoy the right 'in accordance with applicable law' would not leave it open for a party-state subsequently to decide *whether the right should actually be given.*" R. WILSON, UNITED STATES COMMERCIAL TREATIES AND INTERNATIONAL LAW 11 (1960).

the phrase is superfluous and is only included in agreements "as a matter of caution." But if the phrase is really superfluous, how can one read into it a note of "caution." Moreover, it would be difficult to interpret as superfluous language which appears to have a clear import. Thus the "laws and regulations in force" in some way limit the value of the promise but cannot be construed to make it entirely worthless. The meaning and extent of the commitment on both parties to issue licenses is thus very unclear. At a minimum, a party agreeing to such a proposal should have adequate knowledge of all the laws and regulations in force governing the issuance of import and export licenses in the territory of the other party, and some assurance that the same laws and regulations will be in effect in the future or that new laws and regulations will not vary greatly from the old ones.

A second shortcoming to this type of provision, applicable equally to the two licensing provisions quoted previously, is that it leaves it to each party to establish any procedural requirement for import licenses that that party believes necessary. No standards are established to forestall the excesses that have in the past been associated with the issuance of licenses. Where a licensing system has been established, whether in connection with a system of import quotas or not, exporting countries should insist that trade agreements include a provision designed to prevent, as much as possible, abuse of that system. An article in widespread use since the early 1920s aimed at dealing with this problem would read: [33]

1. Insofar as prohibitions or restrictions may be enforced in the importation or exportation of any products, the two Parties undertake as regards import and export licenses to do everything in their power to insure:
   (a) that conditions to be fulfilled and the formalities to be ob-

---

[33] See Protocol to the Convention on the Abolition of Import and Export Prohibitions and Restrictions, *done* at Geneva, November 8, 1927, § VII, LEAGUE OF NATIONS, IIA. ECONOMIC AND FINANCIAL 7, at 25 (1928); International Convention Relating to the Simplification of Customs Formalities, *done* at Geneva, November 3, 1923, art. 3 [1925], Gr. Brit. T.S. No. 16 (CMD. 2347) at 6.

served in order to obtain such licenses shall be brought immediately in the clearest and most definite form to the notice of the public;

(b) that the method of issue of certificates of licenses should be as simple and stable as possible;

(c) that the examination of applications and the issue of licenses to the applicants should be carried out with the least possible delay;

(d) that the system of issuing licenses should be such as to prevent the traffic in licenses. With this object, licenses, when issued to individuals, should state the name of the holder and should not be capable of being used by any other person; [34]

(e) that, in the event of fixing of quotas, the formalities required by the importing country shall not be such as to prevent an equitable allocation of the quantities of goods of which the importation is authorized;

(f) that all relevant information concerning the administration of the licensing system, the number and type of import licenses granted over a period and the distribution of such licenses among supplying countries shall be supplied by the importing country to the exporting country upon request.

Conclusion

Despite the strenuous efforts of economic theoreticians and legal draftsmen, no formula has yet been devised and accepted which can negate the discrimination inherent in the use of quantitative import controls. Both global and allocated quotas tend to favor some exporters as against others. Moreover, the operation of a system of controls is highly complicated, usually involving a large grant of discretion to the administrators. In a developing

---

[34] If licenses are transferable, they may all fall into the hands of a single importer, or combination of importers, who might decide that it was more profitable to restrict imports to an amount even less than that provided for in the quota—here monopoly profits would be added to the profits derived from obtaining the license itself. See M. GORDON, BARRIERS TO WORLD TRADE 238 (1941).

Although licenses are not transferable in most countries which utilize them, such provisions have been extremely difficult to enforce.

country where the civil service may be grossly underpaid, this inevitably invites corruption. Nevertheless, most countries operate systems of quantitative import control and in negotiating a trade agreement, developing countries should be aware of the alternative formulations which can, at least, decrease the discrimination to which their trade may be subjected.

IV. Exchange Controls

"Balance of payments crisis" and "developing country" are phrases that seem to go hand in hand. A country's balance of payments is, in simple terms, the sum remaining after deducting the outflow of internationally acceptable payments media from that coming into the country. The balance is in a state of crisis when outgoing payments exceed receipts. Such crises are not uncommon in developing countries mainly because of short-term declines in export proceeds from primary products. For a time, a government may utilize its reserves of such payments media to make up the deficit. And it may seek international assistance in the form of temporary loans of reserve funds. But eventually action must be taken. The traditional prescription is devaluation. The effect of a devaluation is to lower the price of exports and raise the price of imports. The price of the local currency is lowered to a point at which equilibrium between income and outflow is established. This sounds simple enough. But devaluation, like many other courses of action, is easier said than done.

In virtually every country there is a psychological barrier to devaluation. The belief has gained wide currency that to devalue is evidence of a failure on the part of the government. In addition, a devaluation carries with it a redistribution of income within the country. Producers of exports generally benefit, since they receive a greater amount of local currency for each unit of foreign exchange proceeds they earn after the devaluation than before it. On the other hand, consumers of imported products must pay more for those products. Where a developing country imports large amounts of foodstuffs this will result in a rise in food prices. Both the increased incomes to exporters and the increased cost of "essential" imports are effects of devaluation that a government may wish to avoid. Moreover, even if foodstuffs are not imported, a devaluation may result in rising food prices. For increased incomes in the export sector are normally accompanied in a developing country with an increased demand for foodstuffs. In addition, as exporting becomes more attractive, land previously utilized to produce food is switched to growing export crops, so that local food supplies shrink. And the increased cost of food will result in pressure on the nonexport sectors of the economy for additional wages. Thus a devaluation may set off a new round of inflation, negating the benefits of the devaluation.

The final argument against devaluation in a developing country is based on the fact that the principal exports of developing countries are primary products which face a relatively inelastic demand curve. Thus a devaluation may not greatly increase total export earnings. The current exchange rate may be the proper one for maximizing export earnings from primary products. Yet at the same time the current exchange rate may result in an external price for manufactured exports which is too high. That is to say, manufactures cannot be exported at the current rate of exchange, and exportation can only take place if the rate is lowered. And because the costs of manufacturing in developing countries are high, the devaluation necessary to produce a demand for such exports would have to be rather large. In addition, therefore, to a general reluctance on the part of developing countries to devalue, there is an economic dilemma involved in such a course of action.

To enhance the balance of payments position without devaluing, a developing country must pursue a policy which has the same effect—increasing exports and decreasing imports. An alternative focusing on the export side would be to impose an export tax or duty on primary products and use the proceeds to subsidize manufactured exports. Such a policy would avoid the sweeping effects on the economy of a general devaluation of sufficient magnitude to render manufactured exports attractive in world markets. Yet it could allow a substantial reduction in the price of manufactured exports. For example, if Country A's export proceeds from primary products are 90 and from manufactures 10, a 5 per cent export tax on primary product exports would yield $4\frac{1}{2}$ with which to subsidize manufactures, an amount equal to 45 per cent of the total export value of manufactures.[1]

An alternative course circumventing devaluation is the establishment of a system of multiple exchange rates.[2] Multiple rate systems operate to remedy balance of payments difficulties by operating on both imports and exports. Insofar as exports are concerned, exporters of primary products receive less local currency for each unit of foreign exchange earned than do exporters of manufactured goods. For example, exporters of primary products may be compelled to turn their dollar export earnings over to the governments in exchange for local currency at a rate of one dollar to 5 units. Exporters of manufactures, on the other hand, may receive 10 units of local currency for each dollar of foreign exchange. As of December 31, 1966, the Government of Brazil, for example, maintained five different buying rates for export proceeds, with coffee exports receiving less than half the number of cruzeiros per export dollar earned as compared with exports of manufactures. In addition to their use in subsidizing exports, multiple exchange rates also serve to restrict imports. Here the typical pattern is a favorable exchange rate for "essential imports," a medium rate for merchandise imports, and a high rate for luxury imports.

Where the government seeks to maintain a system of multiple exchange rates on imports and/or exports the need for a system

---

[1] See Kaldor, *Dual Exchange Rates and Economic Development*, IX ECONOMIC BULLETIN FOR LATIN AMERICA 215, 220 (1964).

[2] Other possible courses of action are summarized in UNITED NATIONS CONFERENCE ON TRADE AND DEVELOPMENT, REPORT OF THE GROUP OF EXPERTS ON PAYMENTS ARRANGEMENTS AMONG THE DEVELOPING COUNTRIES FOR TRADE EXPANSION, U. N. Doc. TD/B/80/Rev. 1, TD/B/C.3/24/Rev. I, Appendix III (1966).

of exchange controls arises. Exchange controls are the administrative regulations by which the government assures that it can collect and allocate foreign exchange in accordance with its system of multiple rates. An effective exchange control system operates in the following manner: All foreign monies or claims on foreign monies which come into the hands of residents of a country must be sold to the control authorities for local currency at a fixed price. When an importer desires to purchase goods from abroad, he must buy the foreign currency with which to pay for these goods from the exchange control authority. To prevent circumvention of this requirement an exchange control system will require that local currency, except in very small amounts, cannot be removed from the country, where it might be exchanged for other foreign currencies. And all nonresident travelers entering the country with foreign currency will be permitted to exchange it for local currency only at government-authorized exchange offices.[3] To organize and operate such a system involves a considerable administrative effort. Nonetheless, the opportunity to avoid, at least temporarily, the problems of devaluation have rendered multiple exchange rate systems popular in developing countries.[4]

The use of multiple exchange rate systems is not without its shortcomings. By granting preferred rates to imports of foodstuffs and capital equipment, the use of multiple rates discourages local food production and encourages overexpansion of manufacturing capacity. Moreover, the determination of which goods are essential and therefore entitled to a favorable exchange rate on importation and which are not essential is not an easy question to decide. The problem is complicated because of the pressure by local importers on the exchange control authorities

[3] The explanation in the text is simplified to illustrate the high points of an exchange control system. Most systems involve minute control over all international transactions and holdings of foreign claims. For a more detailed description see I. J. MEADE, ON THE THEORY OF INTERNATIONAL ECONOMIC POLICY 265–68 (1951).

[4] See de Vries, *Multiple Exchange Rates: Expectations and Experiences,* 12 I.M.F. STAFF PAPERS 282 (1965). Twenty-eight developing country members of the IMF maintained multiple exchange rate systems in 1967.

to have goods handled by the importers classified as essential. Finally because of the administrative problems involved, many developing countries must allocate a substantial portion of their scarce administrative talent to operating the system. For these reasons multiple rates are generally considered as a transitional measure on the road to devaluation, as opposed to a true alternative to that course of action.

A country maintaining a unitary exchange rate may also resort to exchange controls to cope with its balance of payments difficulties. The exchange control system is generally the same as in the case of multiple rates, but incorporates even more administrative control. For the multiple rate system contains a degree of automaticity absent in a controlled unitary rate system. Goods which the authorities do not wish to see imported under a multiple rate system must be paid for with exchange purchased at a most unfavorable rate. Where a unitary rate is maintained, however, the exchange rate does not, by itself, act to cut down any category of imports, or encourage any particular type of export. In a unitary rate system, imports are therefore controlled by the use of quantitative import controls and exports are encouraged by subsidies to exporters. Because unitary rate systems make necessary the highest degree of administrative complexity, and carry with them extensive systems of quantitative import controls they are the least desirable form of exchange control system, and seem to exist primarily because of the political fears and fetishes surrounding devaluation. Countries maintaining such systems are under constant pressure from the international monetary authorities to loosen up on their exchange restrictions or, as a second-best alternative, to adopt systems of multiple exchange rates. Nonetheless, most developing countries maintain a unitary exchange rate with restrictions on trade payments.

EXCHANGE CONTROLS AND
MOST-FAVORED-NATION TREATMENT

Since the Depression, export-minded countries have recognized that exchange controls could be an effective method of interfering with the importation of their products. In their trade agreements they have attempted to insure that an exchange control system, if one exists, will not discriminate against their exports. To achieve this end, the initial approach has been to seek most-favored-nation treatment in regard to the establishment and administration of exchange controls. "If either Party maintains or shall establish a control of foreign exchange, that Party will accord to the other Party the most general and complete application of the most-favored-nation principle." [5]

The difficulty with this formulation is that the concept of the most-favored-nation is of limited value in dealing with problems of exchange control. This is so because of the nature of the world's money supply. The world's currencies can be divided into two rough groupings: the externally convertible and those whose convertibility is limited or which are inconvertible. The convertible currencies are those which can be exchanged, one for the other, on the world money markets at a predictable and reasonably stable price. This being so, if a country maintains controls on one convertible currency, it must maintain them on all such currencies. Thus there is little to be gained by limiting importers' supplies of U.S. dollars, but not German marks, since American, or any other exporters would gladly accept marks in payment for exports, as the marks could be sold by the exporter for dollars

---

[5] See Trade Agreement between the United States and Brazil, *done* at Washington, February 2, 1935, U.S. EXECUTIVE AGREEMENT SERIES No. 82 (1936), art. VI, quoted in S. Metzger, *Exchange Controls and International Law,* in LEGAL PROBLEMS OF INTERNATIONAL TRADE 311, 314 (P. Proehl ed. 1959).

This type of provision was the first step in the evolution of American trade agreement practice on exchange control. See J. Viner, *Trade Relations Between Free-Market and Controlled Economies,* in LEAGUE OF NATIONS PUBLICATIONS, II. A. ECONOMIC AND FINANCIAL 51 (1943).

in the money market. If, then, most-favored-nation treatment merely requires that if exchange controls are established for dollars, they must also be established for marks, the requirement is of negligible value, since this would be done anyway in a logical exchange regime. The only situation where most-favored-nation treatment could be useful is where a country maintains exchange controls on convertible currencies, but not on inconvertible ones. Suppose, for example, Country A imposed exchange controls on imports from convertible currency areas, but not on purchases paid for in Russian rubles. Would the most-favored-nation rule require that controls be extended to rubles? Apparently not. For the most-favored-national principle only requires that equal treatment be granted in *similar situations*. But Russian rubles are not similar to convertible currencies for they can only be used to purchase Russian goods.[6] Moreover, even if one argues that "money is money" and that to apply exchange controls to hard currencies and not to soft currencies is discriminatory, there is a strong case for such discrimination. The case may be illustrated by assuming that Country D, a developing country, "has, compared to demand for it, a relatively small supply of the hard currency of country A (dollars) and a relatively large supply of the soft currency of country B . . . [rubles] then a nondiscriminatory policy, requiring that the restrictions against imports from B be as severe as those against imports from A, would prevent . . . [D] buying some goods from B which it wanted and which B was prepared to sell. But it would not thereby permit any increase in . . . [D's] purchases from A because B's currency could not be spent in A." [7] Thus, "to insist on nondiscrimination would

---

[6] This distinction also applies to countries in the French Franc Area and to certain Sterling Area countries. Thus French francs in a country which is a member of the Franc Area are *not similar* to convertible currencies in those countries, because the common pool of reserves distinguishes French francs from other convertible currencies. This is somewhat confusing since, for example, French francs in the hands of a German importer are freely convertible into marks or U.S. dollars.

[7] G. Patterson, Discrimination in International Trade, The Policy Issues 1945-1965, 25–26 (1966) (footnote omitted).

be to reduce trade below what it could otherwise be among the nonconvertible (soft) currency countries without thereby expanding it with the hard currency areas." [8]

What then is the value of the most-favored-nation clause with regard to exchange controls? It is simply this. If all convertible currencies are controlled, most-favored-nation treatment will require that in allocating the controlled foreign currencies, no consideration will be given to *the country of origin of the goods* to be purchased with the exchange. Thus, in allocating dollars, marks, francs, etc., the controlling country will not tie the allocation to the purchase of the products of a particular country. To the extent that such an occurrence is feared, most-favored-nation treatment will have relevance in an exchange control situation.

EXCHANGE CONTROLS AND EQUITABLE TREATMENT

Discrimination of this type is not what countries are afraid of when they see exchange controls established in one of their principal export markets. What they really fear is that exchange will not be allocated to buy the *kinds of products* which they have traditionally exported to the exchange control country. To illustrate, assume that Country *A* maintains a convertible currency, and that Country *B* is acquiring that currency in payment for exports to *A*. *A* might naturally hope that some of its payments for imports will be returned to it in the form of payments for exports to *B*. *A's* traditional exports to *B* have been radios, cotton textiles, and motor vehicles. But *B* has decided, as part of its development program, to begin producing its own cotton textiles and, following the imposition of its exchange control regime, announces that it will allocate only a minute portion of its available foreign exchange to finance imports of cotton

[8] *Id.* at 25.

textiles. In such a case, *A* not wishing to interfere with the execution of *B*'s development plan has two choices: *A* can cut down on its imports from *B* by the amount *B* has cut its textile imports from *A*, or *A* can request a commitment from *B* that *B* will purchase additional quantities of radios or motor vehicles or some other product produced by *A*. In the interests of increased international trade, both *A* and *B* will normally opt for the latter choice. If they do, the following provision might be included in their trade agreement:

If either Party brings into force any form of control of foreign exchange, it shall administer such control so as to insure that the other Party will be granted a fair and equitable share in the allotment of foreign exchange and in this regard it shall be guided in the administration of its control by the principle that as nearly as may be determined, the proportion of total foreign exchange available for commercial transactions alloted to the other Party shall be no less than that employed for the purchase of products of the other Party in a representative period prior to the entry into force of the control.[9]

Note that this provision is similar in concept to the approach taken with regard to quota restrictions discussed in Chapter III.

[9] See Commercial Agreement between the United States and Sweden, *done* at Washington, May 25, 1935, art. IX, 161 L.N.T.S. 109, 115-7 (1935), cited in Metzger, *supra* note 4, at 315.

The provision quoted in the text represents the "middle stage" of the evolution in the American approach to exchange controls. Starting with the provision quoted in the text at note 3 *supra*, the formulae employed were, in order: (1) "a fair and equitable share" of available foreign exchange; (2) exchange controls to be administered so as not to disadvantage United States commodities *vis-a-vis* third countries; (3) the provision in the text; (4) imports of American commodities would receive MFN treatment "with respect to rates of exchange, taxes or surcharges, or rules and formalities connected with exchange control" as *"any like* import from any third country"; (5) the same language as (4) except the word "like" was omitted; (6) no secret allotments of exchange; (7) no exchange control measures which would involve "the use of exchange rates higher than those which would result from the free operation of supply and demand in the market." Viner, *Trade Relations between Free-Market and Controlled Economies,* League of Nations, II.A. Economic and Financial at 51 (1943). Professor Viner criticized those standards as lacking in logic and specificity. See *id* at 52. Nonetheless, he noted that these provisions "represent . . . the most important, if not the sole, contribution made by any country to protect world trade against the injurious effects of the exchange controls of other countries when used as an instrument of trade regulation. . . ." *Id.* at 53.

The difference is that where quota restrictions are involved, trade agreement provisions seek to preserve the market for *particular products,* whereas with exchange controls, the aim is to preserve *overall foreign exchange earnings* regardless of which export products generate them.

Notice also that there is no explicit commitment in this provision that the "other Party" will maintain its level of imports from the party imposing the exchange controls. Nonetheless, it seems reasonable to imply a reciprocal obligation on the part of the "other Party" that present imports of the "other Party" should approximate the same proportion of its total imports as during the base period. If during the base period, B imported goods from A valued at $15 out of a total import volume of $75, and if B imposes exchange controls so that it now has available for total imports only $60, the clause quoted in the text assures A that of B's total import volume of $60, A will obtain $12. As noted, the clause says nothing about B's share of A's market. If during the base period A imported goods from B valued at $20, out of A's total import volume of $100, reciprocity would require that A continue to maintain the same import ratio even in the face of B's exchange control regime which is reducing the volume of A's exports to B. Not to imply such a condition would permit A to cut off all imports from B, while B remained bound to import from A. To read such an implication into this provision is not to require that A take positive action to maintain the level of B's imports, but only that it also deal in a "fair and equitable" manner in view of the fact that the explicit obligation of the clause rests only with the party imposing exchange controls. The provision acts roughly to preserve each party's share of the other's market despite the imposition of exchange controls. And it limits the decline in total world trade due to the imposition of exchange controls.

Limiting the Scope of Exchange Controls

A third approach to the problems posed by exchange controls, as in the case of quantitative restrictions on imports, is to include in the trade agreement a provision prohibiting exchange controls or narrowly limiting the circumstances in which exchange controls may be imposed. Where both parties to a trade agreement are members of the International Monetary Fund, they may agree to accept any exchange controls which are permitted by the Fund authorities. "Nothing in the present Agreement shall preclude either Party from imposing such exchange restrictions as are consistent with the rights and obligations it has or may have as a contracting party to the Articles of Agreement of the International Monetary Fund." [10]

Article VIII of the Fund Agreement prohibits "restrictions on the making of payments and transfers for current international transactions," the latter being defined to include all "payments due in connection with foreign trade . . ." [11] To this blanket prohibition there are only three exceptions. The first deals with the "scarce currency" provisions of Article VII, 3 (b), and is of little importance. The second permits exchange controls during a "transitional period" and was originally intended to provide for postwar readjustments.[12] The provision is extremely important to developing countries, for IMF practice has evolved in such a way that "[a] member availing itself of the transitional arrangements . . . is authorized, for balance of payments reasons, to maintain and to adopt to changing circumstances those restric-

[10] See Agreement on Commerce between Japan and Peru, *done* at Tokyo, May 15, 1961, art. II, 451 U.N.T.S. 30, 32 (1963).

[11] Article VIII 2(a); art. XIX (i)(1), 2 U.N.T.S. 39, 66, 104 (1947).

[12] Article XIV 2, 2 U.N.T.S. 39, 92 (1947). Thus when a party to a trade agreement consents to accept controls permissible under the IMF Agreement, it accepts not only those which the Fund specifically approves, but also those which were in effect at the time the other party joined the Fund. This should not prove too great a burden in practice since during the discussions which take place when a party seeks membership in the Fund, any restrictions of which the Fund disapproves will probably be eliminated from a new member's exchange control regime.

tions or payments and transfers for current international transactions which were in effect when the country became a member of the Fund." Seventy-six developing country members of the Fund maintained restrictions on current transactions under this provision on December 31, 1967. The third exception, for countries which are no longer in a state of transition, permits members to maintain controls with the "approval of the Fund."

By including in a trade agreement a provision accepting those exchange restrictions permitted by the IMF agreement, the Parties in effect leave the question of the justifiability of the restrictions to the Fund authorities. This resolution of the question would appear the most desirable one. The IMF is a neutral third party whose experience and expertise place it in a unique position to evaluate the need for exchange restrictions. This has been recognized in the General Agreement on Tariffs and Trade which places the resolution of such questions in the hands of the IMF. In addition, the IMF is dedicated to the liberation of trade transactions from exchange controls, and exerts considerable pressure on its member countries towards this end. Thus, in agreeing to abide by what is acceptable to the IMF, a country whose exports have suffered from the imposition of exchange restrictions has allied itself with an agency to whom such restrictions are also anathema.

Some countries, however, are not members of the Fund, or prefer to use their own judgment as to the legitimacy of exchange controls. In such circumstances they may incorporate in their trade agreements a provision limiting the imposition of exchange controls to circumstances in which the balance of payments problems of one of the parties are relatively serious.

In order to safeguard its external financial position and its balance of payments, either Party may restrict the quantity or value of merchandise permitted to be imported by means of quantitative restrictions and/or exchange controls. Import restrictions instituted, maintained or intensified by a Party under this article shall not exceed those necessary:

(1) to forestall the imminent threat of, or to stop, a serious decline in its monetary reserves, or

(2) in the case of a Party with very low monetary reserves, to achieve a reasonable rate of increase in its reserves.[13]

Needless to say, problems are raised by this "low reserves" provision determining what constitutes a "serious decline" and how low reserves must fall before they are considered "very low." The Contracting Parties to the GATT, which contains this provision, have laid out some ground rules. In measuring a "serious decline," parties are to consider the "size of the country, its need for reserves, the variability of its trade and the size of the reserves." [14] It has also been "pointed out that a country exporting principally a small number of products would, in like conditions, probably be considered to have need for greater reserves than a country exporting a large variety of products, particularly if the exports were exhaustible or subject to considerable fluctuations of supply or price. A country actively embarked on a programme of economic development which is raising levels of production and foreign trade would probably be considered to have need for greater reserves than when its economic activity was at a lower level." [15] Despite these attempts to fill in the vast open spaces of this provision, the experience of the GATT members has been that it is a "rubber clause not setting any real limits." [16] Moreover, its very nebulous character would seem to lay the perfect basis for a disagreement between the parties.[17] For these

[13] See GATT, 55 U.N.T.S. 188, 228 (1950), art. XII. See also Trade Agreement between New Zealand and Malaya, *done* at Wellington, February 3, 1961, art. V (3), 447 U.N.T.S. 251, 256 (1962); Treaty of Friendship, Commerce and Navigation between the United States and Japan, *done* at Tokyo, April 2, 1953, art. XII (2), 206 U.N.T.S. 143, 206 (1955).

[14] GATT, ANALYTICAL INDEX 62 (Rev. ed. 1966).

[15] *Id.* at 63.

[16] Linder, *The Significance of GATT for Under-developed Countries,* V. PROCEEDINGS OF THE UNITED NATIONS CONFERENCE ON TRADE AND DEVELOPMENT 502, 520 (1964).

[17] Parties which are not members of the IMF, but which are willing to accept its judgment, might avoid some difficulties by adding to such a balance of payments provision a further clause agreeing to refer the determination of any disbute on this matter to the Fund. See art. XV (2), GATT, 55 U.N.T.S. 188, 246 (1950).

reasons, such provisions would probably best be omitted from any future trade agreements.

Finally, any article dealing with exchange controls should provide a definition of the term:

The term "exchange controls" as used in the present Article includes all restrictions, regulations, charges, taxes, fees, or other requirements imposed by either Party which burden or interfere with the making of payments, remittances, or the transfer of funds or of financial instruments between the territories of the two Parties.[18]

ADVANCE DEPOSITS

Advance deposit requirements are sometimes found in countries maintaining exchange control regimes.[19] Under the advance deposit system an importer must place with the central bank or its agent local currency equal to a specified percentage of the value of the goods to be imported at a time prior to importation. Once importation is completed the sum is returned to the importer. Brazil at one time maintained such a system. Importers desiring to purchase certain categories of foreign-made products were required to deposit in the Bank of Brazil, 150 days prior to importation, a sum equal to 150 per cent of the value of the merchandise. In exchange for this deposit, the Bank issued notes bearing interest at the rate of 6 per cent. Since importers could gain a larger return by utilizing their funds in other ways, the cost of imported goods was increased by the difference between the return they could have had, and the 6 per cent paid by the Bank.[20] In form and effect then, advance deposits are very similar

---

[18] See Treaty of Friendship, Commerce and Navigation between United States and Germany, *done* at Washington, October 29, 1954, art. XII (5) 273 U.N.T.S. 3, 20, (1957).

[19] Thirty-three developing country members of the IMF maintained advance deposit requirements as of December 31, 1966.

[20] The notes were usually sold by the importers in the market, but at 60-70% of their face value. See *Hearings on H.R. 9990 before the House Comm. on Ways and Means,* 87th Cong. 2d Sess., at 176 (1962).

to customs duties. The main difference is that they are usually a temporary device, designed to meet a specific situation. Their relation to exchange controls is that they have been widely used as a short-term measure to reduce the volume of imports during the transitional period when countries are dismantling their exchange control systems. Thus, they will be found with increasing frequency in developing countries as those countries progress to the point where they feel that exchange controls are no longer necessary for the orderly implementation of their development programs.

Discrimination in the application of advance deposit requirements can be guarded against by including in trade agreements a most-favored-nation provision of the type discussed in Chapter II which encompasses both customs duties and "charges of any kind."

CLEARING AND PAYMENTS ARRANGEMENTS

In a world where most countries maintain exchange controls and where the currencies of many of these countries are not acceptable as a means of payment in international commerce, new methods had to be devised to increase trade and yet minimize the need for convertible foreign currencies as a medium of exchange. The most popular techniques by which this has been accomplished are by the use of clearing and payments arrangements. Both continue to be of importance to developing countries.

CLEARING ARRANGEMENTS

A clearing arrangement provides that balances arising out of import and export transactions between two countries will be used solely for the purpose of financing trade between those countries. The need for international transfers of foreign exchange is reduced through the use of clearing accounts.[21] In practice what happens is that a special clearing account is opened in a local bank into which importers make payments for goods imported from a particular country and from which exporters receive payment for goods shipped to that country. Since all transactions in the clearing account are in local currency, the offsetting entries replace the usual international transfers of funds.[22] To illustrate, a typical clearing arrangement is established in Article 4 of the Trade Agreement between the Government of India and the Government of the Polish People's Republic, *done* at New Delhi, April 3, 1956.[23] Under this provision the Polish State Bank established an account in a commercial bank in India. This account was in Indian rupees. When an Indian merchant exports goods to Poland, he receives payment in rupees by means of a check drawn on the account of the Polish State Bank at the Indian commercial bank. In turn, when Polish exporters ship goods to India, they receive payment in Polish currency from the Polish State Bank. The Polish State Bank recovers an equivalent sum in Indian rupees from the Indian importer and adds those rupees to its account in the Indian commercial bank. Under this agreement international transfers of foreign exchange

[21] Some countries exclude from the operation of clearing arrangements certain of their export products which are in demand and can easily be sold for convertible exchange on the world market. Norway has done this with regard to its exports of nickel, Chile with regard to copper. See de Looper, *Current Usage of Payments Agreements and Trade Agreements*, IV IMF STAFF PAPERS 339, 349 (1955).

As of December 31, 1967, of the 107 members of the IMF, 51 were parties to bilateral clearing and/or payments agreements. Of these most were developing countries. The members of the IMF were parties to 309 bilateral clearing and/or payments arrangements. Of these agreements, 224 were with centrally planned countries, 35 between developing countries. There is a trend away from the use of clearing arrangements on the part of some centrally planned countries. See, e.g. the Trade and Payments Agreement between Brazil and Czechoslovakia, done in June 1960, which was amended in 1968 to provide for trade payments in convertible currencies; Article 2 of the Trade Agreement between Turkey and Albania, *done* at Ankara, April 19, 1967, reprinted as Decree No. 6/8309, TURKISH OFFICIAL GAZETTE No. 12, 640, July 6, 1967 (unofficial translation).

[22] There is nothing really novel or recent about clearing arrangements when one considers that they have formed the basis of commercial banking for hundreds of years.

[23] See INDIA'S TRADE AGREEMENTS WITH OTHER COUNTRIES 219-220 (1957).

are kept to an absolute minimum if not eliminated altogether.[24]

A clearing arrangement will totally eliminate the need for international transfers between parties provided that their trade is in balance, i.e., imports from one equal in value imports from the other. But because of difficulties in production and transportation, as well as seasonal variation in needs, trade is not usually in complete balance between two countries. To refer to the Indian-Polish arrangements, during any given short-term period, demands on the Polish account at the Indian commercial bank may exceed existing balances. This would occur if exports to Poland were running ahead of Polish exports to India. When this occurs, one possible course of action is to require that exporters wait for their payments until the balance of the clearing account has been built up through payments for imports. This was the usual situation in the 1930s; in some cases the waiting period was several months. Since everyone found this an unsatisfactory situation, the obvious cure was to permit a deficit to be run in the clearing account. Just as in the case where one overdraws a private bank account, the deficit in the clearing account was really an extension of credit from the bank to the importing country. In the jargon of international economics the sum by which a clearing account may be overdrawn is known as a "swing credit," "swing" because the balance may run in favor of either party at some point during the life of the arrangement.[25] If the amount of the swing credit is exceeded, agreements provide for various remedies which are available to the creditor country. In

[24] The Polish State Bank also maintains an account with the Reserve Bank of India. Any time that the account of the Polish State Bank with the Indian commercial bank runs low in rupees it may be replenished by the Polish State Bank drawing on its account with the Reserve Bank of India. At times when the balance in the Polish account in the Indian commercial bank is high, the Polish State Bank may transfer its surplus rupees to its account in the Reserve Bank of India and convert them into sterling. This may also happen if, at the expiration of the Agreement, there is a balance in the Polish State Bank account at the Indian commercial bank.

[25] For a "swing credit provision," see art. IV of the Payments Agreement between the Federal People's Republic of Yugoslavia and the State of Israel, *done* at Jerusalem, December 11, 1958, reprinted in Appendix B to this chapter.

some cases the creditor has a right to demand that any balance above the swing credit be paid in gold, convertible currency, or goods.[26] In others he has the right to limit trade with the debtor country by the imposition of controls. A third remedy provides that such problems will be dealt with by a "commission" composed of representatives of both parties.[27]

Clearing arrangements have been subjected to severe criticism by many commentators. Since a clearing arrangement enables countries to maintain a substantial volume of trade with their mutual debts offsetting one another thus tying up only a minimum amount of scarce foreign exchange, governments often "prefer" that importers purchase goods from clearing partners. Thus the pattern of trade is distorted from what it would otherwise be if importers were permitted to seek supplies from any source. Furthermore, there is a long history of clearing agree-

[26] See art. IX (4) of the Trade and Payments Agreement between the Government of Ceylon and the Government of the People's Republic of China, *done* at Peking, September 19, 1957, reprinted in Appendix A to this chapter. See also Viner, *supra* note 4 at 31 n.l. "A clause in the Argentine-Brazil Trade Agreement of 1941, apparently unique in the history of trade agreements, provides that annual trade balances . . . between the two countries exceeding a certain amount may only be collected by means of an increase in purchases by the creditor country. If such a clause were widely adopted and could be carried out both in the letter and in the spirit whatever tendency trade-bargaining between two countries on a bilateral-balancing basis has to restrict the total volume of foreign trade *as between the two countries* might be largely removed, since there would be avoidance of the two main trade-restrictive methods by which under existing practice bilateral balancing is achieved, namely, restriction of imports by the 'debtor' or import-surplus country, and restriction of exports by the 'creditor' or export-surplus country."

[27] There is yet a fourth possibility for liquidating balances in clearing accounts, the use of balances in settlements with third countries. If Country A has a positive balance with Country B and a negative balance with C, a three-party arrangement might be made in which B would ship goods to C in satisfaction of B's debt to A. The European Payments Union had such an arrangement between its members. See de Looper, *supra* note 20, at 348. The Council for Mutual Economic Assistance (COMECON) maintains such a system. Balances are settled through the International Bank of Economic Cooperation. See M. KASER, COMECON 137 (1965). Developing countries have been parties to such arrangements. The "Hague Club" and the "Paris Club" were schemes "whereby Brazil and Argentina, respectively, were permitted to spend their earnings from any of their European partners in the Club in any of the other partner countries." G. PATTERSON, *supra* note 6, at 103, note 61. See also art. VII of the Payments Agreement between the Federal People's Republic of Yugoslavia and the State of Israel, *done* at Jerusalem, December 11, 1958, reprinted in Appendix B to this chapter.

ments being used as a means for the exploitation of the weak by the strong. In such cases what happens is that the stronger of the two parties begins by buying up large quantities of products, usually needed agricultural or other primary commodities, from the weaker party. This, in itself, is a cause for some jubilation in the foreign trade offices of the smaller country until it begins to realize that it must import equal amounts of goods from the other party in order to liquidate the clearing balances. To the extent that those balances are not promptly liquidated, the weaker state finds that it is financing the imports of the stronger.[28] Moreover, the weaker country may find that the goods the stronger is offering for sale are either overpriced or useless—or both.[29] This technique was the primary weapon in the economic exploitation of the Balkan States by Nazi Germany during the 1930s. And in more recent years, developing countries have found themselves exploited in much the same way. Ghana, for instance, was forced to liquidate clearing balances by accepting "enough alarm clocks . . . to wake up all of Africa for 10 years.' " [30] Clearing arrangements have also been criticized on more general grounds. For they have been used as a stopgap measure to postpone taking more drastic steps to bring a chronic balance of payments deficit into line. And they have been cited as a primary cause of inflation in countries

---

[28] And it is frequently extending this financing at no charge to the borrower. See the Payments Provision of the Trade and Payments Agreement between the Government of Ceylon and the Government of the People's Republic of China, *done* at Peking, September 19, 1957, art. IX (1), reprinted in Appendix A to this chapter.

[29] Overpricing may be direct or it may take place as a result of overvaluing the exchange of the stronger country. The exchange rate established in the arrangement will be a crucial factor in determining trade flows and the value of the clearing arrangement. It is for this reason that many clearing agreements contain a clause providing a gold equivalent for each country's currency, as protection against a devaluation by one of the parties. See R. SAWYER, COMMUNIST TRADE WITH DEVELOPING COUNTRIES: 1955-1965, at 58 (1966).

[30] "Ghana: Proud, Dynamic, But No Rice in the Shops," N. Y. Times, January 31, 1966, at 46, col. 1.

Ghana's predicament is strangely reminiscent of the one Yugoslavia found herself in the 1930s when, in order to liquidate huge credit balances with Germany, she was forced to accept "enough German aspirins to cover her requirements ten years ahead." P. EINZIG, BLOODLESS INVASION 26 (1939).

which grant swing credits to allow a deficit country to continue purchasing goods. This result occurs because the swing credit is usually created by the central bank of the exporting country and central bank credits are the principal source of new money in most countries.[31]

These arguments have not operated to prevent developing countries from entering into clearing arrangements with each other, particularly on a multilateral basis and as part of an overall program of closer economic cooperation.[32] Thus over 80 per cent of the intraregional transactions of the Central American Common Market are carried on under clearing arrangements through settlements in a regional clearing house (Camara de Compensacion Centroamerica) established in 1961. And the Economic Commission for Latin America (ECLA) has long advocated a multilateral clearing arrangement among the member states of the Latin American Free Trade Area as a means of strengthening intraregional trade cooperation. The purposes of such an arrangement would be to: "(1) promote transactions in area currencies; (2) eliminate the need for financial dealings through intermediate countries located outside the zone; (3) provide credit for the member countries (prudently limiting it to instances of transitory disequilibrium in their over-all balance of payments); and (4) serve as an instrument to enable the monetary authorities in the area to maintain periodical contact with each other." [33] In particular, the ECLA argument in favor of a clearing arrangement runs along the following lines. The freeing of trade among LAFTA coun-

---

[31] To avoid this effect central bankers advocate the abolition of the swing credit system in favor of a method of financing exports by medium-term borrowing on the capital market.

[32] In addition to those discussed in the text, clearing arrangements are under discussion in West Africa between Guinea, Ivory Coast, Liberia, and Sierra Leone, and between the members of the Arab Common Market. For details of these and other arrangements, see REPORT OF THE GROUP OF EXPERTS, PAYMENTS ARRANGEMENTS AMONG DEVELOPING COUNTRIES FOR TRADE EXPANSION, U.N. Doc. TD/B/80/Rev. 1, TD/B C.3/24/Rev. 1, Appendix II (1966).

[33] LATIN AMERICAN ECONOMIC INTEGRATION 12 (M. Wionczek ed. 1966).

tries will result in some of them running a trade deficit within the area. Under the Treaty of Montevideo, a deficit country has the right to slow down the dismantling of its trade barriers so as to ease its plight. And surplus countries are to speed up the elimination of their trade barriers against imports from deficit countries. But this process takes a lot of time and the respective negotiations are likely to end with each side harboring ill will. In the interim, deficit countries might be forced to protect their payments position by the imposition of new trade restrictions. To avoid these lengthy negotiations and retrogressive steps ECLA proposed the creation of a regional clearing mechanism with credits to be made available to deficit countries.[34] Efforts at concluding a regional arrangement, however, were "vigorously opposed" by the International Monetary Fund,[35] principally because the Fund viewed the step as retrogressive in the direction of bilateralism, since many of the LAFTA member states had currencies which were, in theory at least, freely convertible.[36] Nonetheless, the LAFTA countries have proceeded to create a multilateral clearing system, based on individual reciprocal credit agreements between the central banks of the LAFTA countries.

[34] The argument is expounded in detail and discussed in Siegel, *Payments Systems for the Latin American Free Trade Association,* in M. WIONCZEK, *supra* note 32, at 239, 240-241.

[35] Mikesell, *The Movement toward Regional Trading Groups in Latin America,* A. HIRSCHMAN, LATIN AMERICAN ISSUES 125, 147 (1961).

[36] See J. Lindeman, Preferential Trading Systems in Latin America 39 (International Economic Consultants, Washington, D.C., 1960). The arguments pro and con are summarized in M. WIONCZEK, *supra* note 32 at 87-89. These arguments are additional evidence of the eternal quality of many of the pressing issues of the day. See Siegel, *Payments Systems for the Latin American Free Trade Association,* in WIONCZEK, *supra* note 32 at 239, 240. "Indeed, the recent debates between ECLA, on the one hand, and United States officials and the International Monetary Fund, on the other, are very reminiscent of the classic controversies that arose in the nineteenth century between protection-minded young republics, such as the United States, and free-trade-oriented industrialized countries, such as Great Britain." See also Vernon, *A Trade Policy for the 1960s,* 39 FOREIGN AFFAIRS 458, 466 (1961), quoted in *id* at 84 note 15. "But the conditions imposed [on the underdeveloped countries] by the IMF, seen through the eyes of the outside observer, have run too much in the tradition of the banker and too little in the tradition of the entrepreneur. They have too easily subordinated the objectives of growth to those of stability."

The system entered into effect between Argentina, Chile, Columbia, Mexico, Paraguay, and Peru on July 1, 1966, with the central bank of Peru acting as the clearing agency.[37]

PAYMENTS ARRANGEMENTS

The second device used to help the problem of the scarcity of convertible foreign exchange is the payments arrangement, which is similar to a clearing arrangement in that it segregates the funds involved in transactions between two countries from the general foreign exchange earned through the sale of exports. The difference between clearing and payments arrangements is that while clearing arrangements virtually eliminate the need for foreign exchange, payments provisions seek to protect only against the *loss* of foreign exchange in trade.[38] Remittances between importers and exporters in countries which are parties to payments arrangements are made in the usual way—involving foreign exchange. What payments arrangements do is attempt to balance imports against exports so that the amounts of foreign exchange used in the import and export transactions will be approximately equal. A tightly drawn payments provision would read:

Whenever any system of exchange control is in operation in Country *A*, the conditions under which foreign currency shall be made available in any year shall be such as to secure that there shall be available, for the purpose of meeting current remittances from Country *A* to Country *B*, the full amount of the exchange arising from the sale of products of Country *A* in Country *B*.[39]

[37] A proposal for an Asian Payments Union involving clearing arrangements has also been widely discussed. See SUPPLEMENT TO 29 INT. FIN. NEWS SURV. 332 (1967).

[38] It should be noted that the distinction between clearing and payments arrangements drawn here is not always adhered to in practice. At times the term payments arrangement is applied to what has been described in this chapter as a clearing arrangement, the only difference being that the "payments" arrangement covers "noncommercial" remittances. When the terms are used in this manner, a clearing arrangement deals only with payments for goods. An arrangement which covers remittances for transport charges, insurance costs, and repayments of loans, etc. is termed a payments arrangement. See Appendix A to this chapter.

[39] The provision in the text is derived from Art. 2 of the famous Runciman-Roca Agreement, Additional Convention Between the United Kingdom and Argentine to the Treaty of Friendship, Commerce and Navigation concluded at

In this provision Country *B* wanted to preclude the possibility of *A*'s selling in *B*'s market without restriction and using the exchange thus earned to purchase goods in countries *C, D,* and *E*. But the provision goes much further than that. *A* cannot use earnings of exports to *B* to amortize loans from lenders in other countries, or from institutions like the World Bank. This is a particularly stringent provision for a developing country to accept, since the debt service burden of the developing countries is rising and will continue to rise as development quickens. In such circumstances, *B* might alter the provision to read that, instead of the "full amount," only 60 or 70 or 80 per cent of the "exchange arising from" shall be available for current remittance to *B*. Even here, however, a developing country may feel that its freedom is being unduly restricted. Nonetheless, where one party to a trade negotiation maintains a convertible currency and the other does not, the former may insist on such a provision as the price for the latter's maintaining an exchange control system.[40] Though it may thus be forced to accept a payments

---

Buenos Aires, February 2, 1825, *done* at London, May 1, 1933, 143 L.N.T.S. 67, 71 (1933), quoted in M. GORDON, BARRIERS TO WORLD TRADE 190 (1941). A more specific arrangement is included in the Agreement between Greece and Sweden regarding Commercial Exchanges between the Two Countries, *done* at Athens, January 17, 1935, 157 L.N.T.S. 9 (1935). Paragraphs 1 and 2 of that Agreement provide in part:

    I. The Swedish Government undertakes to recommend Aktiebolaget Svenska Tobaksmonopolet [Swedish Tobacco Monopoly] to purchase during the year 1935 as much Greek tobacco of the 1934 crop as is compatible with its requirements.

    II. All foreign exchange accruing from:
        (1) Purchases of tobacco of the 1934 crop . . . ;
        (3) Purchases . . . of Greek goods other than tobacco of the 1934 crop imported into Sweden; shall be used solely for purchasing Swedish goods for importation into Greece.

[40] Payments agreements came into wide use in the 1930s when debtor states introduced exchange control systems in an effort to preserve their shrinking exchange earnings for use in purchasing necessary imports. Creditor states which also bought from the debtor states more goods than they sold them insisted that the debtor states enter into payments agreements which provided that a portion of the debtors export earnings be set aside to liquidate the claims of the creditor. See *Enquiry into Clearing Agreements,* LEAGUE OF NATIONS, II.B. ECONOMIC AND FINANCIAL 6, at 25 (1935).

arrangement, a developing country would do well to seriously ponder its implications.

Finally, it should be noted that while the above-quoted clearing and payments provisions were integral parts of trade agreements, it is not uncommon to find separate clearing and payments agreements. Where this is the case, the trade agreement between the parties would contain a provision such as the following: "Any payments to be made between Country *A* and Country *B* shall be governed by the provisions of the payments agreements concluded on [date]."

A typical payments agreement is reproduced in Appendix B to this chapter.

APPENDIX A

PAYMENTS PROVISION OF THE TRADE AND PAYMENTS AGREEMENT BETWEEN THE GOVERNMENT OF CEYLON AND THE GOVERNMENT OF CHINA, *Done* AT PEKING, 19 SEPTEMBER 1957 [41]

. . . . .

ARTICLE IX

The two Contracting Parties agree that the payments arrangements between the two countries under this Agreement shall be in accordance with the following terms:

(1) The Government of China shall open two accounts in the Central Bank of Ceylon, Colombo, styled Government of China Account "A" and Government of China Account "B."

The Government of Ceylon shall open two accounts in the People's Bank of China, Peking, styled Government of Ceylon Account "A" and Government of Ceylon Account "B."

The above accounts shall bear no interest and shall be free of charges.

(2) Payments for the purchase of commodities which the two Contracting Parties have undertaken to import and export in terms of the yearly protocol referred to in Article IV of this Agreement and payments for the relative incidental expenses, shall be made through the "A" accounts mentioned in paragraph (1) above.

---

[41] 337 U.N.T.S. 148, 150, 152 (1959). This is, in fact, a clearing arrangement. See note 37, *supra*.

Payments for other purchases and the relative incidental expenses as well as other payments approved by the Foreign Exchange Control authorities of both countries shall be made through the "B" accounts mentioned in paragraph (1) above.

The phrase "relative incidental expenses" shall mean the expenses of services in connection with the exchange of goods such as transport charges including charter hire of ships and connected expenses, insurance, arbitration awards, warehousing and customs fees, agents' commissions, advertising, brokerage, and other such charges.

(3) The accounts specified in paragraph (1) above shall be maintained in Ceylon Rupees.

(4) Any residual balances in the "A" accounts specified in paragraph (1) above, outstanding on 31st March of the succeeding year, shall be settled by payment in Pound Sterling or any other currency mutually acceptable immediately after the accounts have been reconciled.

Payments in respect of contracts entered into under the annual protocol of any year, which are made after 31st March of the succeeding year shall be brought to account under the "A" account of the succeeding year.

(5) The balances in the "B" accounts specified in paragraph (1) above shall be reviewed once every quarter by the two Contracting Parties for the purpose of ensuring that trade between the two countries progresses in balance.

Any balances in the "B" accounts remaining outstanding at the end of each calendar year, shall be settled as far as possible by delivery of goods during the first three months of the succeeding year. Any residual balances in the "B" accounts still remaining outstanding on 31st March of the succeeding year, shall be settled by payment in Pound Sterling or any other currency mutually acceptable immediately after the accounts have been reconciled.

(6) The exchange rate for settlement of balances contemplated in paragraphs (4) and (5) above shall be the middle of the Central Bank of Ceylon's buying and selling rates for Pound Sterling or other currency at the time of payment.

· · · · ·

APPENDIX B

PAYMENTS AGREEMENT BETWEEN YUGOSLAVIA AND ISRAEL, *Done* AT JERUSALEM, 11 DECEMBER 1958 [42]

[42] 386 U.N.T.S. 283 (1961).

ARTICLE I

The National Bank of the Federal People's Republic of Yugoslavia, acting on behalf of the Government of the Federal People's Republic of Yugoslavia, shall open on its books a noninterest-bearing account in U.S. dollars (as unit of account) [43] in the name of the Bank of Israel, acting on behalf of the Government of the State Israel.

ARTICLE II

The account referred to in Article I shall be credited with the counter value of goods delivered from Israel to Yugoslavia and with all incidental charges relating thereto.

The account shall be debited with the counter value of goods delivered from Yugoslavia to Israel and with all incidental charges relating thereto. The account shall also be credited or debited in respect of any other transactions effected between the two countries and agreed upon by the two Contracting Parties.

ARTICLE III

All payments provided for in Article II shall be carried out in conformity with the foreign exchange control regulations in force in the two countries.[44]

ARTICLE IV

The National Bank of the Federal People's Republic of Yugoslavia and the Bank of Israel shall execute each other's payment orders irrespective of whether there are funds available in the account referred to in Article I, provided that the balance outstanding on that account shall not exceed one million U.S. dollars.

. . .

ARTICLE V

All payment orders issued by either Bank in pursuance of Article II shall be expressed in U.S. dollars.

. . .

ARTICLE VI

The National Bank of the Federal People's Republic of Yugoslavia and the Bank of Israel shall agree upon the technical procedures to carry out the provisions of the present Agreement.

ARTICLE VII

Either Contracting Party may offer to transfer to the account referred to in Article I balances standing to its credit in a clearing

---

[43] Where the currency of the parties is not widely used in international trade, it is common to use a third currency, usually the U.S. dollar, as a unit of account. See L. TOWLE INTERNATIONAL TRADE AND COMMERCIAL POLICY 655 (2d ed. 1956).

[44] See pp. 79-80 *supra*.

account with any third country and vice versa. Such transfer shall require the prior approval of the other Contracting Party and of the third country concerned.

. . .

ARTICLE IX

Upon termination of this Agreement, any balance appearing on the account referred to in Article I, shall be settled by the debtor country through the delivery of goods and the supply of services of equivalent value. Any balance remaining unsettled six months after the termination of the Agreement shall be settled through payment in transferable Pounds Sterling or any other transferable currency agreed upon by the two banks.

V. Internal Restrictions

Internal Taxes

In Chapter II mention was made of the fact that "import duties are like taxes . . . the effect of which is to increase the cost of imported articles to the consumer." We now deal with the converse of this proposition, taxes which are like import duties. Internal excise taxes which discourage the purchase of imported goods came into their own in the 1930s as a means of offsetting the reductions in customs duties resulting from tariff negotiations. They continue to remain in wide use today, both as a means of protecting local industries and as a device for raising revenue.

Although internal taxes can be used tot discriminate between the products of different foreign producers, their principal use has been to prejudice imports of any origin which compete with domestically produced goods. For example, at one time Cuba levied a 9 per cent tax on the sale of imported newspapers. Norway has taxed the exhibition of newsreels in its cinemas, but exempted domestically produced newsreels from the tax.[1] For countries which exported newspapers and newsreels to Cuba and Norway respectitvely, the proper course was to enter into trade

[1] U.S. Department of State, Memorandum on the Use of the General Agreement on Tariffs and Trade to Remove Restrictions and Discriminatory Practices against United States Trade, 84th Cong., 2nd Sess. 56, 58-59 (1956). More recently in the United States, the State of Tennessee attempted to impose a license of $1,500 on manufacturers, processors, and packers of imported meat. The legislation was struck down as in conflict with the GATT. See "U.S. Opposes Curbs on Imported Meat," N. Y. Times, November 4, 1965, at 10, col. 3.

agreements which would provide for the elimination of these discriminatory taxes. In such negotiations exporters would seek something more than most-favored-nation treatment, since such treatment only requires that importing states treat all similar imports equally. Cuba and Norway were already doing that. Therefore, the exporters had to aim for *national* treatment, which requires that Cuba must treat imported newspapers and Norway foreign newsreels in the same manner as their own. This request for national treatment would not be unusual, since national treatment is the international standard with respect to internal taxes and restrictions. Thus it is generally accepted among trading nations that any distinction between imported and domestic goods should be effected through customs duties which are *highly visible*. Discrimination by internal restriction is much less visible and is therefore thought to be "not cricket." Moreover, states may consider their tax systems an "internal affair" which should not be subject to international negotiation. By granting each other national treatment as to internal taxes, they in effect prevent these taxes from discriminating against imports, and shift any necessary negotiations to customs tariffs where there is a long history of revision based upon international agreement. The final and most important reason for national treatment is to prevent internal taxes being used to wipe out the effects of a reduction in the customs duty.

National treatment for internal taxes and restrictions may be provided for in a trade agreement in the following language:

The products of either Party imported into the territory of the other Party shall not be subject, directly or indirectly, to internal taxes or other internal charges of any kind in excess of those applied, directly or indirectly, to like products of national origin or of any other origin nor shall they be accorded treatment less favorable than that accorded to like products of national origin or any other origin in respect of all laws, regulations, and requirements affecting their internal sale or use. The term "like product" includes products which are directly competitive with or substitutable for the imported product.[2]

In view of what has been said about the lack of value of a guarantee of most-favored-nation treatment with regard to internal taxes and regulations, it may appear strange to the reader that the quoted provision provides for such treatment ("or any other origin") as well as national treatment. This language is necessary, however, to provide for the case where an imported item is not produced in the importing country. In such a situation there is no "treatment" upon which a "national" standard can be based. If most-favored-nation treatment is not provided for and if imports come from two or more countries it would be possible for the importing state to discriminate between foreign sources of supply. Where there are domestic producers the national treatment standard will usually prove to be the guarantee which is more valuable. For domestic producers can be expected to fight against the imposition of an excise tax on their product. In doing this they will be fighting the battle of an exporter on whose product the tax would also fall. Thus, by securing national treatment the exporter gains not only the lowest rate of tax, but also an ally better situated than he to press for either the reduction or total elimination of the tax.

Where the importing country does not itself produce a product of the type imported, it may be necessary to provide that national treatment extends to "directly competitive or substitutable" products. To illustrate, suppose Country A produces butter and imports oleomargarine. Would tax on the sale of oleomargarine, but not on the sale of butter, be commensurate with the national

---

[2] See arts. III (1) and (2) GATT, 55 U.N.T.S. 188 204, 206 (1950). This provision would cover, *inter alia*, action like the distribution of signs reading "only domestic beef sold here" by the Government of the State of Alabama in the United States. Alabama was prohibited from following this practice by a United States Court which held that it violated United States GATT obligations. See "U.S. Opposes Curbs on Imported Meat," N. Y. Times, November 4, 1965, at 10, col. 3.

Internal taxes and other internal regulations are occasionally dealt with in separate articles. See General Treaty on Central American Economic Integration, *done* at Managua, December 13, 1960, arts. VI, VII, 1 UNITED NATIONS, MULTILATERAL ECONOMIC CO-OPERATION IN LATIN AMERICA, U.N. DOC. E/CN 12/621, at 5 (1962).

treatment standard? If the national treatment were limited to "like" products, the question would be debatable. To avoid such ambiguities, the trade agreement provision has been extended to cover "directly competitive or substitutable products." This seemingly narrow point may be of some significance to those developing countries which export beverage crops. Coffee, in particular, has been subjected to high rates of internal taxation in some countries of Western Europe.[3] Since coffee is not produced in those countries, the question of national treatment does not appear to arise. But if coffee is "directly competitive" with, or "substitutable for" soft drinks, beer, and wine, the rates of taxation on those beverages may establish a case of discrimination against coffee.[4]

An alternative formulation for dealing with internal taxes is found in Article IV of the Agreement Establishing a Free Trade Area between the United Kingdom and the Republic of Ireland: [5]

(1) Neither party shall—
  (a) apply directly or indirectly to imported goods any fiscal charges in excess of those applied directly or indirectly to like domestic goods, or otherwise apply such charges so as to afford *protection* to like domestic goods; or
  (b) apply fiscal charges to imported goods of a kind not produced or not produced in substantial quantities in its territory in such a way as to afford effective protection to the domestic production of goods of a different kind which are substitutable for the imported goods, which enter into direct competition with them, and which do not bear, directly or indirectly, in the importing territory fiscal charges of equivalent incidence; and the party shall give effect to these obligations in a manner laid down in paragraphs (2) and (3) of this Article

[3] See S. WEINTRAUB, THE FOREIGN-EXCHANGE GAP OF THE DEVELOPING COUNTRIES 11 (1965) (customs duties and fiscal charges on coffee amounted to 127% ad valorem in Germany, 174% ad valorem in Italy).
[4] The Havana Charter contained an interpretive note which provided that an internal tax "which is applied to a product not produced domestically in substantial quantities shall be treated as a customs duty. . . ." for purposes of tariff negotiations. *Ad Article* 17, C. WILCOX, A CHARTER FOR WORLD TRADE 320 (1949).
[5] [1966] Gr. Brit. T.S. 31 (CMD. 3026) at 10.

(2) . . .

(3) (a) The effective protective element in any charge shall be eliminated

    (i) by the Government of the United Kingdom not later than . . .

    (ii) by the Government of Ireland on or before . . .

Either party may implement the provisions of this sub-paragraph by reducing a fiscal charge applicable to imported goods, by imposing a new fiscal charge applicable to imported goods, or by raising an existing fiscal charge applicable to domestic goods. (Emphasis added.)

This article provides for national treatment in the traditional language. It also provides for the elimination of any *protective* element in an internal tax. At first glance this language might appear redundant, since the same fiscal charges levied on domsetic and imported goods would not ordinarily provide protection for the domestically produced goods. Here, however, it is well to recall the discussion in Chapter II regarding specific duties where it was noted that specific duties penalize low-priced goods. So here, if the tax is in a specific amount, rather than ad valorem, and if domestic goods are of high quality, while similar goods which are imported are of lower quality, the same tax will fall unequally on the two types of goods, to the detriment of the lower-priced goods. Thus not only must tax treatment be equal on its face, it must also "apply" in a manner so as not to afford protection to domestic producers. To illustrate the situation in which this added language would be most useful, take the case of the taxes levied on automobiles by several Western European countries. The tax rates vary according to the horsepower of the automobile, a standard which on its face makes no distinction as to the country of origin. In France the tax is called a *use tax*. Automobiles with a physical horsepower of 5 are liable for an anual tax of $12.15. For cars with a horsepower of 16, the fee is $30 per year. Above 16 horsepower, however, the annual tax jumps to $202. The cars above 16 horsepower are virtually all American products. A similar situation prevails in Italy, where a *road tax* is levied. For a car of 12 horsepower, the annual tax is $29. But for a small American car, the Ford Falcon, the tax is $166. And for a Ford Galaxie, with 45 horsepower, the tax is $379 per year.[6]

An altetrnative method of dealing with internal taxes is found in the Treaty Establishing the Central American Common Market. Article VI of that Treaty provides:

If the goods traded are liable to internal taxes, charges or duties of any kind levied on production, sale, distribution, or consumption in any of the signatory countries, the country concerned may levy an equivalent amount on similar goods imported from the other Contracting State, in which case it must also levy at least an equivalent amount for the same respective purposes on similar imports from third countries.

This provision goes further than a requirement of national treatment. It seeks the elimination of internal taxes on imported goods and in effect penalizes a member state which maintains such a tax system by the reciprocal imposition of taxes on its exports. The provision suffers from one obvious shortcoming. The reciprocal taxes may only be levied on "similar" goods. Normally, states do not export "similar" goods to each other, so that to retain the apparent intent of the article it would be necessary to interpret the word "similar" to mean goods of *similar value* rather than those which are *similar in kind*. But even here, the effect of an equal levy on goods of similar value may be far different as a result of demand conditions. What the draftsmen really aimed for was giving the party affected by the internal taxes the right to impose

---

[6] See *Hearings on H.R. 9990 Before the House Comm. on Ways and Means,* 87th Congress, 2d Sess. 1545 (1962); Mathews, *Non-Tariff Import Restrictions: Remedies Available in United States Law,* 62 MICH. L. REV. 1295, 1326 (1964).

In addition to the general provision suggested above, particular problems like automobile use taxes can be dealt with separately in articles such as the following:

With regard to automobiles produced in Country *A* and imported into Country *B*, Country *B* shall, in levying use, road or other internal taxes by whatever name, on automobiles, seek to provide that [such taxes, if based upon horsepower, shall not exceed $.......... per unit of horsepower] [the highest rate levied shall not exceed more than .... times the lowest rate]

The Kennedy Round negotiations included intensive discussions about automobile taxes. According to reports, the negotiations "succeeded in breaking . . . the automobile tax system" referred to in the text. See "Non-tariff Curbs Take Bigger Role," N. Y. Times, June 11, 1967, § 3, at 1, col. 8, at 5, col. 3.

taxes which have an equivalent *effect* on the other party. But this is not the easiest formula to articulate, nor is the goal of "equivalent effect" as objectively determinable as "equivalent amount" and "similar goods." Futhermore, this provision allows the injured party to impose countervailing taxes *provided* that these taxes are imposed on imports from third countries. If, as is normally the case, in the trade agreements between the injured party and third countries there is a provision calling for national treatment with regard to internal taxes, this would require that the injured state also impose the countervailing taxes on its domestic production. But internal pressures may make this an undesirable course of action. Thus, the requirement that the injured party has the right to impose countervailing taxes only if such taxes apply to imports from a third country may render that "right" ephemeral.

One final point on internal taxes. Since customs duties are normally subject only to the requirement of most-favored-nation treatment, whereas internal taxes must meet the higher standard of national treatment, in the past exporting parties have sought to classify certain charges as internal taxes, even though the importing country considered the charges "customs duties." The problem is illustrated in the following passage which describes various fiscal charges in Latin America:

Special taxes having primarily a fiscal objective cover a wide range and are based on varying criteria. Prior to its last customs reform, which reduced the different import charges formerly in effect to a single levy consolidated on the basis of value, Argentina collected a "statistical" duty (i.e. one whose proceeds are used in financing statistical processing), a duty to finance the 'forestry plan,' and another corresponding to the 'iron and steel plan.' Brazil applies a special levy for customs handling, another that goes to a fund for a port improvement, and yet another for the rehabilitation of the merchant marine. Chile enforces similar provisions through special import taxes under the 'highway law' and the 'unloading law'; it also maintains one relating to freight charges. . . . Paraguay imposes, among other duties, a sales tax on all imported goods. In addition to her 'maritime freight law,' which establishes a percentage levy on freight charges, Peru has nine other provisions of a similar nature; . . .[7]

The converse may also occur. An exporting country may make tariff cuts and seek in exchange reductions on charges in the importing country which the former claims are tariffs but the latter claims are internal taxes. To distinguish between the two it has been suggested that customs duties "(a) . . . are collected at a time of, and as a condition to, the entry of the goods into the importing country, and (b) they apply exclusively to imported products without being related in any way to similar charges collected internally on like domestic products. The fact that these charges are described as internal taxes in the laws of the importing country [would] not in itself have the effect of giving them the status of internal taxes. . . ." [8]

The artificially high prices charged to consumers where the import and internal distribution of a product is in the hands of a state enterprise are closely related to internal taxes. Where the enterprise from which the consumer buys is owned by the government, the difference between the cost of the merchandise to the enterprise and the price to the consumer, in a private market economy the profit, is an internal tax in everything but name. States desiring to export merchandise in such situations have recognized this to be the case and have attempted to provide in their trade agreements that where goods are marketed internally by state enterprises the party maintaining such enterprises shall: (1) give notice to its trading partners of the amount of the "markup" that such goods are subject to; (2) be prepared to negotiate over the level of the "markup" as though it were a customs duty

---

[7] Magariños, *Integregration Instruments and LAFTA Achievements*, in LATIN AMERICAN ECONOMIC INTEGRATION 124, 128 (M. Wionczek ed. 1966).

[8] GATT, ANALYTICAL INDEX 21 (Rev. ed. 1966).

The problems discussed in this chapter relate to internal taxes levied on imported goods. Internal taxes are also levied on locally produced goods which are exported—where they have the same effect as export duties. The most-favored-nation provision at pages 36-37 of Chapter II applies to internal taxes levied on goods which are exported. See GATT, REPORT OF THE SECOND SESSION 4 (1948).

or an internal tax. Such provisions have not been a great success.[9] For the markup between the cost of the article and its final
selling price is not solely profit (i.e., tax) but represents, in addition, the costs of transport, distribution, warehousing, etc. And a
party questioning the high markup on its goods is rarely, if ever,
able to produce figures calling into question the other party's
calculations of these costs. Nonetheless the problem remains a real
one. At the first UNCTAD Conference, the member countries
recommended that the "centrally planned countries . . . reduce
. . . the margin between the import price and the resale price
of manufactures and semi-manufactures imported from the developing countries. . . ." [10]

PREFERENTIAL FREIGHT RATES

Preferential freight rates for local commodities have been used as
a means of discriminating against imported goods. Country *A*
might, for example, charge rail freight of $2 per ton to haul
locally grown wheat for 100 miles, while the rail charge for imported wheat to travel the same distance might be $5 per ton.
One way in which this problem has been dealt with is to add the
word "transportation" after the words "internal sale, offering for

[9] There are, however, some precedents. "In 1933 the United Kingdom obtained
from Norway a pledge as to the maximum prices at which British whiskey would
be sold to consumers by the Norwegian state liquor monopoly." Viner, *Trade
Relations between Free Market and Controlled Economies*, LEAGUE OF NATIONS,
II. A. ECONOMIC AND FINANCIAL, at 74 (1943).

[10] See Report of the Second Committee, Annex E to the FINAL ACT OF THE
UNITED NATIONS CONFERENCE ON TRADE AND DEVELOPMENT, in I PROCEEDINGS OF THE
UNITED NATIONS CONFERENCE ON TRADE AND DEVELOPMENT 143, 155-56 (1964). But
see SECRETARY-GENERAL OF THE UNITED NATIONS CONFERENCE ON TRADE AND DEVEL-
OPMENT, TOWARDS A NEW TRADE POLICY FOR DEVELOPMENT 93, 94, U.N. Doc.
E/CONF. 46/3 (1964): "It has been suggested that, in view of the different role
of tariffs in the two economic and social systems, consideration should be given
to the possibility of reducing internal prices in socialist countries as a counterpart
to the lowering of tariffs by private-enterprise countries. This, however would not
bring about the desired result. A lowering of prices in socialist countries would not
by itself promote higher imports, as a reduction of tariffs does in private-enterprise
countries. The level of imports in socialist countries depends upon the provisions
made in the economic plans, which are in turn based on expected exports."

sale, purchase" in the provision quoted on page 115. A more detailed treatment would provide that: "As regards the importation and exportation of the products of either Party, the charges and fees of all types for transport by rail or any other form of internal transport applied by either of the Parties shall not be higher than those which it applies to or may apply to its own products or to the products of any other country dispatched under the same conditions, to the same destination and via the same route." [11]

MARKING REQUIREMENTS

Most countries maintain a form of discrimination against foreign-made goods by requiring that imported goods be marked with their country of origin. The purpose of such requirements was made clear in a remarkably candid opinion of the United States Customs Court, where it was noted that "The purpose of Congress in enacting the [marking] provision was to make competition with the domestic manufacturer more difficult and expensive, and if compliance with its requirements should render articles less desirable to purchasers, or should be more expensive and difficult, such fact could not defeat the intention of Congress, which was to reduce, if not prohibit, competition with American manufacturers." [12] In accordance with this philosophy, the American marking law, which provides for a duty of 10 per cent on goods not properly marked, has been strictly enforced. An importer of books printed in France was penalized because the dust covers on the books were not marked with the country of origin, even though the books themselves were properly imprinted. A manufacturer of candy had to pay $2,000 because a shipment of

[11] See Commercial Convention between Finland and France, done at Paris, July 13, 1921, art. 10, 29 L.N.T.S. 445, 453 (1924); Provisional Agreement concerning Commerce and Navigation between Bulgaria and Poland, done at Sofia, April 29, 1925, art. X, 60 L.N.T.S. 103, 111 (1927).

[12] Burstein & Sussman v. United States, 47 TREAS. DEC. 342, 343 (1925), quoted in G. ELLIOTT, TARIFF PROCEDURES AND TRADE BARRIERS 219 (1955).

almonds for use in his product arrived in the United States marked "Portucues" instead of "Portuguese." [13]

Countries which find marking requirements burdensome may seek to include in their trade agreements a provision similar to Article IX of the General Agreement on Tariffs and Trade:

1. Each Party shall accord to the products of the other Party treatment with regard to marking requirements no less favorable than the treatment accorded to like products of any third country.
2. Both Parties agree that their laws and regulations relating to the marking of imported products shall be such as to permit compliance without seriously damaging the products, or materially reducing their value, or unreasonably increasing their cost.[14]

The usual means of reducing the impact of such requirements has not, however, been through trade agreements. Rather the approach has been for exporting states to familiarize themselves with the marking requirements of importing nations and to ensure that all exports are properly marked before leaving the country. Where, however, marking "requirements . . . [go] beyond the obligation to indicate origin," such requirements will be considered a violation of the provision quoted above.[15]

---

[13] See L. TOWLE, INTERNATIONAL TRADE AND COMMERCIAL POLICY 540 (2d ed. 1956). To eliminate these barriers to trade, the Government of Czechoslovakia, supported by the Governments of Australia, Canada, Chile, Cuba, Czechoslovakia, and France, sought to have the Havana Charter incorporate a provision abolishing marks of origin. The proposal was opposed by Belgium, Luxembourg, the United Kingdom, and the United States. See meeting of the Technical Sub-Committee of the Drafting Committee of the Preparatory Committee of the International Conference on Trade and Employment, January 31, 1947, U.N. Doc. E/PC/T/C. 6/30, at 3.

[14] GATT, III BASIC INSTRUMENTS AND SELECTED DOCUMENTS 17 (1958). See also the International Convention for the Abolition of Import and Export Prohibitions and Restrictions, *done* at Geneva, November 8, 1927, art. III, LEAGUE OF NATIONS, IIA. ECONOMIC AND FINANCIAL 7, at 7 (1928), ("Should the High Contracting Parties, in pursuance of their legislation, subject the importation and exportation of goods to certain regulations in respect of . . . the imposition of marks . . . , they undertake that such regulations shall not be made a means of disguised prohibition or arbitrary restriction.")

[15] See ANALYTICAL INDEX, *supra* note 8, at 24.

MIXING REQUIREMENTS

The final type of internal restrictions which may substantially limit the market for imports are "mixing" requirements. Mixing requirements usually apply to nonprocessed or semiprocessed agricultural products, and provide that not less than a specified proportion of the final product must be composed of goods of domestic origin. There are two types of mixing requirements. The first has been termed "linked-utilization." An example would be the requirement, almost universal in Europe during the 1930s, that a specified minimum amount of domestic wheat flour must be used in all bread.[16] The second type of mixing requirement is "linked-purchasing." This is illustrated by the Malaysian requirement that importers must purchase one ton of rice from official (local) stocks for each ton they wish to import. Another case is the requirement that Argentine rubber importers must purchase one ton of domestically produced synthetic rubber for each ton of natural rubber imported.

Mixing requirements are, of course, another in the long list of devices which may be used to discriminate against imports. They are particularly nefarious as a means of circumventing an obligation to give imports national treatment with respect to internal taxes. To combat the discriminatory effect of mixing requirements, the logical first step would be to see whether this can be accomplished by requiring most-favored-nation treatment. But the most-favored-nation concept will not be of use in situations where, as here, all foreign exporters are discriminated against. Nor is the concept of national treatment of much utility since the very pur-

---

[16] Mixing requirements came into wide use during the 1930s as a means of cutting down on imports, when countries were prohibited from imposing import quotas because they had ratified the Convention for the Abolition of Import and Export Prohibitions and Restrictions, *done* at Geneva, November 8, 1927, LEAGUE OF NATIONS, II.A. ECONOMIC AND FINANCIAL 7 (1928). When the Convention failed to secure the number of ratifications required for it to enter into force, the countries which had ratified it began to restrict imports more directly i.e., by means of import quotas. See M. GORDON, BARRIERS TO WORLD TRADE 290-292 (1941).

pose of such mixing requirements is to discriminate against imported products. The only satisfactory solution is to include in a trade agreement a provision prohibiting mixing requirements. "[Neither Party] shall establish or maintain any internal quantitative regulations relating to the mixture, processing, or use of products in specified amounts or proportions which requires, directly or indirectly, that any specific amount or proportion of any product which is the subject of the regulation must be supplied from domestic sources." [17]

This provision should act to prevent the imposition of mixing requirements to protect local producers. It is possible, however, that where a product is not produced locally, and imported from two or more countries, internal restrictions might be used to discriminate between the sources of supply. Here is a case where the most-favored-nation principle would operate effectively. The usual approach, however, is to provide as follows: "No internal quantitative regulation relating to the mixture, processing or use of products in specified amounts or proportions shall be applied in such a manner as to allocate any such amount or proportion among external sources of supply." [18]

Conclusion

The brief survey of internal restrictions on the importation of goods does not exhaust the field. In fact, there seem no limits to the ingenuity with which governments will at times seek to protect their local markets. There are, for instance, countries which prohibit the advertising of whiskey, ostensibly on the grounds of maintaining the public health. The effect is to protect

[17] Article III(5), GATT, III Basic Instruments and Selected Documents 9 (1958). This provision has been interpreted to permit "the entry of . . . [a] product at a rate of duty lower than the normal tariff rate, provided the product is mixed or used with a certain proportion of a similar product of national origin. . . . [since] the use of a percentage of the local product is not made compulsory, nor is the product in any way restricted." Analytical Index supra note 8, at 25.
[18] Article III(7), GATT, III Basic Instruments and Selected Documents 9 (1958).

local producers of substitute beverages. The field of sanitary, health, and security regulations is discussed in detail in Chapter X. The present chapter has sought to identify only the more common types of internal barriers which, with the completion of the Kennedy Round, are destined to receive an increasing amount of attention.

VI. STATE TRADING

The barriers to trade discussed thus far have involved the placing of governmental hurdles between the exporter and the importer. These barriers range from the levying of duties which increase the price of imported goods to quantitative restrictions which may amount to absolute prohibitions on imports. In this chapter a different genus of import restriction will be discussed. For in the case of state trading there is no need for the government to impose a barrier between importer and exporter, since the government itself assumes one of those roles. It is thus the government acting as an importer which decides directly what goods will be purchased from abroad. So, too, where there is state trading in export goods it is the government itself which decides what goods will be exported to what places and at what prices.

WHAT IS STATE TRADING?

In any discussion of state trading, it is essential at the outset to attempt to define the term. This is not an easy task since the line between state trading and state regulation of private trading is extremely hazy. In many so-called free economies government regulation is, or can be made, so all-embracing that it virtually imposes decisions on private importers. Thus precise government control over imports and exports could be accomplished without much difficulty by a sophisticated use of the devices discussed in Chapters II to V. How, then, is one to identify a state trading situation? It has been suggested that government may be considered to have definitely crossed the line where there is "direct participation by the government (or its agent) in foreign trade including those activities in which the government (or its agent) holds title to exports before transactions and acquires title to imports." [1] This "title" test has all the attractions of simplicity but suffers its drawbacks. Aside from the ambiguities involved in "taking title," this definition does not elaborate on what other acts of "direct participation" might give rise to evidence of state trading. Perhaps the needed elaboration is supplied by a definition which identifies state trading as a situation where the government not only determines, directly, or through an organization under its complete control, what goods will be bought and from what sources but also negotiates the price to be paid or offered and the other terms of sale. It may be said therefore that when the traditional functions of the importer or exporter are exercised by a state enterprise, that is state trading.

Assuming that this issue can be resolved, the next problem is deciding exactly what is a government agent, a state enterprise, or an organization under the "complete control" of the government. Where the economy of a country is centrally planned the issue is not complicated, since the purchaser or seller makes no secret of the fact that it is a government agency. But suppose, in a free economy, the government holds a majority of the shares in a corporation. Is that corporation a state enterprise? [2] And what if the government holds less than a majority but maintains effective control? Suppose the government holds no shares but has made substantial loans to a corporation and the loan agreement has laid down certain conditions which may, in effect, amount to

---

[1] ECONOMIC COMMISSION FOR FAR ASIA AND THE FAR EAST, STATE TRADING IN COUNTRIES OF THE ASIA AND THE FAR EAST REGION, U.N. Doc. E/CN. 11/665 at 1 (1964) (footnote omitted).

[2] In litigation in a U.S. Court, the Anglo-Iranian Oil Company was granted the immunity of a foreign government "on the ground that the British Government held a controlling interest in its voting stock and that the purpose of the company was to ensure oil supplies for the British Navy." W. FRIEDMANN, THE CHANGING STRUCTURE OF INTERNATIONAL LAW 351-352 (1964). (The case was styled Re Investigation of World Arrangements with Relation to Production, etc., of Petroleum, 107 F. Supp. 628 (D.D.C. 1952).)

"substantial" control of the corporation? These questions are particularly relevant in developing countries where, because of a lack of available private capital or expertise, or because the government as a matter of policy has decided upon the construction of a "socialist economy," most enterprises engaged in overseas trade have both government capital and government directors.

The Charter of the International Trade Organization attempted to deal with the question of what is a state enterprise. Article 31 of the Havana Charter provided that "[t]his Article shall apply to any enterprise, organ, or agency in which there is effective control by a Member government." The Charter then continued with two alternative proposals which could be added to the foregoing sentence. *"Alternative A* or over whose trading operations a Member government exercises effective control by virtue of the special or exclusive privileges granted to the enterprise. *Alternative B* or over whose trading operations a government is, under the arrangements providing for the special or exclusive privileges granted to the enterprise, legally entitled to exercise effective control." [3] While giving a bit more meaning to the term "state enterprise," the proposed Article opened the Pandora's box of "effective control." [4] Where government officers constitute a majority of the board of directors, and where the board is *de jure* the principal policy maker for an enterprise, a clear case of effective government control of an enterprise may be made out. But suppose the government directors are a minority on the board but retain a veto power over certain aspects of management, e.g., decisions to purchase goods above x amount in value, decisions on hiring of

[3] REPORT OF THE DRAFTING COMMITTEE OF THE PREPARATORY COMMITTEE OF THE UNITED NATIONS CONFERENCE ON TRADE AND EMPLOYMENT U.N. Doc. E/PC/T/34/ Rev. 1 at 27 (1947).

[4] An early draft of the I.T.O. Charter found state trading where the government exercised "substantial" control over an enterprise. At the suggestion of the United Kingdom delegate to the meeting of the Sub-committee on State Trading of Committee II of the Preparatory Committee of the International Conference on Trade and Employment on November 9, 1946, U.N. Doc. E/PC/T/C.II/47 at 2, the word "substantial" was dropped in favor of the word "effective." The United States representative then proposed the phrase "'a substantial measure of effective control.'" *Id.* at 3. But the delegate from New Zealand immediately pointed out that "in order to be effective, control must be substantial." *Ibid.*

management personnel. Is the government in "effective control"? Or take the case where the goverment directors are private citizens appointed by the government, is this a clear case of effective government control? Perhaps it was because it raised questions of this nature that the ITO Charter provision was not included in the General Agreement on Tariffs and Trade.

The Preparatory Committee for the GATT believed that the term "state enterprises" "did not require any special definition; it was generally understood that the term includes, *inter alia,* any agency of government that engaged in purchasing or selling." [5] While the latter part of this statement is undoubtedly correct, a government agency is clearly a state enterprise, the real issue is whether enterprises which are not identifiable as government agencies may also be state enterprises. Apparently they may, for Article XVII of the GATT deals with state enterprises and "any enterprise," which is granted "exclusive or special privileges." Precisely what privileges need be granted to make an enterprise a state enterprise is not made clear in the Agreement. Presumably, the privileges refer, at a minimum, to the exclusive right to import or export certain goods.[6] Thus the GATT aimed at avoiding the "effective control" miasma of the ITO Charter. For it would be relatively easy to identify enterprises given a monopoly over imports or exports. But the issue was somewhat clouded by Paragraph 1(a) in *Ad Article* XVII of the GATT. For that paragraph provides that "[g]overnmental measures imposed to assure standards of quality and efficiency in the operation of external trade. . .but which do not empower the government to exercise control over the trading activities of the enterprise in question, do not constitute 'exclusive or special privileges.' " According to this, if a govern-

---

[5] GATT, ANALYTICAL INDEX 91 (Rev. ed. 1966).

[6] The point was a little clearer in an early draft of the I.T.O. Charter which provided, *inter alia,* ". . . if any Member grants exclusive or special privileges, formally or in effect, to any enterprise to import, export, purchase, sell, distribute, or produce any product . . ." See meeting of the Drafting Sub-Committee on State Trading of Committee II of the Preparatory Committee of the International Conference on Trade and Employment, November 16, 1946, U.N. Doc. E/PC/T/c.II/53 at 1 (1946).

ment grants to Enterprise A the exclusive right to import certain goods and justifies such action on the grounds of "efficiency in the operation of external trade" Enterprise A will be considered a state enterprise only if the government is "empowered" to exercise "control" over the trading activities of Enterprise A. Since one can safely assume that if questioned, most governments would defend the granting of monopoly import or export rights to any enterprise as a means of promoting efficiency in their external trading operations, in effect the GATT, while in theory abandoning the ITO definitions, has included them. The key question thus remains whether the government is empowered "to exercise control over the trading activities of the enterprise in question." [7]

Despite the deviation incorporated in *Ad Article* XVII, the basic GATT definition seems to move in the right direction. For the essence of state trading is a *combination of state control and monopoly*. And of those two components, *monopoly* would seem the more significant. For, as has been noted above, state control over foreign trade is quite extensive in the market economies and a distinction based on this criterion alone would be a fragile one indeed. Its justification would have to lie in the fact that in the state trading situation, state control also means that the barriers to trade remain hidden within the confines of the government bureaucracy. On the other hand, the monopoly element of state trading seems a much more clear-cut basis for distinguishing between market economies and state trading systems. The point may be illustrated by imagining an economy in which trade is conducted by state enterprises, but where there is more than one

---

[7] The question is sometimes put in the converse: "To what degree do state enterprises enjoy autonomy from government control?" It is difficult to see how this formulation aids in finding a solution to the question. Here again the question is what weight is to be given form, and, if the answer is little, how to discover whether control is being exercised informally and/or confidentially. See Viner, *Trade Relations between Free-Market and Controlled Economies*, LEAGUE OF NATIONS, II. A. ECONOMIC AND FINANCIAL, at 73 (1943). "If the State monopolies are set up as separate administrative units with substantial autonomy, and without close integration with the agencies in charge of political and commercial policy, this may in practice constitute a substantial barrier to the use of their operations for political or trade-bargaining purposes, but other countries can never be confident that such will be the case."

state enterprise in each line of endeavor, so that there is competition between the enterprises. In such a case, it is a safe assumption that the competition between state enterprises would lead them to behave very much like private importers. As long as there is no yardstick to measure the efficiency of a bureaucratic organization, that organization is liable to suffer all of the ills which have been associated with such endeavors. But where there is such a yardstick, in the form of a competing bureaucracy, the competitive atmosphere brings about the same kind of situation as that prevailing in the private markets. Thus in considering whether a state trading situation exists, the better starting point would be a determination of whether the organization enjoys a monopoly position in the market in question, rather than beginning with the search for "effective cotrol" by the state.[8]

From the complexity of the problem it can be appreciated that there is no readily available test which will identify state trading in all its forms. Nonetheless, discussion of the problems raised by state trading can continue on the assumption that there are some situations which are clear cases of state trading. One should, however, be aware of the fact that what is said relative to them applies equally well to situations where there is state trading in fact but not in form.

---

[8] For a recent attempt at defining a state enterprise, see The Agreement Establishing a Free Trade Area between the United Kingdom and Ireland, art. XIV (5) [1966] Gr. Brit. T.S. No. 31 (CMD 3026) at 15. ("For purposes of this Article 'public undertakings' means central, regional or local government authorities, public enterprises and any organizations other than the foregoing by means of which either party, by law or in practice, controls or appreciably influences imports from or exports to the territory of the other.")

As far as exports are concerned, an added factor in determining whether a state enterprise is more "state" than "enterprise" has recently come to light in the reforms in Czechoslovakia which are taking the export trade out of the hands of trading corporations and placing it with joint stock companies formed by industrial enterprises. See Economic Intelligence Department, Barclay's Bank, Ltd., East Europe, June 1967. One can safely assume that an export organization tied to producers is more likely to behave "commercially" than an independent trading organization which can always blame the producer for making the wrong goods if those goods do not sell. This is in fact the basis for the Czech reform.

Why State Trading?

Governments engage in state trading for a variety of reasons. For the centrally planned economy, such a system is the only practical way in which the economic plan can be effectively implemented.[9] The reasons for the presence of state trading in free market countries are somewhat different. In a large number of countries tobacco and alcohol are imported and marketed by state organizations because the sale of such commodities provides the government with a substantial source of revenue. State trading in narcotic products, alcohol, and pharmaceuticals is frequently maintained to protect the health of the country's cititzens. Similarly, trade in arms and ammunitions is generally subject to state trading for purposes of national security. Finally, many agricultural products are sold by state enterprises, e.g., marketing boards, which form part of a comprehensive system of regulation of agriculture designed to support and/or stabilize farm income.

For developing countries, the last reason is perhaps the most important. To protect their local growers from the fluctuations of world market prices, government marketing boards have been established which purchase primary commodities from farmers and market them in bulk throughout the world. In addition to its stabilizing function, government marketing of primary products is an administratively easy way to tax producers of such products. Government trading has also been used in developing countries, however, as a means of getting the indigenous population into businesses formerly in the hands of expatriates. The Ceylon Cooperative Wholesale Establishment, a government corporation,

[9] See Allen, *State Trading and Economic Warfare*, 24 LAW & CONTEMP. PROB. 256, 258 (1959). There is also an ideological basis for state trading. "Foreign trade in the U.S.S.R. and in the People's Democracies is conducted on the basis of a state monopoly. This is a necessary corollary, of a system in which the main export resources as well as the imported commodities constitute public property." Sergeyev, *Economic Principles of the Foreign Trade of Socialist States*, INTERNATIONAL TRADE THEORY IN A DEVELOPING WORLD 277, 282 (R. Harrod & D. Hague ed. 1964).

has thus been used as a device for "Ceylonizing" foreign trade. And the direct nationalization of foreign-owned businesses usually means the conversion of formerly private companies into state enterprises. Finally, developing countries have established state trading corporations for the express purpose of dealing with other countries which employ state trading. For example, the Nepal Trading Company Limited was established to deal in imports from the Soviet Union and the People's Republic of China. And in negotiations between India and the Soviet Union, the latter expressed a desire to do business with Indian state trading organizations rather than with private importers and exporters. For all of these reasons state trading plays an important role in the external trade of developing countries.[10]

STATE TRADING AND MOST-FAVORED-NATION TREATMENT

With state trading such a widespread and growing practice, it may be somewhat surprising to discover that it remains a highly controversial subject in international trade. This was not always the case. The system itself has been present in the world about as long as taxes have.[11] And in the International Convention for the Abolition of Import and Export Prohibitions and Restrictions,

[10] In a recent study the Economic Commission for Asia and the Far East lists the following "aims and purposes" of state trading (in addition to those already mentioned in the text) by countries in the region:
(a) to ensure adequate and regular supplies at reasonable and stable prices of essential commodities to meet local demand;
(b) to secure better prices for export and import products through increased bargaining power;
. . . . .
(f) to secure the advantages of bulk transactions;
. . . . .
(h) to facilitate the import of goods financed under foreign aid programmes;
. . . . .
(k) to raise revenues for the treasury;
(l) to facilitate sanitary and public health controls.
See STATE TRADING, *supra* note 1, at 1-2.
[11] See Allen, *supra* note 9, at 256. *Trade Barriers in the ECAFE Region*, ECONOMIC COMMISSION FOR ASIA AND THE FAR EAST, THE ASIAN DEVELOPMENT BANK AND TRADE LIBERALIZATION, U.N. Doc. E/CN 11/707 at 112 (1965).

done at Geneva, November 8, 1927, there was no attempt to generally prohibit "restrictions applied to products which, as regards production or trade, are or may in future be subject within the country to State monopoly or to monopolies exercised under State control." [12]

In a protocol to the Convention, however, it was made clear that the state trading permitted was the kind which created "monopolies each of which applied only to one or more specific articles." This language was apparently inserted to prevent the Convention from being interpreted as a recognition of the legitimacy of the action of the Soviet Union which adopted state trading as the means by which it conducted *all* of its foreign trade. This became all the more clear when, in 1933, state trading was condemned as "fundamentally irreconcilable" with "the most-favored-nation principle." [13] While such a system could be tolerated with regard to a few goods, or agricultural products in general, the principle Western trading nations opposed the idea of state trading as the normal means by which imports and exports should be regulated. This opposition continues in part because the practice is associated with the West's Cold War enemies and in part because state trading is considered an inherently discriminatory means of conducting foreign trade.[14] A third voice has, however, entered the state trading dialogue. Free of Cold War prejudices, and having found state trading to be of value in the implementation of their development policies, the developing countries have pressed for recognition of state trading as a legitimate means of conducting foreign trade. They seized the opportunity offered by the first

---

[12] LEAGUE OF NATIONS, II.A. ECONOMIC AND FINANCIAL 7, at 9 (1928) (art. 4 (8)).

[13] Royal Institute of International Affairs, *Memorandum on the Most-Favored-Nation Clause as an Instrument of National Policy* 23 (1933), quoted in Domke and Hazard, *State Trading and the Most-Favored-Nation Clause*, 52 AM. J. INT'L L. 55, 59 (1958).

[14] A different type of political objection is that as state trading involves the "substitution of government business for private business" it involves "a process of transformation of private quarrels into international quarrels . . . . This transformation of private quarrels into government quarrels is dangerous for peace." Viner, *International Relations between State-Controlled National Economies*, XXXIV Papers and Proceedings of the 56th Annual Meeting of the American Economic Association, Supplement to 34 AM. ECON. REV. 315, 318 (1944).

United Nations Conference on Trade and Development to pass the following resolution:

DIRECT PARTICIPATION BY GOVERNMENTAL TRADE ORGANIZATIONS IN FOREIGN TRADE

The Conference

Recognizing that direct participation by governmental trade organizations in foreign trade, including those trading activities in which the Government or its agent holds title to exports before transactions and acquires title to imports, is being pursued by many developing countries with mixed economies for the purpose of expanding their foreign trade,

Noting that government participation in foreign trade is assuming increasing importance in a number of developing countries,

Further noting that these developing countries are achieving satisfactory results by trading through this method,

Realizing that participation by Governments of developing countries in foreign trade could be an effective instrument and consistent with the promotion of international trade and development,

Recommends:

(a) That direct participation by governmental trading organizations in foreign trade as defined above be recognized and accepted as one of the effective methods and instruments of promoting the foreign trade of a number of developing countries;

(b) That developed countries should not discriminate against trade with developing countries on the ground that their governmental trading organizations directly participate in trade as a public policy.[15]

The resolution was adopted by a vote of 89 to 1, with 21 abstentions. The opposing nation was the United States. The group of countries which abstained included all the countries of Western Europe except France and Norway.

If we leave political considerations aside, there are two propositions underlying Western objections to state trading. First, state trading is inherently discriminatory. This is a shorthand way of saying that decisions to purchase and sell goods are being made on a basis other than pure economics. The most important "other

---

[15] *Final Act of the United Nations Conference on Trade and Development*, adopted June 15, 1964, Annex A.VI.4, reprinted in I PROCEEDINGS OF THE UNITED NATIONS CONFERENCE ON TRADE DEVELOPMENT 64 (1964).

bases" are domestic politics and foreign relations.[16] Thus, goods tend to be purchased from "friendly" sources rather than the "cheapest" sources.[17] This offends the principle of comparative advantage which is the polestar of Western trade theory. Nations which engage extensively in state trading practices, principally the centrally planned economies of Eastern Europe, would deny that they make it a practice of buying from more expensive, but friendlier, sources. The Western countries, however, reply (and this is the second proposition underlying their objections to state trading) that because of the nature of the system it is not possible to determine when a state trading enterprise is discriminating.[18] For where trade is in private hands and an exporter can produce

---

[16] In the realm of domestic politics one can point to the example of the French Tobacco monopoly (Régie) which is "obligated to help implement politically-determined national socio-economic policies, such as subsidization of the French tobacco farmer, or cultivation of relations with African territories in which France has a special interest. Its criteria [for purchases] are hardly those of autonomous commercial enterprises not bound by such obligations." Walker, *The Effects of Existing or Proposed International Trade Treaties and Agreements Upon Foreign Trade Between the USSR and the USA*, THE LAW OF U.S.-U.S.S.R. TRADE 79, 90 (1965).

[17] At one time the Soviet Government published its administrative orders directing that trade with certain countries be curtailed.

"Thus, after the assassination of the Soviet representative at a conference in Lausanne in 1923, the Soviet Government published in its collection of laws an order to its trading agencies to cease purchasing in Switzerland because the assassin was not punished. And again, in 1935, purchases of cheese in Uruguay were terminated following severance of diplomatic relations."

Domke and Hazard, *supra* note 13, at 67.

Publication of such information has ceased in recent years. But there are "skeptics who doubt that the orders no longer appear within Soviet administrative circles." *Ibid*. (Footnote omitted.)

Professor Kindleberger has pointed to the "readiness" of the Soviet Union "to buy fish when Iceland was unable to sell its catch to the West, or to absorb Egyptian cotton, Cuban sugar, and similar surpluses elsewhere when there was a political advantage to be gained from it, without initially questioning whether the commodities would readily fit into domestic requirements or could be resold elsewhere at a profit or a tolerable small loss." C. KINDLEBERGER, FOREIGN TRADE AND THE NATIONAL ECONOMY 159-160 (1962).

[18] "In dealing with . . . state monopolies the governments of the countries of market economies are hampered by the inherent difficulty of distinguishing between normal commercial considerations and the impact of state policy, by frequent lack of information on such matters as the actual field of competition open to their traders (e.g. the size of the total import programme for an individual product and the extent of its subdivision by area, the extent to which the sum of trade agreement quotas exceeds actual import plans for a particular product, and

and transport a desired product of similar market acceptability at a lower price than the products of competing nations, he can expect large sales in an importing market since private importers may be expected to purchase those goods which will yield them the greatest *profit*. This is so because all private importers, of whatever nationality, are in business to make money. Where these sales do not come about, the exporter would naturally look to the customs duties, quantitative restrictions, etc., of the importing country, which are the usual means of discriminating against the exports of a particular nation. The important point here is that these import barriers are visible, so that an exporter can determine whether his products are being discriminated against. But where the state is the importer, the profit motive may be inoperative. So that even if all import restrictions were administered without discrimination, the efficient exporter could not be certain of selling his product. In fact, import restrictions are no longer necessary, as importing is controlled by the state making the ultimate decision of whether or not to buy. And the factors which go into the state's decision to buy will be highly confidential.[19] In these circumstances it is practically impossible for the exporter to determine why his product has not been purchased by the state import agency. Moreover, the helplessness of the exporter in such

so forth—all justified in the eyes of the authorities of the countries of planned economies as matters of commercial secrecy) and by the fact that the criteria of national development plans—to which foreign trade plans are subordinated—are seldom either fully explained on the one side or appreciated on the other." UNITED NATIONS ECONOMIC AND SOCIAL COUNCIL, WAYS AND MEANS OF PROMOTING WIDER TRADE CO-OPERATION AMONG STATES, U.N. DOC. E/3389 at 15 (1960).

[19] Professor Berman believes that the lack of access to information regarding how the state decides to buy "is probably due primarily to the international political situation, and only secondarily (if at all) to the inherent nature of a state administered and centrally planned system of foreign trade. . . . In particular, the contents of the foreign trade plans, and even the nature of the planning process, are not available to businessmen of other countries. It is therefore impossible for a foreign businessman to make the same kind of independent, informed estimate of market developments in the Soviet Union that he can make of market developments in Italy or Switzerland." H. Berman, *Legal Aspects of Trade Between Planned and Free Economies* 16 (Introduction) (mimeo 1958) (footnote omitted).

If Professor Berman's view is correct, it would appear that the "commercial considerations" clause should provide adequate protection against discrimination

a situation is compounded by the fact that in a market economy there will usually be several importers dealing in his type of merchandise, so that even if one or more are uninterested, he still has a very good chance of breaking into the market, whereas state trading in a product generally means that there is only one buyer, the state enterprise.

STATE TRADING AND COMMERCIAL CONSIDERATIONS

The first approach of the principal exporting nations in dealing with state trading was to seek a guarantee that state enterprises would behave in their purchasing and selling as private importers and exporters. In their trade agreements countries sought to implement this policy by inserting an article providing that state enterprises must be guided in their purchases and sales "solely by commercial considerations." This type of provision first appeared in the Protocol to the Temporary Commercial Agreement between His Majesty's Government in the United Kingdom and the Government of the Union of Soviet Socialist Republics, *done* at London, April 16, 1930: [20]

In concluding the present Agreement the Contracting Parties are animated by the intention to eliminate from their economic relations all forms of discrimination. They accordingly agree that, so far as relates to the treatment accorded by each Party to the trade with the other, they will be guided in regard to the purchase and sale of goods, in regard to the employment of shipping and in regard to all similar matters by commercial and financial considerations only and, subject to such considerations, will adopt no legislative or administra-

---

by state trading enterprises where the countries engaging in state trading are willing to grant access for the collection of market data. This situation obtains in most developing countries. United States objection and Western reluctance in general to grant the seal of legitimacy to state trading practices in developing countries at UNCTAD would therefore seem to be grounded in their disagreement with the Berman position, or a purely emotional reaction to "state trading" in general.

[20] 101 L.N.T.S. 409, 418 (1930). See Domke and Hazard, *supra* note 13, at 58.

tive action of such a nature as to place the goods, shipping, trading organizations and trade in general of the other Party in any respect in a position of inferiority as compared with the goods, shipping and trading organizations of any other foreign country.

The language of the "commercial considerations" clause has been refined since its introduction in 1930, and today a widely used version reads as follows:

Each Party undertakes (a) that enterprises owned or controlled by its Government, and that monopolies or agencies granted exclusive or special privileges within its territories, shall make their purchases and sales involving either imports or exports affecting the commerce of the other Party solely in accordance with commercial considerations, including price, quality, availability, marketability, transportation and other conditions of purchase or sale, which would ordinarily be taken into account by a private commercial enterprise interested in purchasing such products under the most favorable terms; (b) that such other Party shall be afforded adequate opportunity, in accordance with customary business practice, to compete or participate in such purchases and sales.[21]

In practice the "commercial considerations" clause has not been a great success. For, as noted above, it is difficult, if not impossible, for exporters to obtain the kind of information that would enable them to determine whether the state enterprise is basing its actions on purely "commercial considerations." [22] This is especially

[21] See Treaty of Friendship, Commerce and Navigation between the United States and Germany, *done* at Washington, October 29, 1954, art. XVII, 273 U.N.T.S. 3, 24 (1957); Agreement concerning Tariff Questions between the United States and Finland, *done* at Washington, March 18, 1936, art. IX, 172 L.N.T.S. 97, 103 (1936). Sometimes accompanying this provision in a trade agreement is one which exempts certain governmental activities from the "commercial considerations" standard.

Each Party shall accord to the other Party fair and equitable treatment as compared with that afforded to any third country, with respect to:
(a) imports of products for immediate or ultimate consumption in governmental use and not otherwise for resale or use in the production of goods for sale;
(b) the awarding of concessions and other governmental contracts;
(c) the sale of any service sold by the government or by any monopoly or agency granted exclusive or special privileges.
See Treaty between the United States and Germany, *supra* at 24, art. XVII(2).

[22] The GATT made an attempt at creating an obligation on the part of a country employing state trading to supply affected parties with information to determine whether decisions are being made solely on commercial considerations. Article XVII(4)(c) thus provides that

true for developing countries which usually lack the elaborate consular and trade representation in the importing country necessary to obtain information on the manner in which state enterprises are operating. Moreover, the "commercial considerations" clause contains an inherent contradiction. For state traders are monopolies, and it would be strictly in accordance with "commercial considerations" for them to pursue monopoly buying and selling policies. A " 'discriminating monopsony' . . . instead of buying only in whatever market happened to have the lowest prices, as a competitive private trader would endeavor to do . . . [would buy] at higher prices in markets with elastic supplies and lower prices in markets with inelastic supplies, and instead of endeavoring to equalize its purchase prices in different markets it [would seek] . . . to equalize as between the different markets its marginal expenditures per unit, or the net additional outlays for additional units of purchase after allowance for the effect of its purchases on prices." [23] Thus to require a state trader to follow commercial considerations in his purchases and sales is to require him to behave like a private monopolist. But this is not enough. For the market system of allocating trade according to comparative

---

The CONTRACTING PARTIES may, at the request of a contracting party which has reason to believe that its interests under this Agreement are being adversely affected by the operations of an enterprise of the kind described in paragraph 1(a), request the contracting party establishing, maintaining or authorizing such enterprise to supply information about its operations related to the carrying out of the provisions of this agreement.
The Article goes on, however, to provide:
(d) The provisions of this paragraph shall not require any contracting party to disclose confidential information which would impede law enforcement or otherwise be contrary to the public interest or would prejudice the legitimate commercial interests of particular enterprises.
GATT, III BASIC INSTRUMENTS AND SELECTED DOCUMENTS 33 (1958).
Despite these provisions and the "commercial considerations" clause, "in the view of a number of countries, the provisions of the GATT do not provide a realistic and effective basis for the development of trade relations between State trading countries and other contracting parties . . . ."
The Developing Countries in GATT, V PROCEEDINGS OF THE UNITED NATIONS CONFERENCE ON TRADE AND DEVELOPMENT 430, 458 (1964).
[23] Viner, Trade Relations between Free-Market and Controlled Economies, LEAGUE OF NATIONS II.A. ECONOMIC AND FINANCIAL, at 77 (1943).

advantage is premised on the existence of competition in the market place.

Finally, the "commercial considerations" clause has been subject to a rather broad interpretation. A Swiss government representative has maintained that the phrase must include "the question of public taste." And in the discussions on the Havana Charter, it was the view of the Indian Government that the words should "include long-term interests, e.g., the need for the development of trade with a specified country because of the other commercial benefits which may result from such a development." This interpretation, if widely accepted, would put an end to the utility of the clause once and for all.

State Trading and Balanced Trade

Because the "commercial considerations" clause has generally been considered unworkable, many countries have abandoned their efforts to make state enterprises behave as private traders and have instead focused on the actual volume of imports by state enterprises regardless of how decisions to purchase are made. Thus a free market country will grant a state trading country most-favored nation treatment in exchange for the state trading country agreeing to purchase a specific amount of goods. The Exchange of Notes constituting an Agreement on Commercial Relations between the United States and the Soviet Union, *done* at Moscow, August 4, 1937, illustrates this approach.[24] It provided:

[24] U.S. Executive Agreement Series, No. 105 (1937), quoted and discussed in H. Hawkins, Commercial Treaties and Agreements, Principles and Practice 201-202 (1951).

A more recent illustration is the Five Year Trade Agreement between the United Kingdom and the USSR, *done* at Moscow, May 24, 1959, [1960] Gr. Brit. T.S. No. 34 (CMD 1076) at 2-3. The relevant parts of that Agreement read as follows:
Article 2
(1) The United Kingdom Government *expect* that beginning, in the first year of the present Agreement, there will be a substantial increase in the total volume of imports, under normal commercial conditions, of traditional goods from the Soviet Union to the United Kingdom . . . .

Article 3
The Goverment of the Soviet Union expect that Soviet Foreign Trade Organiza-

One. The United States of America will grant to the Union of Soviet Socialist Republics unconditional and unrestricted most-favored-nation treatment in all matters concerning customs duties and charges of every kind and in the method of levying duties, and, further, in all matters concerning the rules, formalities and charges imposed in connection with the clearing of goods through the customs, and with respect to all laws or regulations affecting the sale or use of imported goods within the country.

. . .

Two. On its part the Government of the Union of Soviet Socialist Republics will take steps to increase substantially the amount of purchases in the United States of America for export to the Union of Soviet Socialist Republics of articles the growth, produce, or manufacture of the United States of America.

In a note accompanying this agreement the Soviet Union stated that:

[T]he economic organizations of the Union of Soviet Socialist Republics intend to buy in the United States of America in the course of the next twelve months American goods to the amount of at least forty million dollars.

While this provision suffers from the fact that the volume of trade between the two countries is limited in an artificial manner,[25] there is assurance that the state-trading country will purchase some goods from the other party. This is an especially important consideration for a developing country which, by granting most-favored-nation treatment, is opening its doors to imports from

---

tions will place, on normal commercial conditions and having regard to Article 2, substantial orders in the United Kingdom for equipment for the manufacture of . . . .
(emphasis supplied.)

[25] Any agreement which provides for a balanced exchange of goods also raises the possibility of discrimination since a given volume of goods must be purchased from the other party despite the fact that similar goods may be available from third countries at a lower price. See C. WILCOX, A CHARTER FOR WORLD TRADE 101 (1949). In its original *Proposals* for the Havana Charter, the United States proposed that each state-trading country enter into a multilateral agreement "in which the minimum quantities of goods to be purchased from all sources would be guaranteed." *Ibid.* This idea was not incorporated in the final version of the Charter.

state trading countries. It is not too difficult to imagine a situation where the developing country might find itself making extensive purchases of consumer goods and industrial equipment from a state trading country while at the same time failing to export a sufficient amount of goods to that country so as to generate the wherewithal to pay for its imports. Provisions such as the one quoted above and the following will protect a developing country against having to liquidate unfavorable trade balances by the use of its foreign exchange reserves.

Deliveries of Goods from Country *A* to Country *B* and from Country *B* to Country *A* shall be effected within the framework of the goods stipulated in the lists marked "A" and "B" attached to this Agreement, forming an integral part thereof, with an annual turnover on each side as follows:

	Millions of dollars
1962	6
1963	8
1964	10
1965	12
1966	14

An alternative technique used by several developing countries has been to include in their trade agreements with state-trading countries provisions requiring that trade be balanced and providing the means for implementing this requirement:

1. Both Parties will encourage the importation of goods from the other country with the aim of achieving a balance of mutual trade.
2. Both Parties agree that if at the end of any twelve-month period from the date of the entry into force of this Agreement imports into one country from the other exceed exports to the latter by more than 15%, the Parties shall meet, upon the request of the Party whose imports exceed its exports, to discuss measures which will assure a balance of trade between the two Parties. Should no agreement be reached within six months of the time the request for the meeting was first made, the Party whose imports exceed its exports shall have the right to take any measures, including the

licensing of imports, imposition of quotas and other means, designed to restore the balance of trade. [26]

BARTER

The ultimate means of insuring balanced trade, and the one which seems to be preferred by some state trading countries themselves, is the barter agreement. In a barter arrangement, goods of one country are exchanged for goods of the other of equal value. Not only does the barter agreement provide a balance of trade, but it also minimizes the need for using foreign exchange in the trade between the two countries, since the barter agreement is usually accompanied by a clearing or payments arrangements. Excerpts from a barter agreement between Ceylon and Mainland China may be found in Appendix A to this chapter.

The experience of developing countries with barter agreements has not been an altogether happy one. Burma, for example, has been troubled in its dealings with state trading countries because of the limited choice of goods it was offered, the poor quality of the goods delivered, the inflated prices of the goods, and delays and irregularities in deliveries. The United Arab Republic has also experienced delays in receiving shipments of cement from the U.S.S.R. which resulted first in the expansion of U.A.R. cement production, and then, after the shipments arrived, the shutdown of those U.A.R. facilities. In the case of Argentina, state trading countries delayed deliveries of goods called for in barter agreement to such an extent that at the end of 1954, Argentina was the

[26] See Trade Agreement between the Republic of Tanganyika and the Union of Soviet Socialist Republics, *done* at Dar es Salaam, August 14, 1963, art. 6(3), and the Exchange of Letters of the same date, para. 3. See also Trade Agreement between Uganda and the Polish People's Republic, *done* at Nairobi, April 20, 1964, art. 2, and Exchange of Letters of the same date, para. 1; Trade Agreement between the Government of Kenya and the Government of the Czechoslovak Socialist Republic, *done* at Nairobi, March 9, 1964, art. 2(2), and the Exchange of Letters of the same date, para. 2.

A requirement of balanced trade will not, of course, always work in favor of a developing country. In 1965, for example, Libya exported goods, mainly crude oil, worth $371 million to the Federal Republic of Germany. Libya imported German goods worth only $31.5 million. See XII AFR. REPORT, February 1967, at 28.

creditor of the U.S.S.R. for $13.6 million, Hungary $12.4 million, Czechoslovakia $11.6 million, and of Poland for $5.6 million.

These problems having been noted, it remains to be stated that barter arrangements are not inherently bad. On the contrary, in 1953 Ceylon had a barter agreement with China similar to the one quoted in Appendix A. As it worked out, Ceylon obtained rice at about two-thirds the world market price, while disposing of its rubber at a price *60 per cent above* the world price. In part Ceylon's success was due to the fact that it was exchanging a primary commodity for a primary commodity, thus largely eliminating the problem of the quality of the goods it was receiving. So it does appear possible to make a success of a barter arrangement. The prime rule for success seems to be that *barter arrangements should be used to dispose only of those goods which cannot be sold for convertible foreign exchange.* Thus, developing countries must learn to resist the temptation of bartering away their cash crops in exchange for increased trade with the centrally planned countries. Their interests would be better served by selling these crops on the world markets for convertible currencies and then, if they so desire, using the convertible currencies to make their purchases from the East. The only exception to this rule is when a barter arrangement will bring a higher "price" than would a sale for foreign exchange. But the "price" must be carefully examined—especially where it consists of manufactured goods. With these principles in mind, developing countries can successfully expand their trade both among themselves and with state trading countries by means of barter arrangements.[27]

The application of these principles has led to recent growth in barter trade between developing countries and Western trading nations. Usually these deals have been part cash, part commodity. Thus "English Electric has taken Egyptian cotton as part payment for a power station and Handley Page has sold £5 million-worth

[27] 1966 witnessed an exchange of formerly flared gas by Iran for a steel mill to be supplied by the Soviet Union. Brazil was able to exchange unsaleable coffee for cargo vessels built in Poland.

of aeroplanes against Brazilian coffee." [28] Such transactions have
enabled exchange short developing countries with surplus commodities to obtain in exchange for those commodities such items
as tractors and medium-sized agricultural processing, textile, and
chemical machinery.

CONCLUSION

The legal aspects of state trading and attempts to deal with it in
trade agreements are extremely complex matters. Much discussion
of the subject has begun with the assumption that state trading
situations are easily identified. This is not the case. Nor will it be
in the future. For evolutionary changes in many of the centrally
planned countries are altering traditional state enterprises in a
number of ways. The establishment of profit incentives may cause
many state enterprises to be more responsive to market conditions
and less subject to political "guidance." This may, however, result
in conduct much more similar to a private monopoly or monopsony than has hitherto been the case. The crucial change will
undoubtedly be the creation of two or more state enterprises
competing in the same field. Here a bureaucratic desire to show
better results than those exhibited by a competing organization
may make the behavior of state enterprises resemble that of private
companies to a remarkable degree. Finally, there is the move away
from state enterprises towards enterprises "owned and managed"
by the workers. Are those to be considered state enterprises? Again
the answer would seem to be yes if they are granted a monopoly
position by the government; no, if there are competing organizations. In the long run, the changes in state trading will most likely
render unnecessary the heretofore unsuccessful search for a legal
formula by which state trading and nondiscrimination can be
reconciled. In the interim, two courses of action seem desirable
for those planning external trade with a nation maintaining some
form of state trading. The maximum effort must be made to

[28] "Barter is Respectable" 218 THE ECONOMIST 428 (1966).

ensure that the criteria for decisions to buy or sell on the part of state trading organizations be made available to the other party and/or the public at large. In addition, some minimum commitment with regard to purchases should be secured from the state trading country.[29] By recognizing the problems involved in state trading, and attempting to deal with them in the manner proposed, developing countries can both enhance their own trading positions and the general development of the public law of international trade.

APPENDIX

Excerpts from the
Trade and Payments Agreement between Ceylon and China, *Done*
at Peking, 19 September 1957 [30]

. . .

ARTICLE IV

The two Contracting Parties shall, before the end of October of each year, conclude a protocol of the commodities to be exchanged between the two parties in the following calendar year. This protocol shall specify:

(1) The aggregate value together with the names and approximate quantities of the commodities which the two Contracting Parties will *undertake* to import and export during the year covered by the protocol and,

(2) The aggregate value together with the names and approximate quantities of the commodities which the two Contracting Parties will *endeavor* to import and export during the year covered by the protocol. (emphasis added)

. . .

Protocol Relating to the Exchange of Commodities between
Ceylon and China in 1958, Done at Peking, 19 September 1957

. . .

ARTICLE I

The Government of the People's Republic of China undertakes to buy and the Government of Ceylon undertakes to sell Ceylonese com-

---

[29] "One of the main features of Poland's accession [to the GATT in 1967] was an agreement to expand its trade with GATT members by 7 per cent per annum." XX Int. Fin. News Surv. 402 (1968).

[30] 337 U.N.T.S. 137, 148, 150, 162-66 (1959).

modities of the guaranteed value set out in Schedule "A1" of this
Protocol; and the Government of Ceylon undertakes to buy and the
Government of the People's Republic of China undertakes to sell
Chinese commodities of the guaranteed value set out in Schedule
"A2" of this Protocol. A variation of 5 per cent more or less in the
guaranteed values specified in Schedules "A1" and "A2" is permissible
under this Protocol.

ARTICLE II

The Government of Ceylon and the Government of the People's
Republic of China will endeavor to expand trade between their countries on the basis of maintaining a balance between the values of
imports and exports, and do their utmost to increase their respective
imports and exports to the extent of the values set out in Schedules
"B1" and "B2" attached to this Protocol.

. . .

SCHEDULE "A1"

Aggregate value of commodities which Ceylon undertakes to export
to China and China undertakes to import from Ceylon: Rs. 95,000,000
(Ninety-Five Million Ceylon Rupees).

Name of Commodity	Approximate Quantity
Rubber	30,000 metric tons
Other Commodities	unspecified

SCHEDULE "A2"

Aggregate value of commodities which China undertakes to export
to Ceylon and Ceylon undertakes to import from China: Rs. 95,000,-
000 (Ninety-Five Million Ceylon Rupees).

Name of Commodity	Approximate Quantity
Rice	200,000 metric tons
Steel	
Coal	
Cement	
Dried Chillies	
Garlic	
Potatoes	
Onions	
Other Commodities	unspecified

SCHEDULE "B1"

Aggregate value of commodities which Ceylon will endeavor to
export to China and China will endeavor to import from Ceylon:
Rs. 165,000,000 (One Hundred Sixty-Five Million Ceylon Rupees).

(This figure includes the value of commodities listed in Schedule A1.)

Name of Commodity	Approximate Quantity
Rubber	50,000 metric tons
Coconut Oil	5,000 metric tons
Cocoa	200 metric tons
Other Commodities	unspecified

SCHEDULE ''B2''

Aggregate value of commodities which China will endeavor to export to Ceylon and Ceylon will endeavor to import from China: Rs. 165,000,000 (One Hundred Sixty-Five Million Ceylon Rupees) (This figure includes the value of commodities listed in Schedule A2.)

Name of Commodity	Approximate Quantity
Rice	270,000 metric tons
Cotton Textiles	15,000,000 yards
Tea Chests	1,000,000 sets
Steel	20,000 metric tons
Cement	40,000 metric tons
Automobile tyres	10,000 sets
Dried Chillies	5,000 metric tons
Newsprint and paper	4,000 metric tons
Garlic	1,500 metric tons
Potatoes	10,000 metric tons
Green gram	4,000 metric tons
Onions	4,000 metric tons
Machinery and equipment	
Chemicals	
Coal	
Other commodities	unspecified

VII. Export Subsidies and Dumping

In the introduction to Chapter III note was taken of the fact that development seems to go hand in hand with balance of payments crises. In response to such a situation developing countries usually act to reduce imports and/or expand exports. Import controls raise problems which have been discussed earlier. And even if those problems could be overcome, there is a limit on how low total imports can be reduced. Moreover, from a global point of view, import restriction is undesirable in that it tends to reduce the volume of world trade. The better solution to a developing country's balance of payments problems, from the country's point of view as well as that of the world economy, is the expansion of exports. In Chapter III the popularity of multiple exchange rate systems was attributed, in part, to their use as an export promoting device. From this point of view, multiple exchange rate systems are nothing more than a means of export subsidization.

In addition to increasing its foreign exchange earnings, a developing country will subsidize its exports so as to lower the prices of the same products to its own citizenry. Many plants in developing countries have a production capacity in excess of local demand. If this surplus capacity can be used to produce goods for export, overhead costs per unit will ordinarily decrease, enabling the producer to lower his price at home, while at the same time gaining the added revenues from exports.

EXPORT SUBSIDIES

Professor Haberler has drawn a useful distinction between *compensatory* export subsidies and *pure* export subsidies. *Compensatory* export subsidies are a means of assistance given to producers who are placed by their governments under some unique disadvantage relative to their foreign competitors, e.g., because they are subject to special taxation in their home country. To illustrate, suppose that in Country *A* each pair of shoes produced is subject to an excise tax of 10 per cent payable by the manufacturer. Such a tax does not exist in country *B*. Both *A* and *B* export shoes to Country *C*. In the competition for markets in Country *C*, shoes produced in *A* will be at a disadvantage as compared with those produced in *B*, since *A*'s shoes must include in their cost of production the 10 per cent excise tax. To allow shoes from Country *A* to compete in world markets on an equal footing with those produced in other countries, the Government of Country *A* will grant a rebate to producers in Country *A* of the excise tax paid on each pair of shoes exported.[1] This rebate is a compensatory export subsidy. *Pure* export subsidies, on the other hand, go further than to compensate for governmental handicaps under which exporters suffer. They seek to confer positive advantages on

---

[1] Neutral as they may appear, compensatory export subsidies may be of assistance to exporters. If Country *A* taxes producers by means of an indirect tax and Country *B* taxes through direct taxes, e.g., income taxes, *A* can clearly rebate the tax on products exported. Trade agreement provisions permitting such rebates, see p. 204 *infra*, have been interpreted, however, so as not to permit the rebate of direct taxes on the theory that "the burden of indirect taxes is always and wholly shifted forward to the ultimate consumer and that such burden is reflected in the price of the product, whereas . . . direct taxes are never shifted forward but are always wholly absorbed by the factors of production, and thus do not affect the price of the product." *Report of Committee on International Trade and Investment*, Report of the Fifty-Second Conference of the International Law Association 369, 389 (1967). This theory has now come under heavy attack, *Id.* at 389-90. See also Cooper, *National Economic Policy in an Interdependent World*, 76 YALE L. J. 1273, 1289-90 (1967). The issue is current at the time of this writing in that the EEC plans to utilize a value-added tax as its principal means of public finance. American exporters fear that rebates of this new tax will put them at a disadvantage. See *VAT Is Not Unfair*, 226 THE ECONOMIST 56-57 (1968).

exporters relative to their foreign competitors by reducing the costs of production for export and marketing abroad below what they would be in the absence of government action. It is these pure, rather than compensatory, export subsidies which have created problems in international trade.

Pure export subsidies originally took rather simple forms. One type was very much like the shoe illustration above where the Government refunded internal taxes paid on goods which were to be exported. The pure subsidy element came in because the refunds exceeded in amount the taxes which had actually been paid. A second type was very similar and entailed a refund of customs duties paid on imported raw materials used in the manufacture of a product which was exported, again the refunds were in excess of the duties actually paid. In time, more sophisticated means of subsidizing exports were devised. Lower internal freight rates were charged on goods for export, exporters were granted government loans below market rates of interest, and monopolies were granted to certain favored exporters. The high point in the sophistication of export subsidies probably came with the activities of the German Government prior to 1934. At that time German bonds were selling abroad at substantial discounts from par, due to inflation in Germany. Exporters were permitted to use part of the foreign exchange proceeds from the sale of German products abroad to purchase these bonds in foreign markets, and then to sell the bonds in Germany at par value. The gains accruing to exporters from these bond sales were their export bounties.

Present-day export subsidy programs have generally followed the path of indirection. For developing countries direct cash payments to exporters place a great burden on the revenue-raising ability of the government which is generally not up to the task. Thus Indonesia uses a currency retention system which permits an exporter to keep a portion of his foreign exchange earnings for use in importing certain categories of goods. A related system, in force in Pakistan, is to grant to exporters bonus vouchers entitling the holder to import goods not otherwise licensed for importation.

As is the case with many currency retention schemes, the bonus vouchers may be freely sold, so that the exporter receives the "quota profits" involved in an import restriction system as his subsidy. These systems accomplish the purpose of export subsidization without the strain on the government revenue collecting machinery which would be caused by cash payments to exporters.[2] Like exchange controls, however, export subsidies utilize administrative talents which might be usefully put to work elsewhere in a developing country.

The great objection to subsidization as a useful means of export promotion for developing countries is that it benefits the rich at the expense of the poor. Manufactured exports are sold in the markets of the developed countries at "less than cost," and the "losses" are borne by the developing countries. This analysis is the basis for the proposal made at the UNCTAD that the developed countries grant preferences to the developing countries on imports of manufactures. The object of this proposal is to shift the cost of subsidizing the manufactured exports of developing countries to the developed countries.[3] To illustrate how this would work, assume that Country A, a developed country, produces one barrel of metal screws, and sells them to consumers in its own country at a cost of 100. Assume further that the world market price for one barrel of screws, the price at which other developed countries are willing to export screws, is 80. To protect its screw industry, Country A levies a tariff of 25 per cent ad valorem on imports of screws, thus raising the price of imported screws in A to 100. Further assume that B, a developing country, also produces screws and can offer them for sale at 90. With the world market price at 80, B is not going to export screws at a price of 90. To sell screws

---

[2] Indirect subsidization schemes, however, eliminate one of the attractions of subsidies as a means of promoting exports. That attraction is visibility. Where subsidies are a charge on the general revenues, the public is normally made aware of their existence by the annual legislative discussions concerning the budget. Such visibility tends to keep subsidies within politically acceptable limits. Where subsidies are indirect, the public rarely appreciates how expensive a new industry is to protect and promote.

[3] H. JOHNSON, ECONOMIC POLICIES TOWARD LESS DEVELOPED COUNTRIES 181 (1967).

in the world market B must subsidize its screw manufacturers to the point that they can profitably offer screws for sale at 80. Alternatively, if A grants B a preference, and eliminates its tariff on screws imported from B, the latter can now export screws to A without subsidy and can actually raise the price of its screws from 90 to 100.[4] B would thus receive a windfall of 20 on each barrel of screws exported to A (10 represented by the price increase and 10 by the price of B's screws above the world market price), and A would lose the tariff revenue on imports of screws. What is in effect happening is that the customs duties formerly collected by A on imports of screws are now being transferred to B in the form of a higher price for B's screws. As B's industry gets on its feet, and is able to offer screws at prevailing world market prices, the preferences and the consequent revenue transfer will be eliminated. In the meantime, however, a good portion of the costs of subsidization is borne by consumers in A.[5]

Even if a preference scheme comes into effect, export subsidies will continue to remain important in the trade between developing countries. For developing countries will continue to join together in regional trading areas, within which the establishment of manufacturing industries will be allocated to the constituent member states. Initially the output of these enterprises will include the costs of infancy and will thus cost more than equivalent products heretofore imported from outside the region. To reduce the level of increased prices due to the commencement of production within the region, developing countries are very likely to turn to subsidization of these infant industries. The question is again one of who bears the costs of infancy—the consumers or the taxpayers in the country where the goods are produced? This question points up the necessity for close cooperation in financial

---

[4] Alternatively, B could continue to offer screws for sale at 90, and knock out A's domestic producers. Such action would not be politic in the short run, however, and B would probably be well advised to lower the price of its exports gradually to allow for the reallocation of the factors of production in A's domestic screw industry into other fields where A holds a comparative advantage.

[5] This simplified example is drawn from the brilliant analysis of the case for preferences in H. JOHNSON, *supra* note 3, at 181-195.

matters between the members of the regional trading area. Such cooperation may in this case, involve reverse transfers so as to equitably share the burden of regional development.[6]

Absent a special relationship such as a preference system or a customs union, export subsidization has traditionally been viewed as an "illegitimate" practice in international trade. Export subsidies were opposed by importing states which viewed them as an attempt to neutralize the effect of the tariff walls which had been erected to protect local industry.[7] And competing exporters took the view that subsidized exports were a form of unfair competition which gave to the exporting countries a larger share of the market than they would "rightfully" have. Both types of injured parties attempted to deal with the problems caused by export subsidies in their trade agreements.

COUNTERVAILING DUTIES

The first line of attack on the export subsidy system was to include in the trade agreements and commercial treaties of the late 1800s provisions pledging each party not to grant export subsidies. These pledges were "wholly ineffective." International efforts to meet the problems having thus failed, each country fell back on unilateral action. In an effort at least to protect their domestic producers from what they considered the unfair competition of subsidized foreign imports, countries enacted legislation providing for "countervailing duties." An example is Section 303 of the United States Tariff Act of 1930 [8] which provides that:

Whenever any country . . . shall pay or bestow, directly or indirectly, any bounty or grant upon the manufacture or production or export of any article or merchandise manufactured or produced in such coun-

---

[6] For a detailed discussion of this point, see Cooper and Massell, *Toward a General Theory of Customs Unions for Developing Countries*, 73 J. POL. ECON. 461 (1965).

[7] From a global viewpoint, the offsetting of tariff protection by export subsidization may be a desirable step leading to freer trade and a more optimal allocation of world resources.

[8] 19 U.S.C. § 1303 (1965).

try . . . then upon the importation of any such article or merchandise into the United States, . . . there shall be levied and paid . . . in addition to the duties otherwise imposed by this . . . [Act] an additional duty equal to the net amount of such bounty or grant, however the same be paid or bestowed.[9]

The appearance of countervailing duty legislation raised a furor among the countries granting export subsidies. They claimed that countervailing duties were a violation of the principle of most-favored-nation treatment and therefore could not be imposed on products originating in countries to whom such treatment had been promised in trade agreements. In response, the Attorney General of the United States issued an opinion stating that countervailing duties were compatible with the most-favored-nation obligations, apparently on the ground that countervailing duties were not "duties" at all, but internal regulations which were not covered by the most-favored-nation clause.[10] This opinion, however, was attacked by many scholars. Their argument ran as follows. When a nation subsidizes its exports, it is not discriminating against any particular country. The subsidy applies to exports of that product to any and all countries and would therefore not violate the principle of most-favored-nation treatment. But, when an importing nation levies a countervailing duty, that duty is levied on the products of a particular country, and since that country is being treated differently than other countries, the most-favored-nation principle is violated. The battle was still raging in the 1920s when the League of Nations established a committee for the Codification of International Law which considered the issue and found that, although countervailing duties "seem by the weight of authority" to violate the most-favored-nation clause, something had to be done to protect states against subsidized foreign exports. Their conclusion was that "it is generally allowed that countervailing duties are permissible, even though they are

---

[9] Additional examples of such legislation can be found in GATT, ANTI-DUMPING AND COUNTERVAILING DUTIES 141 et seq. (1958).

[10] Discussed in J. VINER, INTERNATIONAL ECONOMICS 315 (1951). See also R. SNYDER, THE MOST-FAVORED-NATION CLAUSE 118-130 (1948).

in technical violation of the clause, if they are used justly and as a matter of necessity." [11] This enquiry seems to have put an end to the matter and the acceptance of the compatibility of countervailing duties with most-favored-nation treatment is evidenced by the inclusion of provisions regarding both points in the General Agreement on Tariffs and Trade.[12]

As noted above, early attempts to outlaw export bounties and subsidies resulted in failure. In the Havana Charter the "free traders" made one more try at outlawing export subsidies.[13] The provision was not incorporated in the original version of the GATT.[14] In 1955, however, the GATT was amended to include a prohibition on export subsidies other than subsidies relating to the export of primary products.[15] The provision, however, did not enter into effect until 1962.[16] And even then, it only applies to members which specifically accept its provisions.[17]

---

[11] *Report of the Sub-Committee on the Most-Favored-Nation Clause*, adopted by the Committee of Experts for Progressive Codification of International Law, April 1927, reprinted in Supplement to 22 AM. J. INT'L L. 134, 148 (1928).

[12] One writer has raised the intriguing question of whether in some circumstances the imposition of a countervailing duty might not be required to honor a most-favored-nation commitment. Suppose Country *A* has promised most-favored-nation treatment to Country *B*, the latter being an exporter of shoes to *A*. Country *C*, eager to enter the shoe exporting business, pays a bonus to its producers of $1 (U.S.) per pair of shoes exported. Thus cushioned, *C*'s producers lower the price of their shoes and are able to knock *B* out of *A*'s market. Could *B* demand that *A* impose a countervailing duty on *C*'s shoes, arguing that to do nothing aids and abets *C*'s subsidization scheme and thus denies *B* most-favored-nation treatment? The point is raised in *Note, Dumping and "Most-Favored-Nation" Treatment*, 75 SOL. J. 875, 876 (1931) cited in Ehrenhaft, *Protection Against International Price Discrimination: United States Countervailing and Antidumping Duties*, 58 COLUM. L. REV. 44, 57 n. 79 (1958). See also pp. 160-61 *infra*.

[13] See Havana Charter Article 26 (1), C. WILCOX, A CHARTER FOR WORLD TRADE 262 (1949).

[14] There is no evidence as to the reason for this omission. In 1948, when it was again proposed to incorporate the prohibition in the agreement, the Working Party found that "practical difficulties" prevented their recommending this step. See GATT, ANALYTICAL INDEX 84 (Rev. ed. 1966).

[15] Artile XVI: 4, GATT, III BASIC INSTRUMENTS AND SELECTED DOCUMENTS 31 (1958).

[16] See ANALYTICAL INDEX *supra* note 14, at 89.

[17] See Declaration of November 19, 1960, Giving Effect to the Provisions of Article XVI: 4, GATT, 9S BASIC INSTRUMENTS AND SELECTED DOCUMENTS 32, 33 (1961). The declaration entered into force November 14, 1962. The developed countries of Western Europe, North America, and Japan have adhered to it.

TRADE AGREEMENT PROVISIONS

The usual approach to the question is to say nothing about subsidies in the trade agreement,[18] but instead to specifically permit the imposition of countervailing duties where subsidization occurs.

No countervailing duty shall be levied on any product of either Party in excess of an amount equal to the estimated bounty or subsidy determined to have been granted, directly or indirectly, on the manufacture, production, or export of such product in the country of origin or exportation, including any special subsidy to the transportation of a particular product. The term "countervailing" shall be understood to mean a special duty levied for the purpose of offsetting any bounty or subsidy bestowed, directly or indirectly, on the manufacture or production or export of any merchandise.

The provision applies to bounties granted "directly or indirectly." This language is aimed at countering the more sophisticated form of subsidization, examples of which have been discussed above. If something has the *effect* of subsidizing an export, then it is a bounty no matter how remote it may be from the particular transaction in question.

Notice also that this provision covers bounties or subsidies granted "on the *manufacture, production,* or *export* of such product . . ." In the debates over the drafting of the Havana Charter, a distinction was made by the development countries between production subsidies and export subsidies.[19] Production subsidies, also termed domestic subsidies, were made available to producers of goods for both the home and export markets. Export subsidies,

[18] But see Treaty of Commerce, Establishment and Navigation between the United Kingdom and Japan, *done* at London, November 14, 1962, art. 18, [1963] Gr. Brit. T.S. No. 53 (CMD. 2085) at 12-13. (". . . [6] The provisions . . . of this Article shall not prevent the payment by either Contracting Party of subsidies exclusively to producers in any territory of that Contracting Party, including payments to producers derived from the proceeds of internal taxes or charges applied consistently with the provisions of paragraphs . . . and subsidies effected through government purchases of national products.')

[19] Meeting of the Preparatory Committee of the International Conference on Trade and Employment, Committee II, November 1, 1946, U.N. Doc. E/PC/T/ C.II/37 at 8 (U.S.), 10 (U.K.).

on the other hand, were payments, etc., which affected only the costs of exported goods. The evil associated with export subsidies was that they resulted in an item being "sold in foreign markets at a lower price than it is sold at home. . . ." [20] This distinction is preserved in GATT Article XVI:4 which prohibits export subsidies. Nothing, however, is said about production subsidies. In fact, the draftsmen seem to have taken great pains to see that such subsidies are not interfered with, for only those export subsidies are prohibited which result "in sale of such product for export at a price lower than the comparable price charged for the like product to buyers in the domestic market"—a backhanded but specific way of saying that subsidies which affect the price of both domestic and exported products, i.e., production subsidies—are not so prohibited. The logic of the distinction is none too clear. For products which were subsidized at the production stage will wreak as much havoc on the law of comparative advantage when exported, as those subsidized by low-cost loans to exporters, etc. This is clearly recognized by GATT Article VI which permits, as noted, the imposition of countervailing duties when exports are subsidized at the manufacturing or production stages.[21] Furthermore, production subsidies act to limit imports, an evil recognized in GATT, Article XVI:11. This latter fact, however, may give a clue to the rationale for an otherwise illogical distinction. For if a country is determined to have, for example, a domestic shoe industry, and to establish it requires tinkering with the concepts of free trade and comparative advantage, major trading nations may have expressed a preference that such industries be nurtured by subsidies rather than import restrictions. This preference is apparently based on the fact that subsidies tend to lower the

[20] DEPARTMENT OF STATE, HAVANA CHARTER FOR AN INTERNATIONAL TRADE ORGANIZATION 8 (1948).

[21] "The fact that the granting of certain subsidies was authorized by provisions of Article XVI of the General Agreement clearly did not debar importing countries from imposing, under the terms of Article VI, a countervailing duty on the products on which subsidies had been paid." *Report on Anti-dumping and Countervailing Duties,* GATT, 9S BASIC INSTRUMENTS AND SELECTED DOCUMENTS, 194, 200 (1961).

price of a product on the domestic market, while the shelter afforded by import barriers tends to result in higher prices.[22] Thus
the burden of fostering the domestic industry is borne by the
taxpaying public in general, as opposed to just consumers of
shoes. In sum, when viewed in terms of their effect on exports
logic may require prohibition of both production subsidies and
export subsidies. Production subsidies may, however, play a useful role as a protection against imports.

Following the general provision concerning countervailing
duties, it is not unusual to find a short paragraph in a trade agreement making an exception for compensatory export bounties.

No product of either Party imported into the territory of the other
Party shall be subject to a countervailing duty by reason of the exemption of such product from duties or taxes borne by the like product
when destined for consumption in the country of origin or exportation, or by reason of the refund of such duties or taxes.

Finally, one of the perennial struggles between the advocates
of freer trade and those concerned primarily with nourishing domestic industry is over the point at which various offsetting devices
will begin to operate. The possibility that countervailing duties
might be used as a protectionist device so as to deprive the other
party of trade opportunities has never been far from the mind
of most exporters.[23] To calm their fears, most trade agreement
clauses dealing with countervailing duties provide:

Neither Party shall levy any countervailing duty on the importation
of any product of the other Party unless it determines that the effect-
of the subsidization is such as to cause or threaten material injury to
an established domestic industry, [or to traditional patterns of domestic trade,] or is such as to retard materially the establishment of
a domestic industry.

[22] See Meeting of Committee II of the Preparatory Committee of the International Conference on Trade and Employment, November 1, 1946, U.N. Doc.
E/PC/T/C.II/37 at 8.
[23] Countervailing duties are to be regarded at most "as exceptional and temporary measures." *Report on Anti-dumping and Countervailing Duties*, GATT, 8S
BASIC INSTRUMENTS AND SELECTED DOCUMENTS 145 (1960).

The first question raised by this limitation is the use of the word "threaten." The language clearly refers to the immediacy of the threat, its magnitude being covered by the companion word "material." Similar language in American legislation has been construed to mean that to constitute a "threat" the contemplated action must be "clear, imminent [and] specific." [24] This interpretation reflects the American bias towards free and unrestricted trade. Developing countries who fear that they will be on the receiving end of charges of "dumping" when they export their manufactures and semi-manufactures to the developed countries would, of course, gain were this interpretation universally accepted. On the other hand, countries whose primary concern is the protection of their own commerce and industry would press for a much broader interpretation.

The issue of how great an injury must be before it will be considered "material" is another open question.[25] Some content may be given to the term by reference to the interpretation of similar language by the United States Tariff Commission. The Commission has interpreted the work "material" as meaning more than the "loss of sales by a few competitors." [26] By requiring "material" injury the draftsmen are said to have meant to permit and encourage competition in the market up to the point that imports of subsidized goods are actually destroying competition. The Commission has quantified this language in a test which requires a market invasion of more than 7 to 10 per cent before it will find material injury. While a domestic industry in the United States may be able to withstand such a degree of subsidized competition, the same will not usually be the case in a developing country, where the market is generally small and there is a constant fight to attain even the minimum production required by econo-

---

[24] See Baier, *Substantive Interpretations under the Antidumping Act and the Foreign Trade Policy of the United States,* 17 STAN. L. REV. 409, 455 (1965).

[25] Some light is shed on the issue by Article 3 of the Agreement on Implementation of Article VI of the GATT, *done* at Geneva, June 30, 1967.

[26] See Baier, *supra* note 24, at 441.

mies of scale. At the outset, therefore, a developing country may want to delete the word "material" from a provision concerning countervailing duties. Alternatively, such a country might propose that if x per cent of the market is captured by subsidized imports, that country may impose countervailing duties. Needless to say, if the developing country were more concerned with placing its own subsidized exports in the other party's market, it would take the opposite approach.

Finally, what is an "industry"? It has been suggested that in this context the term should encompass all organizations producing the "like commodity." [27] The GATT draftsmen also indicated that the term " 'includes such activities as agriculture, forestry, mining, etc. as well as manufacturing.' " [28] Here again one is plagued with a term which has been puzzling courts dealing with, e.g., anti-monopoly laws, for generations and there is only a limited content that can be given to the term absent a specific situation.

Note that by restricting the imposition of countervailing duties to situations where there is injury (or, at least, the threat thereof) to *domestic* industry, the importing country is prohibited from imposing countervailing duties solely to place one foreign source of supply on an equal footing with another. This may be a significant limitation on the freedom of action of an importing developing country. Suppose, for example, that Country *A* has traditionally supplied the market in developing Country *B* with a substantial proportion of *B*'s bicycles. In addition, *B* receives a considerable amount of foreign aid and technical assistance from *A*. If Country *C* subsidizes its bicycle producers, so that they are able to sell in *B*'s market at prices far below the price of *A*'s bicycles, what action can *B* take to aid *A*? Under the provision

---

[27] *Report on Anti-dumping and Countervailing Duties*, GATT, 8S Basic Instruments and Selected Documents 145, 150 (1960).

[28] Report of the United Nations Conference on Trade and Employment, Section 24, at 74 quoted in Analytical Index, *supra* note 14, at 35. See also Article 4 of the Agreement on Implementation of Article VI, *supra* note 25.

quoted above—none. But by including the bracketed phrase "to traditional patterns of domestic trade" such a situation can be covered.[29] This result depends on the words "domestic trade" being interpreted to cover trade in both locally produced and imported goods. This interpretation is not illogical, since if "domestic trade" merely meant "trade in domestically produced goods," the situation would be covered by the injury to "domestic industry" phrase. For action which harmed trade in locally produced goods would inevitably injure the industry which produced them. But if the new phrase is really meant to protect foreign producers why not say so directly? Two reasons why it is desirable to take a more circuitous route to this end come to mind. First, such an approach would be a departure from traditional practice in this area—and this, in itself, is a formidable obstacle. Second, the other party to the negotiations might protest that there is no place in a trade agreement for provisions protecting third parties which are strangers to the agreement. B and C are negotiating a trade agreement whose purpose is to govern trade relations between them, not to confer gratuitous benefits on A. B, by invoking the "domestic trade" formula, could partially meet these arguments by shifting the focus from A to B's traders who distribute A's products. While a party may question the legitimacy of B seeking to protect A while negotiating with C, B would be on far stronger ground if B argued that what he was really trying to do was to protect his own importers. Here he can exert a legitimate interest akin to that already accepted with regard to B's industry. B may or may not be overly concerned about A's exports to B, but B is surely concerned about B's importers who distribute A's products.

---

[29] The GATT also attempts to cover third countries—although somewhat circumspectly—but there the test is the "material injury" to A's industry, rather than displacement in B's market. See Article VI (5), GATT, 55 U.N.T.S. 188, 214 (1950). See also *Report on Anti-dumping and Countervailing Duties, supra* note 21, at 198; L'HUILLIER, LES RELATIONS ÉCONOMIQUES INTERNATIONALES 152 (Paris, 1962), cited in G. CURZON, MULTILATERAL COMMERCIAL DIPLOMACY 123 (1965); Article 12 of the Agreement on Implementation of Article VI, *supra* note 25.

From *A*'s point of view, if he fears subsidized competition in *B*'s market, *A* should seek to include in *his* trade agreement with *B* a clause providing that

Both Parties recognize that industries in each country engaged in trade with the other country may be materially injured by the competition of subsidized exports from third countries. They agree that, if after consideration, it is established that such injury is being caused or threatened, to take such action as is necessary to remedy the injury or prevent the threat of injury.[30]

D U M P I N G

Closely related to the issues raised by the export subsidy system is the question of dumping. Dumping is probably the most misused term in the vocabulary of international trade. The proper meaning of the term is the sale of a product in *foreign markets* at a price below that for which it is sold in the *market* of the country *where* it is *produced*. To illustrate, assume a manufacturer produces shoes in Country *A* and sells them in that country for $10 per pair. If he also exports shoes of the identical kind to Country *B*, but sells them in Country *B* for $5 per pair, they are being "dumped" in Country *B*. The crucial point is that dumping has *nothing to do* with the prices prevailing for shoes of similar type and quality in Country *B*. Failure to appreciate this fact has lead to the widespread misunderstanding as to the meaning of dumping. For most laymen consider goods are dumped when they are sold in a foreign market at prices below those prevailing in *that* market. But this is not in itself dumping. In order for there

[30] See Trade Agreement between New Zealand and Malaya, *done* at Wellington, February 3, 1961, art. X, 447 U.N.T.S. 251, 258 (1962). This agreement also provides that: "Each Government undertakes that it will at any time, on written request, consult with the other Government before accepting commodities offered by third countries from government stockpiles or under programmes of surplus disposal or other non-commercial agreements." Art. XII, *id.* at 260.

to be dumping, it must be shown that goods are being sold in the foreign market below the price at which they are sold in the home market.[31]

Shoes "dumped" in Country B may be offered for sale at prices below, equal to, or above the prices prevailing in Country B for shoes of similar quality. Suppose that shoes of "fine quality" sell for $10 per pair in Country B. Country A produces such shoes, and sells them in its own country for $15 per pair. A decides to dispose of some of its unsold stock by exporting it to B where it offers "fine quality" shoes for sale at $12 per pair. Obviously A is going to find very few customers, since consumers in Country B can already buy "fine quality" shoes for $10 per pair. Thus, although dumping is theoretically possible at prices above those prevailing in the importing country, it will not ordinarily take place in those circumstances. When one hears of "dumping" what is normally happening is that goods are being sold at a price below that prevailing in the country of origin *and* at a price equal to or, more probably, below that prevailing in the importing country. To make the situation more concrete, again assume that fine quality shoes are selling in Country B at $10 per pair. In Country A, locally produced fine quality shoes sell for $15 per pair. A, however, is willing to export fine quality shoes to B at a price of $6 per pair. Clearly, the shoes are being dumped, i.e. sold below the market price prevailing in the producing country, and they are

---

[31] Various devices have been used to conceal the fact that dumping is taking place. One format is "hidden dumping by associated houses." Here an exporter in Country A will own an importing firm in Country B. The exporter sells his product to the related importer at a price at or above that prevailing in Country A. The importer then markets the product in Country B at a price below that prevailing in A (i.e. below his "cost"). The losses incurred by the importer are made up by capital transfers from the associated exporter. In effect the goods are being dumped. The margin of dumping is the difference between the price of the product in Country A and the price at which the associated importer sells the goods in County B. See *Ad Article* VI, Paragraph 1 (1). GATT, 55 U.N.T.S. 188, 296 (1950). Another means of concealing dumping is to charge the same price as in the domestic market, but give export customers better terms of sale, e.g., longer credit terms, reduced packing and transport charges, or higher grade goods. See J. VINER, DUMPING: A PROBLEM IN INTERNATIONAL TRADE 17 (1923).

also being sold at a price below that prevailing in the market of the importing country.

Dumping is widely condemned.[32] Yet is it necessarily bad? The effect of this transaction has been to lower the price of fine quality shoes to consumers in Country *B* from $10 to $6. This would appear to be an effect which everyone would favor. Why then is dumping viewed as an illegitimate trade practice? To find an answer it is necessary to refer briefly to the classical theory of international trade. That theory postulates that each country will export those products of which it is a relatively efficient producer. When a country exports goods at prices below those prevailing in its own market, there is a suspicion that that country is not really an efficient producer of those goods. It would appear that profits made from the sale of goods at high prices on the local market are being used to *subsidize* exports [33] so that the price of the exported

---

[32] See *Special Principle Nine* adopted at the first United Nations Conference on Trade and Development: "All countries shall refrain from all forms of dumping." *Final Act of the United Nations Conference on Trade and Development,* June 15, 1964, Annex I in I PROCEEDINGS OF THE UNITED NATIONS CONFERENCE ON TRADE AND DEVELOPMENT 23 (1964). 107 countries voted in favor of this principle, none opposed, 9 abstained. *Ibid.*

Economists have refined the term "dumping" and have given their approval to some forms subject to blanket condemnation at UNCTAD. The classic categories are *sporadic, intermittent,* and *continuous.* See VINER, *supra* note 31, at 23-31. It is only intermittent dumping—and only then if done with predatory intent—which is condemned. See Baier, *supra* note 24, at 449. It is, of course, somewhat easier in theory than in practice to distinguish between the three types of dumping. And the "attempt to prescribe only predatory dumping . . . [is] exceedingly difficult, if not completely impractical." *Id.* at 452. No wonder then that governments have simply agreed to condemn "all forms of dumping."

[33] Such a practice may be profitable both as a means of increasing export markets and as a scheme to maximize monopoly profits on the domestic side of the operation. Mercantile traders were familiar with these practices: "I have known the different undertakers of some particular works agree privately among themselves to give a bounty out of their own pockets upon the exportation of a certain proportion of the goods which they dealt in. This expedient succeeded so well that it more than doubled the price of their goods in the home market. . . ." (SMITH, THE WEALTH OF NATIONS, Book IV, Chapter V, quoted in VINER *supra* note 31 at 36 n. 1.)

It is important to note, however, that the conditions which make dumping a profitable enterprise are not easily found. First, the producer must have a

goods is kept "artificially" below what it "should" otherwise be. This price, and the export sales which result from it, then, are not the result of efficient production, but of an imperfect market situation in the producing country. Now theoretically there exists somewhere an efficient producer who is being deprived of his "natural" market, because of this dumping practice. He would be supplying the goods which are being dumped if he did not have to compete with the dumped goods. Thus, as far as the theory is concerned, the evil of dumping is that the efficient producer is being deprived of his "natural" market, because another producer is dumping goods.

From the point of view of the importing country, this displacement of the "natural" supplier by the "dumping" supplier may or may not be cause for concern. It will not be if the importing country is primarily interested in allowing its consumers to purchase goods at the lowest possible price. It will be a matter of concern if the importing state is willing to sacrifice the benefits to its consumers in the interests of perfection of the world economy. By barring dumped goods it would be doing its part in preventing deviations from the operation of the classical theory of international trade. Few nations, however, are so altruistic. Of infinitely more immediate importance to them may be the fact that the "natural" supplier, especially if he is the existing supplier, is a country with whom the importing country may prefer to do business for other than purely economic reasons. Country *A*, for

---

domestic monopoly situation. Secondly, he must be certain that his home market is isolated "from the markets in which his goods are being dumped, lest the cheap goods be reimported and then used to undercut the producers' high home price." Ehrenhaft, *supra* note 12, at 49.

Where the dumping is done with predatory intent, i.e. to crush competition or prevent its birth in the dumped market, with the idea that once this has been accomplished the dumper may then raise his prices and enjoy monopoly profits, it is also necessary that the industry be one which is difficult to enter or reenter. This requirement would seem to cast doubt on the frequent allegations of dumping with regard to textiles, an industry where entry is relatively easy. See C. KINDLEBERGER, FOREIGN TRADE AND THE NATIONAL ECONOMY 131 (1962).

example, may have in the past purchased all its fine quality shoes from Country *C*. Now along comes Country *B* which is willing to dump fine quality shoes at prices well below these charged by *C*. But *A* may desire to continue purchasing shoes from *C*, because *C* is a political or military ally. Or *C* may be a source of considerable financial and technical assistance for *A*. *A* must then decide whether these factors outweigh the benefits to *A*'s consumers to be gained by purchasing dumped shoes from *B*. The issue would be much clearer, of course, if shoes were produced in *A* and *B*'s dumped shoes were undercutting the price received by *A*'s producers. In that case *A* might clearly prefer to protect its own producers at the price of making its consumers pay more for the product. This, in fact, would seem to be the preference in most developing countries which are seeking to build up their manufacturing sector. Thus there are the two situations that a country in whose territory low-priced goods are sold will be concerned about: displacement from the market of traditional suppliers, and injury to local industries.

Now it is important to note that these two situations can come about without dumping. That is to say, a producer may be so efficient that he can sell both at home and overseas at prices far below his competitors. In overseas markets he could thus both displace traditional suppliers and injure local producers. But to allow a state to prohibit the importation of his product in such circumstances would discourage new innovations in production leading to increased efficiency. This would, of course, be extremely undesirable. The international economy is, in theory, willing to accept the displacement of traditional suppliers and the injury to local industry caused by increases in efficiency of production. What it is unwilling to accept is displacement and injury caused by the subsidization of exports by the profits reaped in the market of the producing country, i.e., dumping. Thus, sales in an importing market below prices prevailing in *that* market will "legitimately" call forth governmental action *only* when those sales are the result of dumping.

The usual government action to counteract the effects of dumping takes the form of the levying of an anti-dumping duty. Legislation providing for such duties is in force in many countries,[34] and consists of two main parts: first, a definition of dumping, and, second, the action which may be taken if dumping is found. The substance of these provisions is normally included in the trade agreements of countries maintaining such legislation.

The provisions of this Agreement shall not apply to such special duties as are or may be assessed on importation of products which have been sold at a price less than (a) the price at which such products are sold in the country of origin, or (b) the highest price at which such products are sold in any third country.

There are two important points to notice about this clause. First, it suspends the operation of the most-favored-nation clause ("shall not apply") with respect to anti-dumping duties ("special duties"). This may be important in two circumstances. If there is dumping from more than one source, the most-favored-nation provision would require the imposition of anti-dumping duties equally on all dumped imports in comparable situations. The other situation in which the most-favored-nation principle could operate is with regard to the anti-dumping orders which are issued by the importing country. Assuming that one of several shoe manufacturers in Country X is dumping in Country Y, Country Y may levy an anti-dumping duty (a) on all imports of shoes from Country X, (b) on all imports of shoes from Country X, except those produced by certain specified manufacturers, or (c) on imports of shoes from Country X which are the products of a particular manufacturer. To make the distinctions necessary to the determination involved in (b) and (c) requires, of course, that Country Y possess a considerable body of information about sales of shoes in Country X. Absent this information, the usual situation, Country Y would probably impose an anti-dumping duty on all shoes originating in Country X. But any solution (e.g., (a) and (b), above) which penalized exporters who were not dumping

[34] See GATT, ANTI-DUMPING AND COUNTERVAILING DUTIES 6 (1958).

solely on the ground that they happened to produce in and export from the same country as the dumpers, would be to discriminate against the former solely on the basis of their nationality, a violation of most-favored-nation treatment, so that here again the suspension of the most-favored-nation standard may have a significant effect.[35]

The second point about Provision I is that it offers two definitions of dumping. The definition suggested as alternative (a) is the conventional definition which has been discussed earlier.[36] While sound in theory, however, it suffers from an obvious practical defect. Information on the prices for which goods are sold in the home economy of the alleged dumper may be difficult to obtain. So the practice has arisen of treating as dumped in Country X, imported goods which are sold in Country X at a price lower than they are sold in Country Y or Country Z. Something more must be added to alternative definition (b), however, else virtually every transaction in international trade fall into the dumping category. Clearly there may be sound economic reasons for charging different prices for similar goods in different markets. To allow this, a trade agreement provision on dumping should provide that: "Due allowance shall be made in each case for difference in conditions and terms of sale, for differences in taxation, and for other differences affecting price compatibility."

As the definitional problem is the most important in drafting trade agreement provisions dealing with dumping, it would be well to look at another. The following is based on the GATT: [37]

1. The Parties recognize that dumping, by which the products of one Party are introduced into the commerce of the other at less

[35] See Coudert, *The Application of the United States Antidumping Law in the Light of a Liberal Trade Policy*, 65 COLUM. L. REV. 189, 222-223 (1965).

[36] What has not been mentioned is the fact that by accepting this standard, each Party may be implicitly consenting to permit representatives of the other Party to visit its territory to ascertain the facts concerning the domestic selling price. See *Report on Anti-Dumping and Countervailing Duties, supra* note 21, at 196.

[37] Art. VI, GATT, III BASIC INSTRUMENTS AND SELECTED DOCUMENTS 12 (1958).

than the normal value of the products, is to be condemned if it causes or threatens material injury to an established domestic industry [or to traditional patterns of domestic trade] in the territory of the other Party or materially retards the establishment of a domestic industry. For purposes of this Article, a product is to be considered as being introduced into the commerce of an importing country at less than its normal value, if the price of the product exported from one country to another

(a) is less than the comparable price, in the ordinary course of trade, for the like product destined for consumption in the exporting country, or

(b) in the absence of such domestic price, it is less than either

    (i) the highest comparable price for the like product for export to any third country in the ordinary course of trade, or

    (ii) the cost of production of the product in the country of origin plus a reasonable addition for selling cost and profit.

Notice that in the definition of dumping, a comparison must be made between "the price of the product exported" and the figure defined by subparagraphs (a), (b)(i), or (b)(ii). At the outset the language "the price of the product exported" is ambiguous, since it could be the price at the point of exportation or the point of importation. Common sense, and a knowledge of what dumping is, however, militate in favor of choosing as a basis for comparison the price at which the product left the exporting country—and so this provision has been interpreted.[38] Note further that this price is to be compared first with the domestic price and only *"in the absence of such domestic price"* may the other two standards be turned to. On the other hand, subparagraphs (b)(i) and (b)(ii) are alternatives. The "third country sales" standard [(b)(i)] will be

---

[38] See *Report on Anti-dumping and Countervailing Duties, supra* note 23, at 146. This figure was further refined to mean either the "ex-factory price on sales for export" or the "f.o.b. price, port of shipment." *Ibid.*

Other items sometimes taken into account in computing the export price are "cost of packing and expenses incident to conditioning the merchandise for shipment." Baier, *supra* note 24, at 414.

discussed shortly. The other criterion, based on costs of production, can be expeditiously disposed of. For it seems based on a premise barely tenable—that cost of production figures are more readily available than information on domestic prices. It is well known that governments have a difficult enough time in determining costs of production for purposes of income taxation. How, then, one could expect that a foreign government could obtain such information is difficult to imagine. Nonetheless, there may be situations where all kinds of information is freely available and yet a domestic sales price cannot be established. This would be true, for example, if the quantity sold in the home market were so small as to give an inadequate basis for comparison of prices. Or where a "producer intending to export at prices lower than those current in the domestic sale market . . . refrain[s] from offering for sale commodities identical with those exported at low prices." [39] In such situations, production costs may provide the only measure for determining dumping.

The most useful standard, however, is that of sales to third countries. For developing countries which, as a rule, lack the far ranging diplomatic and consular representation available to their wealthier neighbors, the information gathering necessary to the establishment of the fact of "dumping" presents a formidable obstacle. To require them to justify antidumping action by establishing production costs would be to force developing countries to assume an almost impossible burden. Even to obtain domestic price information may require representation in or near the country of origin. The "third country sales" criterion, on the other hand, greatly expands the sources of relevant information upon which a claim of dumping can be based. To the extent that it does so, it is of benefit to developing countries.

The "third country sales" standard is also of great utility in another way—with regard to sales by states with centrally planned economies. For them the "domestic price" and "cost of produc-

[39] See VINER, *supra* note 31, at 19.

tion" criteria simply will not operate. This is so because resources are allocated in centrally planned economies on the basis of administrative decisions, with the price system playing a secondary and somewhat formal role. In such circumstances measuring dumping in terms of domestic prices becomes an unreal exercise.[40] The only realistic standard is to compare the prices charged externally, i.e., the prices at which the goods are sold to third parties. To illustrate, in 1955 Bulgaria exported nitrogenous fertilizers at the following prices per ton: Mainland China $84.50; Czechoslovakia $61.50; Greece $61; Hungary $90.30; Poland $64.70; and Rumania $92. If these price differentials were not due solely to valid commercial considerations and without establishing the cost of producing such fertilizers in Bulgaria, or the price in Bulgaria, and armed with a provision such as that suggested above, Greece could establish that Bulgarian fertilizer was being dumped in Greece. The margin is the difference between the price at which the fertilizer was sold to Greece and "the highest comparable price for the like product or export to any third country in the ordinary course of trade." In the absence of any special cirucumstances, the highest price would appear to have been that to Rumania, $92 a ton, and since the price to Greece was only $61 a ton, the margin of dumping in Greece was $31 per ton.[41]

[40] This situation has been noted in the General Agreement on Tariffs and Trade. *Ad Article* VI, Paragraph 1 (2), GATT, III BASIC INSTRUMENTS AND SELECTED DOCUMENTS 67 (1958) provides: "It is recognized that, in the case of imports from a country which has a complete or substantially complete monopoly of its trade and where all domestic prices are fixed by the State, special difficulties may exist in determining price comparability for the purpose of paragraph 1, and in such cases importing contracting parties may find it necessary to take into account the possibility that a strict comparison with domestic prices in such a country may not always be appropriate."

[41] Where there are too few sales to third countries to establish a "third country price," the U.S. Government has utilized the standard of "prices charged for exportation by another country shipping the same product." See Comment, *The Antidumping Act: Problems of Administration and Proposals for Change*, 17 STAN. L. REV. 730, 733 (1965). Thus where domestic manufacturers complained against exports of sheet glass from Czechoslovakia, a determination of whether such exports were being dumped was made by comparing the price of the Czech glass with the "Western European price, f.o.b. shipping port, for exportation to the United States, of glass . . . most nearly similar to the . . . [glass] exported

Having defined dumping in terms acceptable to both parties, a trade agreement should then go on to provide for the remedy available to the party which is the "victim" of the dumping. "In order to offset or prevent dumping, a Party may levy on any dumped product an antidumping duty not greater in amount than the margin of dumping in respect of such product. For purposes of this Article, the margin of dumping is the price difference determined in accordance with the provisions of paragraph 1."

At one time there was a move afoot to legalize the use of other measures, including quantitative restrictions, to combat dumping.[42] Justification for such an expansion of remedies would, however, be difficult to find. Since the elaborate calculations required to establish the fact of dumping also yield the figure for the margin of dumping, it would appear that no administrative advantage would be gained by such a move. Perhaps the theory was that countries which dump should be severely penalized, by the banning of their products, so as to end the practice once and for all. In any case, the accepted remedy for dumping is the antidumping duty.

Finally, to restrict the opportunities for the imposition of antidumping duties to those situations where they are really necessary to protect one of the parties from substantial harm, the parties may provide that antidumping duties may be imposed only where the dumping is causing "material injury." The considerations here would be the same as those discussed with regard to "material injury" and countervailing duties.

From the point of view of a developing country, much of the

---

from Czechoslovakia to the United States." *Jalousie-Louvre-Sized Sheet Glass from Czechoslovakia*, 27 FED. REG. 8457 (1962). Without passing judgment on the propriety of this standard, suffice it to say that few countries would be willing to permit their exports to be tested against it, and thus to find it included in a trade agreement would be highly unlikely.

[42] See Draft Report of the Technical Sub-Committee of the Preparatory Committee of the United Nations Conference on Trade and Employment, U.N. Doc. E/PC/T/C.II/54, at 12 (1946).

classic doctrine on dumping heretofore discussed may seem of little relevance. For, as has been pointed out, what an importing country cares about is the price of goods imported into its market, regardless of whether they are being technically dumped or not, and the effect of such imports on the importing country's trade and industry.[43] Several developing countries have recognized that this is the scope of their interest by seeking to include in their trade agreements the following provision:

Notwithstanding any provision of this Agreement, if imports of goods from one Party cause or threaten injury to an established domestic industry or traditional patterns of domestic trade of the other Party or are such as to retard the establishment of a domestic industry in the territory of the other Party, the injured Party shall have the right, after written notification to the other Party, to prohibit in whole or in part, the importation of the products causing or threatening to cause such injury or retardation.

A provision such as this type obviates the necessity of the importing party's looking to prices other than those prevailing in its own market. In point of fact, the provision makes no reference to prices at all, although it seems clearly designed to meet the problems raised by the sale of goods in the local market at some price lower than that viewed as desirable by the importing country. An article of this breadth, however, may not readily be acceptable to most exporting countries.[44] A provision of a similar nature, how-

[43] This is the theory of "market disruption" turned inside out. See pp. 58-59 *supra*. In the present case the markets and infant industries of the developing country are being disrupted by imports. See also art. 23 of the Treaty Establishing a Free-Trade Area and Instituting the Latin American Free-Trade Association, *done* at Montevideo, February 18, 1960, 1 MULTILATERAL ECONOMIC COOPERATION IN LATIN AMERICA, U.N. Doc. E/CN.12/621, at 57, 60 (1962) ("The Contracting Parties may, as a provisional measure and providing that the customary level of consumption in the importing country is not thereby lowered, authorize a Contracting Party to impose nondiscriminatory restrictions upon imports of products included in the liberalization program which originate in the Area, if those products are imported in such quantities or under such conditions that they have, or are liable to have, serious repercussions on specific productive activities of vital importance to the national economy.") On "escape clauses" generally, see I. KRAVIS, DOMESTIC INTERESTS AND INTERNATIONAL OBLIGATIONS (1963).

[44] Such a provision is obviously not compatible with the theory of the allocation of world trade according to comparative advantage.

ever, patterned after Article XIX of the General Agreement on Tariffs and Trade might prove more palatable.

If, as a result of unforeseen developments and of the effect of the obligations incurred by either Party to this Agreement, any product is imported into the territory of one of the Party's in such increased quantities and under such conditions as to (a) cause or threaten serious injury to domestic producers or to the establishment of domestic production in that territory of like or directly competitive products or (b) cause serious disruption of traditional patterns of trade in that product or directly competitive products, the injured Party shall have the right, in respect of such product, and to the extent and for such time as may be necessary to prevent or remedy such injury, to suspend the obligation in whole or in part.[45]

This provision offers more protection to an exporting country in that it limits action by an importing party to the situation where the alleged injury was: (1) the result of unforeseen developments; (2) the result of obligations incurred under the agreement; (3) serious. An "unforeseen development" has been interpreted as one occurring after a trade agreement has been entered into "which it would not be reasonable to expect that the negotiators . . . could and should have foreseen at the time the . . . [agreement] was negotiated.[46] Injury caused by the grant of most-favored-nation treatment or a promise to refrain from imposing quantitative restrictions would result from "obligations" incurred under the Agreement.[47] As to the question of "seriousness, this is "essentially a matter of economic and social judgment involving a considerable subjective element." [48] The most that can be said

[45] The clause was "included in the Charter at the instance of the United States." WILCOX, *supra* note 13, at 182-83. It is known as the " 'Mexican Clause' " since it was first used in a trade agreement between the U.S. and Mexico. See VINER, *supra* note 10, at 353. And the United States has been the nation which has invoked its provisions most often. See ANALYTICAL INDEX, *supra* note 14, at 104-8 (Rev. ed. 1966).

[46] GATT, REPORT ON THE WITHDRAWAL BY THE UNITED STATES OF A TARIFF CONCESSION UNDER ARTICLE XIX OF THE GENERAL AGREEMENT ON TARIFFS AND TRADE 10 (1951).

[47] See ANALYTICAL INDEX, *supra* note 14, at 103.

[48] REPORT, *supra* note 46, at 22.

is that where one party to the agreement protests against the imposition of a restriction on imports because the injury was not "serious," the other party is "entitled to the benefit of any reasonable doubt" since it is the latter which is accused of breaching the agreement.[49]

[49] *Id.* at 23. Another provision, along the same lines, is found in the First Protocol Concerning Trade Relations to Treaty of Commerce, Establishment and Navigation between the United Kingdom and Japan, *done* at London, November 14, 1962, [1963] Gr. Brit. T.S. No. 53 (CMD. 2085) at 74-76:

(1) If the Government of either Contracting Party find that any product of the territory of the other Contracting Party is being imported into the territory of the former Contracting Party in such increased quanities and other such conditions as to cause or threaten serious injury to producers in the territory of that former Contracting Party of like or directly competitive products, that Government, in case they wish to take action under the present Protocol to prevent or remedy such injury, shall give to the Government of the other Contracting Party notice to this effect with a full explanation of the circumstances and the two Governments shall enter into consultation, not later than seven days after such notice is given, with a view to finding a mutually acceptable solution.

(2) If no mutually acceptable solution is found within thirty days after the consultation has begun, the Government of the importing Contracting Party may take action to prevent or remedy the injury referred to in paragraph (1) above, notwithstanding the provisions of Article 17 of the Treaty, provided that such action:

(a) shall not be taken lightly;

(b) shall be limited, so far as administratively practicable, to the specific products in respect of which it is necessary and shall not be more severe than is needed to remedy the injury caused or threatened; and

(c) shall be discontinued immediately either when a mutually acceptable solution is found or when the situation which gave rise to the action is rectified.

The principal difference between this provision and that discussed in the text is the effort made here to protect the exporting state by providing for consultations prior to the imposition of controls. On the other hand, the exporting state has lost the protection of the requirement that controls may only be imposed as a result of "unforeseen developments." This may be a significant loss, for in the provision quoted in the text, an importing state is in effect saying that on the basis of its present knowledge, it is prepared to absorb certain injury to its domestic producers as the price for concessions granted to it in the agreement. Absent the "unforeseen developments" clause, however, an importing state is saying it retains the right to act where imports cause serious injury to its domestic producers, even though this possibility is clearly in the mind of the negotiators at the time the agreement is signed. Since in a trade negotiation it is more probable than not that the parties have explored the likely effects of granting each other most-favored-nation treatment, for example, it is probably true that some injury to domestic producers and traditional suppliers has been foreseen. By including the phrase "unforeseen developments" in the agreements, an importing state expressly agrees to accept such anticipated changes in its pattern of suppliers. By omitting such a phrase, a substantial limitation on the ability of an exporting state to increase its market share may be established.

Another alternative, and one preferred by the centrally planned countries, is a provision on the following lines:

1. Both Parties shall take measures so that the prices for goods to be delivered under the present Agreement will be established on the basis of the world market prices, i.e., prices in the main markets for the corresponding goods.
2. For goods for which no world market price can be established, competitive prices for similar goods of analogous quality shall be applied.
3. In the event of goods being sold under the present Agreement at less than world market prices or competitive prices, the importing country shall have the right to impose a special duty on the goods equal in amount to the difference between the world market price or competitive price, as the case may be, and the actual price for which the goods were sold.[50]

This provision represents a compromise between the interests of the exporting and the importing country. The importing country, more often than not the developing country, is assured that goods will be sold in its market at or near presently existing world prices. This should protect the market from being disrupted by goods sold at "too low" prices. On the other hand, the exporter is assured that if prices in the importing market are at an artificially high level, he can sell his goods at the world market price without having to worry about being accused of dumping.

The reasons why this type of provision is preferred by countries with centrally planned economies have not been articulated. A cynical view would probably be that for most goods there is no "world market price" and therefore such a provision gives centrally planned countries a free hand in selling goods at any price they wish. On the other hand, the reasons for this type of arrange-

---

[50] See, e.g., Trade Agreement between the Republic of Tanganyika and the People's Republic of Bulgaria, *done* at Dar es Salaam, October 5, 1963, art. 11; Trade Agreement between the Republic of Tanganyika and the Union of Soviet Socialist Republic, *done* at Dar es Salaam, August 14, 1963, art. 9; Trade Agreement between Kenya and the Union of Soviet Socialist Republic, *done* at Nairobi, April 29, 1964, art. 12. See also Trade Agreement between the Republic of Ghana and the People's Republic of Bulgaria, *done* at Sofia, October 5, 1961, art. 5.

ment may be more valid. Centrally planned countries have been accused of "dumping" so often that they shy away from the term. Those who have negotiated trade issues with Eastern European countries are doubtless aware that "dumping" is a word best left unmentioned if sensitivities are not to be offended. In addition, the centrally planned countries will readily admit that no standard involving their domestic "prices" has validity. An external stand-ard is thus required. And since the centrally planned countries trade with each other on the basis of world market prices, they much prefer this standard with which they are familiar.

R E - E X P O R T S

The term "dumping" is sometimes used to refer to transactions which do not take place in the market of one of the parties to the agreement. For example, Country *A* may have imported a quantity of cocoa from Country *B* only to find that the cocoa cannot be used in its own country. Country *A* then attempts to sell the cocoa in the world market. In connection with such sales one frequently hears the charge that the goods are being "dumped" on the world market. What is usually meant is that the goods are offered for sale either below the purchase price (i.e., below cost) or below existing world prices. While this is not tech-nically dumping, it may be useful to discuss such practices at this point.

Most developing countries are producers and exporters of primary products. To a very great extent these products are sold on international commodity exchanges for convertible foreign exchange. At times, however, developing countries have engaged in direct barter transactions in which they have exchanged their primary products for other primary products or for manufactured goods. Occasionally a country which has exchanged industrial equipment for primary products finds that it has overestimated its need for the latter, which it resells at prices below existing world prices in order to acquire foreign exchange. This kind of transaction might even be profitable if the industrial goods exchanged for the primary products were "overpriced" so that the foreign exchange proceeds of the sale of the primary commodity exceed those which would have been obtained if the industrial equipment had been sold directly for foreign exchange. Such re-exports and resales ultimately redound to the injury of the developing country, which could have obtained the foreign exchange itself by selling the goods on the world market in the first place. Indonesia has been the victim of such practices. On October 24, 1955, in a speech to the Indonesian Parliament the prime minister stated:

It is an open secret that parallel transactions with the East European countries have brought about a reduction in the overall sale of our foreign exchange. Raw materials we sold these countries are usually retraded in other markets . . . with the result that in the world markets we have to compete with goods originating in our own country. . . .

With barter trade and compensation transactions our exports are usually sold at a lower price than that obtained in the world market. Losses suffered are compensated by increasing prices of articles imported under the transactions. Thus the country loses doubly: on the one hand, it receives less foreign exchange, and on the other Indonesian customers have to pay heavily for increased prices of imported goods.[51]

The simplest way of legally preventing such occurrences is for a trade agreement to provide that: "Both Parties undertake that goods and commodities of one Party imported into the territory of the other Party shall not be re-exported without prior approval of the competent authorities in both countries." [52]

---

[51] Quoted R. MIKESELL and J. BEHRMAN, FINANCING FREE WORLD TRADE WITH THE SINO-SOVIET BLOC 88 (1958). See also pp. 142-44 supra. But see R. SAWYER, COMMUNIST TRADE WITH DEVELOPING COUNTRIES 1955-1965, at 65 (1966) (". . . [T]he rather meagre evidence seems to suggest that although some communist countries have attempted to work out such transactions, the actual volume of such [re-export] sales has been quite limited. . . .")

[52] Item (10) of the "Recommendation on Measures by Countries with Centrally Planned Economies for Expansion and Diversification of Exports of Manufactures and Semi-manufactures by Developing Countries" adopted at the first United Nations Conference on Trade and Development provided: "[The countries with centrally planned economies are] prepared not to re-export goods, purchased in developing countries, unless it is with the consent of the parties concerned." Annex A.III.7, I PROCEEDINGS OF THE UNITED NATIONS CONFERENCE ON TRADE AND DEVELOPMENT 40, 41 (1964).

If the re-export of only one or a few products is likely to cause harm, a more limited provision may be inserted in the Agreement: "The following goods imported from the territory of either Party into the territory of the other shall not be re-exported to a third country without the prior approval of the authorities of the Party in whose territory the goods originated."

A related problem may arise where both of the parties to a trade agreement produce the same primary product and one of the parties sells that product on the world market or to third countries at a price below that prevailing in the world markets with the effect of destroying the market for the other party's product. This is apparently what happened when Bolivia, Indonesia, Malaysia, and Thailand accused the Soviet Union of "dumping" tin and thereby "wrecking" the world market, which resulted in severe economic repercussions in those developing countries which produced tin. Such activities by trade agreement partners could be limited by including in the agreement an article reading: "It is the view of both Parties that sales of certain primary commodities below world market prices are harmful to their respective economies. Both Parties therefore agree that in no case will they sell, or offer for sale the following products at prices (including terms) which are less than the world market prices."

CONCLUSION

Dumping and export subsidization are generally viewed with distaste by the international economic community as practices smacking of "unfair competition." Yet, as has been shown, neither deserves to be condemned outright. Dumping may be a positive benefit to consumers in a particular country and this benefit must be weighed against the negative effects on local producers and foreign exporters. And export subsidies may be the most important device to strengthen the position of the developing countries in the world market for manufactures and semi-manufactures. The choice is not between exports with subsidies and exports without subsidies, but between export subsidies, preferences, import controls and other devices designed to increase the supply of foreign exchange available to developing countries. Viewed in that light, most economists would opt for export subsidies as the most desirable alternative.

VIII. Vessels and Ports

For some countries, a not insubstantial share of their imports are "invisible." That is to say, activities which involve expenditures of foreign exchange, in that way resembling imports, but which do not show up in a country's balance of trade figures. The principal invisibles for developing countries are debt service payments, returns on foreign investments, and ocean shipping (including insurance). The first two do not give rise to the kind of problems ordinarily dealt with in a trade agreement. Shipping, on the other hand, is an activity so closely connected with international trade that problems relating to it have long been considered in trade agreements.

The intimate relation between international trade and ocean shipping is particularly important to the developing countries because of the large amounts of foreign exchange which developing countries expend both to import the goods needed for their development and to export the goods with which imports are financed. Although the figures are not easily obtainable, a survey prepared at the request of the Secretary-General of the United Nations Conference on Trade and Development estimated that ocean freight constituted 10 per cent of the developing countries' total import bill. The developing countries have been concerned about this large outflow of foreign exchange, particularly as it is virtually all going to shipping companies based in the developed countries. And not only have the developing countries been worried about their total freight bill, but they have also been concerned about the structure of freight rates which appear to

be an additional barrier in the path of their economic progress.
A few examples may be cited in support of their case. In 1963
it cost $24 per ton to ship lumber from Mexico to Venezuela.
The rate on shipments of the same type of lumber from Finland
to Venezuela was only $11. In the case of chemicals, the freight
rate was $54 per ton from Buenos Aires to Tampico, Mexico.
But if the same ton of chemicals were first shipped from Buenos
Aires to Southampton, and then trans-shipped to Tampico, the
rate was only $40 per ton.[1] To a large extent these rates are based
on the volume of traffic, the amount of time that must be spent in
port, etc., but there is deep suspicion on the part of many developing countries that these factors alone do not account for the large
disparities in the costs of ocean shipping. Ocean freight rates have
created problems for the developing countries in still another way.
During times of international conflict such as the Korean War and
the 1956 Suez crisis, the major maritime powers diverted a good
part of their merchant marines to serve the national interest,
thereby decreasing the number of ships available to carry goods
to and from many developing countries. The result was that
freight rates on these routes reached astronomical levels. Finally,
developing countries are disturbed about the fact that ocean
freight rates are generally fixed on the basis of the kind of goods
shipped, rather than their weight or volume. When one considers
that developing countries are generally exporters of raw materials,
which bear low rates, and importers of capital goods carrying high
freight rates, one can see the basis of their concern. It appears
to them that the industrial countries have "arranged" the rates so
as to keep raw material costs low in those countries, and the costs
of capital equipment high in the developing countries, with the
aim of "inducing" the developing countries to remain suppliers

---

[1] See S. DELL, A LATIN AMERICAN COMMON MARKET? 101-102 (1966). See also
ECAFE, *Problems of Shipping and Ocean Freight Rates in the ECAFE Region*,
V PROCEEDINGS OF THE UNITED NATIONS CONFERENCE ON TRADE AND DEVELOPMENT
311, 324-25 (1964) (complaints of discriminatory rates adversely affecting the exports
of Burma (beans, pulses, maize), Malaysia (pineapples) and Pakistan (gypsum,
molasses).

of raw materials rather than semimanufactures and manufactures. While charging "what the traffic will bear" is certainly good economics, the developing countries would like to see some change in the direction of basing rates as much as possible on the volume rather than the quality of the goods shipped.[2]

In addition to their concern about freight rates, developing countries complain about the lack of availability of shipping services which prevents them from expanding their markets.[3] In reply shippers argue that there is not a sufficient amount of freight to justify the shipping services desired. But the developing countries suspect that part of the reason is lethargy or conservatism on the part of the companies who are still geared to serving outposts of old empires, and, even worse, a desire on the part of particular maritime powers to continue favoring their former colonial areas.

Since most developing countries are almost wholly dependent on ocean shipping for the export of their products and the import of the goods necessary to their economic development, as well as, in some cases at least, the food supplies on which the well-being of large numbers of their population depend, they are naturally concerned that such shipping services should be controlled by a few developed countries. For them, as for most nations, a national merchant marine is a vital security matter, regardless of the costs involved.

For all of these reasons, developing countries are showing an increasing interest in developing their own merchant fleets, either individually or in conjunction with other developing countries. As part of this program, they are incorporating in their trade agreements provisions which will aid them in attaining this goal.

---

[2] It has been suggested that the growth of "container shipping" will bring an end to the old system and that ocean freight rates will soon be "based on the space taken up by the container, regardless of its contents." "What Comes After Containers," 222 THE ECONOMIST 50, 51 (1967).

[3] See, e.g., *Problems of Shipping and Ocean Freight Rates in the ECAFE Region*, *supra* note 1, at 324 (complaint of China [Taiwan] that trade with Europe has declined substantially due to the absence of regular shipping services.)

Nationality of a Vessel

At the outset of any discussion of the maritime provisions of a trade agreement, it is necessary to consider the question of what is a "vessel of the other party" which will be entitled to the benefits guaranteed in the agreement. The answer is not as simple as might first appear since it is not uncommon for a vessel to fly the flag of Country *A*, be owned by a company organized under the laws of Country *B*, the shareholders of which are citizens of Country *C*.[4] For purposes of the trade agreement does the vessel belong to Country *A*, Country *B*, or Country *C?* The usual trade agreement clause dealing with this question reads: "Vessels under the flag of either Party, and carrying the papers required by its law as proof of nationality, shall be deemed to be vessels of that Party both on the high seas and in the ports, places and waters of the other Party."

According to this provision, the nationality of a vessel is determined by looking at the ship's documents. Those documents will show the country in which the ship is registered, and it is this that determines nationality. The flag requirement is formal only, and merely evidences the country of registry.[5] Under currently accepted standards of international law the other party to the agreement may not go "behind" the flag to see who really owns the vessel. This test satisfies the dual requirements of "high certainty and easy precision in the identification of the national

---

[4] See e.g., Markakis v. Liberian s/s The Mparmpa Christos, 161 F. Suppl. 487 (S.D.N.Y. 1958). (Ship registered in Liberia, owned by a Panamanian corporation, which was controlled by Greek nationals resident in London.)

[5] For a treaty provision dispensing with the "flag" requirement, see Treaty of Commerce, Establishment and Navigation between the United Kingdom and Japan, *done* at London, November 14, 1962, art. 2, [1963] Gr. Brit. T.S. No. 53 (CMD. 2085) at 3–4: ". . . (3) The term 'vessels': (a) in relation to the United Kingdom means all ships *registered* at a port in any territory of that Contracting Party to which the present Treaty applies; and (b) in relation to Japan means all ships carrying the *papers* required by the law of Japan in proof of Japanese nationality." (Emphasis added.)

character of ships." [6] While such practice may result in indirectly conferring benefits on persons who are nationals of neither of the parties to the agreement, any other rule would appear to be fraught with administrative inconvenience and might reduce the order of ocean transport to chaos.[7]

PORT CHARGES AND TONNAGE MEASUREMENT

Upon entering a foreign port, vessels are ordinarily subject to harbor or port dues based on their net tonnage. It is interesting to note that in maritime terminology, net tonnage is a measure of volume rather than weight. A net ton is equal to 100 cubic feet of the internal capacity of a vessel.[8] From this figure, the laws of several maritime states provide for the deduction of space devoted to crew accommodations and propelling power.[9] The majority of other countries, however, include such areas in a vessel's net tonnage.[10] This distinction is important as the countries follow-

[6] McDougal, Burke, and Vlasic, *The Maintenance of Public Order at Sea and the Nationality of Ships*, 54 Am. J. Int'l L. 25, 26 (1960).

[7] Since the end of the Second World War there has been much concern in the international community over the so-called flags of convenience issue. Ships owned by nationals of maritime powers register those ships in Liberia and Panama, for example, to escape the requirements of domestic labor and tax legislation. In an attempt to curtail this practice and at the urging of maritime unions and many shipowners, the Convention on the High Seas, *done* at Geneva, April 29, 1958, U.S. TIAS 5200, [1963] Gr. Brit. T.S. No. 5 (Cmd. 1929) at 3, requires, in art. 5, that there must be a "genuine link" between the state and the ship for the ship to acquire the state's nationality. This requirement has been subject to massive criticism. See McDougal, Burke, and Vlasic, *supra, passim*. The writers conclude that the best rule is still the universally accepted system of attributing nationality through registration and documentation.

[8] See H. Hawkins, Commercial Treaties and Agreements, Principles and Practice 215, note 3 to Chapter III (1951).

[9] Liberia, Panama, and the United States.

[10] See Piper, *Navigation Provisions in United States Commercial Treaties*, 11 Am. J. Comp. L. 184, 198 (1962).

The League of Nations made an attempt to establish a uniform system for tonnage measurement and in 1939 published the Oslo Rules. The Rules were later incorporated into the Convention for a Uniform System of Tonnage Measurement of Ships, *done* in Oslo, June 10, 1947, 208 U.N.T.S. 3 (1955). The Convention has

ing the former system, by decreasing their net tonnage, pay lower harbor dues.

An administrative system has been devised so as to obviate the need for physically measuring the capacity of each ship entering a given port. Instead, certificates of tonnage issued by the party whose flag the vessel flies are customarily recognized and accepted by the port authorities of the other party as proof of the vessel's tonnage. Frequently, this matter is dealt with in a separate agreement between the parties.[11] Where it is not it is customary to include in the Article dealing with vessels, language such as the following: "The certificates concerning tonnage measurements of vessels issued by the relevant authorities of either Party shall be recognized by the relevant authorities of the other Party as equivalent to the certificates issued by the latter."

An alternative formulation is found in Article 13 of the Treaty of Trade and Navigation between the Czechoslovak Republic and the German Democratic Republic, done at Berlin, November 25, 1959: [12]

Tonnage certificates and other ship's papers carried on board the vessel and issued by the competent Czechoslovak authorities shall be recognized by the authorities of the German Democratic Republic. In accordance with this provision, any Czechoslovak vessel carrying a valid tonnage certificate shall be exempt from remeasurement in the ports of the German Democratic Republic, and the net capacity of the vessels as entered in the certificate shall be taken as the basis for computing harbour dues.

The practical effect of the international custom of accepting the other party's tonnage measurement for purposes of computing

---

not, however, entered into force due to lack of agreement among the maritime powers over the rules themselves. In addition to the Oslo Rules and the American System, there is a third general category of rules concerning tonnage measurement —the British tonnage rules. See McIntyre, *Admeasurement of Vessels*, 35 TULANE L. REV. 175, 176 (1960).

[11] See Appendix A to this chapter.

[12] 374 U.N.T.S. 101, 120, 122 (1960).

harbor dues is unequal treatment in some cases. The American system of excluding certain portions of a ship from the area to be measured will result in a lower tonnage figure for an American ship than for an identical foreign ship.[13]

There are lessons for developing countries to be learned here. For they should be free to follow the practice of excluding from their definition of tonnage measurement those areas which other nations have excluded, thus benefiting their shipping by in effect lowering the dues they must pay in each port. On the other hand, when negotiating the mutual acceptability of tonnage measurement certificates, they should go behind the promise of mutual recognition and examine the other party's legislation for defining how tonnage is measured. In addition, if tonnage measurement is to turn on the domestic legislation of the parties, it would be prudent to include in the trade agreement a provision covering the possibility of either party's changing its legislation from that which exists at the time of the agreement. If one of the parties objects to such an "interfering in its domestic affairs," or information concerning that party's system of tonnage measurement is not easily available, an alternative formula would accept tonnage measurement certificates "[s]o long as both Parties follow systems of tonnage measurement which are substantially similar. . . ."[14]

PORT CHARGES AND DISCRIMINATION

Harbor and port charges that are based on tonnage are more than nominal and they loom quite large in the total cost structure of ocean shipping since on any one voyage a ship will normally

---

[13] "The design of ships is greatly influenced and to some extent frozen by tonnage considerations, and, in extreme cases, the safety of the ship itself may be influenced by the desire to realize larger tonnage deductions." Mann. *The Conference on Tonnage Measuremet of Ships* 23 DEP'T. STATE BULL. 471 (1950).

[14] Treaty of Friendship, Commerce and Navigation between Greece and the United States *done* at Athens, August 3, 1951, art. XXI (3), 224 U.N.T.S. 279, 324 (1955).

call at several ports. And such costs multiply even further when one considers that the term port charges include light dues, health dues, buoy dues, entrance dues, wharfage dues, pilotage dues, etc. A different scale of charges for each of these types of dues has been a traditional form of discrimination in ocean shipping. For example, under Brazilian Decree No. 1330 of 1939, American ships entering Brazilian harbors had to pay "manifest charges" of $100 for ships up to 4,000 tons, $10 for each 1,000 tons in excess of 4,000, an additional fee of 50 per cent of the total of the first two charges at the first port of call in Brazil, and a further charge at each subsequent port of call. Brazilian Law No. 420 of April 10, 1937, exempted the national shipping line, Lloyd Brasileiro, from similar charges. Ecuadorian Supreme Decree No. 240 of March 31, 1937, provided that ships flying the Ecuadorian flag paid only 10 per cent as much in lighthouse and pilotage dues as American ships of similar size plying the same routes. On the other hand, the United States Navigation Act of 1884 provided that the tonnage tax which it imposed would apply differently to goods coming from parts of North America and the northern part of South America and to goods coming from all other ports.[15] In addition to direct financial discrimination, some nations have in the past given preference to national ships with regard to berthing facilities. Considering that the daily cost of maintaining a ship in port and that the delays in waiting for berthing facilities ran, in some cases, to three weeks, it can be appreciated that such discrimination could severely limit the competitive ability of foreign shipping lines.

---

[15] See *Report of the Subcommittee on the Most-Favored-Nation Clause* adopted by the Committee of Experts for the Progressive Codification of International Law, April 1927, reprinted in Supplement to 22 AM. J. INT'L L. 132, 147 (1928).

Port Charges and National Treatment

The main practical difficulty with such discriminatory practices was that they were highly visible and easily calculable and thus invited instant retaliation. And it was this latter fact, rather than the fact that such practices were discriminatory, which led to their demise. Thus, in a discussion of the international legal aspects of discrimination in merchant shipping, one starts with the now generally accepted principle of national treatment with regard to access to port facilities. The acceptance of this principle as the standard is evidenced by its incorporation in Article 2 of the Statute on the International Regime of Maritime Ports, *done* at Geneva, December 9, 1923: [16]

. . . every Contracting State undertakes to grant the vessels of every other Contracting State equality of treatment with its own vessels, or those of any State whatsoever, in the maritime ports situated under its sovereignty or authority, as regards freedom of access to the port, the use of the port, and the full employment of the benefits as regards navigation and commercial operations which it affords to vessels, their cargoes and passengers.

Similar provisions are found in many trade agreements. A frequently used formulation provides that:

1. Merchant vessels of either Party shall have liberty, on equal terms with merchant vessels of the other Party and of any third country, to come with their passengers and cargoes to all ports, places and waters of such other Party open to foreign commerce, and navigation. Such vessels shall in all respects be accorded treatment no less favorable than that accorded to like vessels of such other Party and of any third country within the ports, places and waters of such other Party.[17]

[16] L.N.T.S. 285, 301 (1926).
[17] See the Agreement on Commerce between Cuba and Japan, *done* at Tokyo, April 22, 1960, art. VI, 442 U.N.T.S. 261, 281-282 (1962). As an added safeguard, trade agreements sometimes provide that ". . . Parties shall insure that dues and

2. Accordingly, merchant vessels of either Party shall be accorded treatment no less favorable that that accorded to like vessels of such other Party and of any third country with respect to duties of tonnage, harbor, pilotage, lighthouse, quarantine and other analogous duties or charges of whatsoever denomination levied in the name or for the profit of the government, public functionaries, private individuals, corporations or establishments of any kind.

As a rule, trade agreements provide for limitations on the activities of the respective governments which might interfere with the free flow of trade. Paragraph 2 above, however, refers to "charges levied in the name of or for the profit of . . . private individuals, corporations or establishments of any kind." This extension of the coverage of the agreement is a recognition of the fact that in many countries private contractors perform certain tasks with regard to the harboring of vessels. In such cases they are ordinarily operating under a government franchise and will be closely regulated by their governments. Thus, it is not unusual for the parties to promise in their trade agreements that even private contractors will not discriminate against foreign shipping.[18]

The acceptance of the national treatment standard with regard to port facilities has been paralleled by the increased use of more subtle and at the same time more effective devices for discriminating in favor of national shipping. Of prime importance here are so-called "cargo preferences." These are legislative provisions which reserve certain classes or types of cargo to national transport undertakings. For example, Decree-Law No. 444 of Guatemala requires "all state organizations and all persons and companies enjoying import duty exemptions to move the imports concerned

---

charges levied for the use of maritime ports within any of their territories and all by-laws and regulations of such ports shall be duly published before coming into force and that in each maritime port the port authority shall keep open for inspection by all persons concerned a table of the said dues and charges and a copy of the said by-laws and regulations."

[18] To the extent that those private organizations operate on an exclusive or limited franchise basis, they could also be analogised to quasi-governmental organizations. See the definition of state enterprise, *supra* pp. 125-29.

by means of state-owned transport companies." [19] This instance of
a developing country attempting to support its merchant marine
is not unique. Even a nation as wealthy as the United States
requires that 50 per cent of all AID cargoes be shipped on American bottoms.[20]

A more subtle form of discrimination has been practiced by
Colombia. That country, when it maintained a system of multiple
exchange rates, authorized a preferential rate to be obtained for
the purchase of foreign exchange to pay freight charges on imports
if 80 per cent of the capital of the shipping line which transported
the goods was "held" in a country which was a member of the
Latin America Free Trade Area.[21] Countries maintaining trade
controls of this type have a variety of means of discrimination

---

[19] 31 BANK OF L. AND S. AM. F. REV. 279 (1966).

[20] See 46 U.S.C. § 1241(b) (1965). For a discussion of the various types of cargo
preferences enshrined in American legislation, see Olson, *Cargo Preference and the
American Merchant Marine*, 25 LAW & CONTEMP. PROB. 82 (1960).

[21] See 31 BANK OF L. AND S. AM. F. REV. 550 (1966). Note that this legislation
departs from the traditional view that a ship is a vessel of the nation whose flag
it flies. Normally the determination of who "holds" the capital of a shipping line
would be a complicated affair, as the industry is characterized by pyramid holding
companies incorporated in "tax havens." Suppose, for instance, that a ship flying
the flag of Argentina was "owned" by an Argentine corporation, 100% of whose
shares were in turn owned by citizens and residents of Argentina, but the ship was
operated under a bareboat charter by a company which was wholly owned by non-
Argentineans, or that 51% of the shares in the corporation which owned the ship
were "held" by another Argentinean corporation, and the latter was owned 51%
by a corporation chartered in the Bahamas and whose beneficial owners were not
Argentineans, nor resident in the LAFTA area. It may well be that the structure
of the national merchant marines of the LAFTA countries do not raise these
questions. Or the provision may be an attempt to extend preferential treatment to
vessels owned by LAFTA shipping lines, but flying "flags of convenience," e.g.,
Liberia. Because of the complications involved, "ownership" has never been accepted as a test of nationality in international law. See R. RIENOW, THE TEST OF
THE NATIONALITY OF A MERCHANT VESSEL 79-116 (1937).

There are more direct means of discrimination in shipping by utilization of
the exchange laws. For several years Spanish exchange control regulations provided that American ships carrying goods to Spain must collect their freight payments in dollars, and the exchange control authorities "rarely allocated dollars . . .
for payment of ocean freight." The result was that Spanish importers were
"obliged to ship in Spanish vessels." Hearing on Discriminatory Acts of Foreign
Governments Affecting Our Merchant Marine before the Subcommittee on Merchant Marine and Maritime Matters of the Senate Committee on Interstate and
Foreign Commerce, 82d Cong., 2d Sess., at 96 (1952).

open to them. Another approach was the Chilean practice of requiring that applications for import licenses should include the name of the "shipping company to be used." It was alleged that those who specified the name of the national carrier were more likely to receive licenses than those importers who did not. Such schemes have been found far more effective in promoting the national shipping line than attempts to discriminate in port between local and foreign vessels.[22]

Needless to say, such attempts to protect the merchant fleet of a developing country have not been favorably received by the traditional maritime nations. They argue that ocean shipping is an activity peculiarly unsuited to developing countries, since it is a capital intensive industry which requires a high level of technical skill and commercial experience. While this may be true,[23] the argument does not seem to lie well in the mouth of those carriers in the developed countries who are themselves subsidized to a great extent. Moreover, there is some suspicion that what the established shipping lines fear is not so much protected competi-

---

[22] Other means of support include direct government subsidies for operating costs. The Brazilian Government, for example, covers the operating losses of the Lloyd Brasileiro Line. See *Ocean Shipping and Freight Rates and Developing Countries*, V Proceedings, *supra* note 1, at 212, 245. Such direct operating subsidies are not, of course, confined to developing countries. Because wage costs on U.S. flag ships run from three to five times those on competing carriers, the United States Government subsidizes U.S. flag ships to enable them to remain "competitive." See *A Review of Maritime Subsidy Policy in the Light of Present National Requirements for a Merchant Marine and a Shipbuilding Industry* 41–44, Committee on Merchant Marine and Fisheries, U.S. House of Rep., 83rd Cong., 2d Sess. (1954). A less direct form of subsidization employed by many maritime nations is to allow shipowners to depreciate the cost of their ships at a faster than normal rate. See *id* at 56, 88.

[23] The economics of any activity vary, of course, with the "state of the art." With the advent of "container shipping" and the "lighter aboard ship" system, the capital required to compete successfully on prime shipping routes had been increased enormously. At the same time, this "revolution" in shipping is rendering many existing ships "obsolete long before the end of their natural lives." "What Comes After Containers, *supra* note 2, at 51. A similar change in the technology of the airlines industry enabled many developing countries to build up air services with "obsolescent" aircraft. The availability of technically obsolescent ships may give a similar opportunity for developing countries to "legitimately" build up their merchant fleets.

tion, but rather *any* competition which would tend to bring fresh light onto the shadowy practices of the established shipping conferences.

Where the pressure from maritime interests is particularly strong, their governments will normally press for inclusion in the trade agreement of a provision, in addition to the ones noted above, which would prohibit other types of discrimination with regard to shipping. Such a provision in wide use reads as follows:

2. Merchant vessels of either Party shall be accorded treatment no less favorable than that accorded to like vessels of the other Party and of any third country with respect to the right to carry goods and persons that may be carried by vessels to or from the territory of such other Party; and such goods and persons shall be accorded treatment no less favorable than that accorded to like goods and persons carried in merchant vessels of such other Party with respect to (a) duties and charges of all kinds, (b) the administration of the customs, (c) bounties, drawbacks and other privileges of a similar nature.

This paragraph would, at the outset, prohibit cargo preferences such as are incorporated in the Guatemalan legislation referred to above.[24] It would allow carriers flying the flag of either party to

[24] It would also seem to prohibit the American requirement that 50% of AID shipments travel in U.S. "bottoms." *Olson,* supra note 20, at 103, suggests two reasons, however, why this may not be so. First, because the maintenance of a merchant marine is " 'an indispensable factor in our whole defense system' " and trade agreements normally exempt from their general obligations measures necessary to protect the "security interests of one of the Parties." See pp. 218-19 *infra.* Second, the national treatment provisions dealing with maritime affairs refer only to " 'normal' " commercial goods shipments. As to the first point, it would seem that the same argument would be available to most, if not to all, countries. For while the developing countries might not have the global commitments of a power such as the United States, they (unlike such powers) are dependent on ocean shipping for supplying them with the goods necessary to their security. And while it can validly be maintained that national treatment with respect to cargoes did not originally encompass aid, this would seem to be a result of the fact that there was no such thing as aid at the time this standard arose, rather than as a result of some deliberate exclusion. Certainly aid shipments are a normal part of international commerce today, in the sense that they have been taking place for about twenty years and will continue to do so in the foreseeable future. It is thus difficult to see how aid shipments can be excluded from a trade agreement made today which guarantees to the other party national treatment with regard to "the right to carry goods . . . that may be carried by vessels. . . ."

compete for trade on an equal basis with all other carriers, including the national carrier. In addition, such language should be construed to cover more indirect forms of discrimination, such as the Colombian and Chilean schemes cited above, since it is concerned not with the device by which discrimination is practiced, but the "right" of access to cargoes.[25] In this context the word "right" should be construed as equivalent to "opportunity." The latter portion of this provision then goes on to prohibit certain means of discrimination not covered in the provision relating to accessibility to port facilities. In particular it prohibits the imposition of so-called "cargo duties" which may be added to regular customs duties if goods are imported in foreign vessels. The United States, for example, has legislation which provides for a "discriminating duty of 10 per centum ad valorem . . . on all . . . merchandise . . . imported on vessels not of the United States . . . ." [26] The provision suggested above would prohibit the imposition of such duties as well as "bounties, drawbacks" etc., which have a similar effect. In addition, the broad language "charges of any kind" would require national treatment with regard to fees such as manifest charges referred to above, bill-of-lading fees, consular invoice fees and similar impositions which have been used to discriminate in the past.

Where a developing country determines that it is in its national interest to build up its own maritime marine, it will seek to reserve to itself in its trade agreements the power to bestow favorable treatment on the national shipping line.[27] If such a reserva-

[25] The Colombian form of discrimination might also be attacked as violating trade agreement provisions concerning the allocation of foreign exchange, see p. 91 *supra*. Chilean practice might run afoul of a similar provision with regard to import licenses, see pp. 71-72 *supra*.

[26] U.S.C. § 146 (1965).

[27] Such action would not be without precedent. In addition to the examples cited in the text, see *Report of the Subcommittee on the Most-Favored-Nation Clause* adopted by the Committee of Experts for the Progressive Codification of International Law, *supra* note 15, at 150 ("Even in the United States the same spirit was manifested by Section 5 of the Merchant Marine Act (the Jones Act) of 1920, which directed the President to abrogate all of the clauses in treaties which would prevent the United States from discriminating in favour of its own vessels against those of other Powers. No action, however, has been taken pursuant to this resolution.")

tion is acceptable to the trade agreement partner, the provisions suggested above should be modified to render them a guarantee of most-favored-nation treatment rather than national treatment.[28] This would permit, for example, a developing country to exempt its own vessels from tonnage dues, or would allow it to employ cargo preferences to route ocean freight on its own ships. To permit freedom for action of this sort, the above-quoted article could be altered to read:

1. Merchant vessels of either Party shall have liberty, on equal terms with merchant vessels of any third country, to come with their passengers and cargoes to all ports, places, and borders of such other Party open to foreign commerce and navigation. Such vessels shall in all respects be accorded treatment no less favorable than that accorded to like vessels of any third country within the ports, places, and borders of such other Party.

2. Accordingly, merchant vessels of either Party shall be accorded treatment no less favorable than that accorded to like vessels of any third country with respect to duties of tonnage, harbor, pilotage, lighthouse, quarantine, and other analogous duties or charges of whatsoever denomination levied in the name or for the profit of the government, public functionaries, private individuals, corporations, or establishments of any kind.

3. Merchant vessels of either Party shall be accorded treatment no less favorable than that accorded to like vessels of any third country with respect to the right to carry all goods and persons that may be carried by vessels to or from the territory of such other Party; and such goods and persons shall be accorded treatment no less favorable than that accorded to like goods and persons carried in merchant vessels of any third country with respect to: (a) duties and charges of all kinds, (b) the administration of the customs and (c) bounties, drawbacks, and other privileges of a similar nature.

This provision gives the parties the opportunity to discriminate in favor of their own shipping. Where one of the parties to the

[28] Where, as in the case of Colombia, a developing country wished to favor the shipping lines of other developing countries, it would provide that the "most-favored-nation" shall not include those countries or those which are aligned with it in a free-trade area, customs union, or common market. See pp. 224-25 *infra*.

trade agreement protests against the form of such a reservation, an alternative route to the same end would be to include the usual national treatment provision quoted above, but to follow it with an express reservation such as:

4. These provisions shall not apply to any special legislation adopted by the [developing country] Government to protect and develop its national merchant marine.[29]

Finally, there is an increasing tendency in trade agreements between developing countries to divide up the freight traffic which will be the result of the trade between the parties. In some cases the parties have provided that the national shipping line of each will carry 50 per cent of the freight between the respective territories. Other countries have viewed this formula as too rigid. A Latin America Free Trade Area draft agreement on ocean transport proposed that each member state should be entitled to reserve to itself up to 40 per cent of its freight shipments in the area, with first preference on the remainder going to the shipping lines of other LAFTA members. Other developing countries have dealt with the question by first reserving to themselves the power to discriminate in favor of their own shipping by one of the methods outlined above, and have then inserted in their trade agreements a provision such as the following: "Both Parties shall give preference in the transport of their exports and imports to the national shipping lines of the other Party which offer satisfactory rates and conditions."

While such provisions have been included in trade agreements,[30] the principal factor limiting their utility has often been a prior commitment of one of the parties to a third country to grant the vessels of the third country most-favored-nation treatment. Where the parties are not so limited, they might well decide

[29] See Trade Agreement between Cuba and Czechoslovakia, *done* at Havana, June 10, 1960, art. 10, 447 U.N.T.S. 75, 86 (1962).

[30] At the end of 1960, at least twenty developing countries were parties to trade agreements containing this or a similar clause. See *Ocean Shipping and Freight Rates and Developing Countries*, V PROCEEDINGS, *supra* note 1, at 242.

to begin to build a network of agreements containing such provisions so as to retain in the developing areas of the world the sums now flowing to developed countries in the form of freight payments. Should the parties so decide, they would also include in their trade agreement a provision which permitted such preference to be extended to other developing countries, or other members of a particular economic community.

COASTING TRADE

Coasting trade is usually exempted from the coverage of any basic provision concerning nondiscriminatory treatment of vessels. This term is used to cover "the transportation of cargo or passengers from one port to another, both under the same political jurisdiction." [31] The term "coasting trade" is not usually defined in the agreement as its meaning is universally acknowledged. The matter is dealt with in simple straightforward language reading: "The provisions of the preceding paragraphs shall not apply to the coasting trade."

Where a country has several large ports, foreign vessels are usually permitted to call at each port to pick up and discharge passengers and goods going to and coming from foreign countries. This is not technically "coasting trade." To clear up any doubts, however, some agreements provide that immediately after the coasting trade exception:

Merchant vessels of either Party may, nevertheless, proceed from one port to another within the territory of the other Party, either for the purpose of landing the whole or part of their passengers or cargoes brought from abroad, or take on board the whole or part of their passengers or cargoes for a foreign destination.

In addition to reservations regarding the coasting trade, there are sometimes found complementary provisions excepting from

[31] H. HAWKINS, *supra* note 8, at 39.

national treatment participation in the offering of maritime services, "including towage, pilotage, salvage and rescue services." [32]

APPENDIX

EXCHANGE OF NOTES BETWEEN POLAND AND THE UNION OF SOVIET SOCIALIST REPUBLICS CONSTITUTING AN AGREEMENT REGARDING THE RECIPROCAL RECOGNITION OF TONNAGE CERTIFICATES, *Done* AT MOSCOW, 31 MARCH 1936 [33]

Moscow, March 31, 1936

Sir,

With a view to facilitating maritime navigation between the Polish Republic and the Union of Soviet Socialist Republics, I am instructed by my Government to propose to the Government of the Union of Soviet Socialist Republics the following Agreement:

1. Vessels sailing under the flag of the Polish Republic and furnished with measurement certificates issued by the competent authorities of the Polish Republic, which call at the ports of the Union of Soviet Socialist Republics, and, similarly, vessels sailing under the flag of the Union of Soviet Socialist Republics and furnished with measurement certificates issued by the Registry of the Union of Soviet Socialist Republics, which call at the ports of the Polish Republic, shall be exempt from remeasurement in connection with the levying of harbour dues or other charges in port.

   Such dues and charges shall be calculated on the basis of the relevant particulars shown in the vessel's measurement certificate.

2. In the event of the regulations concerning the tonnage measurement of seagoing vessels at present in force in the Polish Republic or in the Union of Soviet Socialist Republics being varied, the question of the reciprocal recognition of measurement certificates issued in virtue of the new regulations above referred to shall be settled through the diplomatic channel.

. . .

In bringing the above to your knowledge, I have the honour to

---

[32] See Treaty of Friendship, Commerce and Navigation between Greece and the United States, *done* at Athens, August 3, 1951, art XXI (6), 224 U.N.T.S. 279, 326 (1955) cited in Piper, *supra* note 10, at note 45.

[33] 186 L.N.T.S. 203 (1938).

request you to inform me whether the Government of the Union of Soviet Socialist Republics accepts the Agreement proposed in the present note.

I have the honour to be, etc.

[Reply note omitted.]

IX. Promoting Trade between the Parties

Most trade agreements contain a preamble which states in general terms the desire of the parties to promote trade between their respective countries. The typical agreement then goes on to attempt to remove the major barriers to trade between the two countries in a manner similar to that discussed in the preceding chapters. Reading further into the agreement, one frequently comes to provisions of somewhat lesser importance. These tend to deal with minor, although nonetheless real, problems arising in the conduct of trade. Furthermore, it is here that one finds the more "positive" side of the agreement, those provisions designed to promote trade rather than to remove barriers to its growth.

Samples

If one has ever waited at a customs clearing station while the officers examined the goods of a commercial traveler, the need for expediting his passage through the customs becomes readily apparent. The commercial traveler is the catalyst of international trade. He goes from country to country, loaded down with his samples, leaflets, catalogs, and other selling paraphernalia attempting to market the wares of the company or companies he represents and thereby increase the exports of his country. He may be the representative of a private business concern or the agent of a government marketing board carrying with him samples of an agricultural product for the consideration of prospective buyers. Harrowing as are the customs for the private tourist, they become infinitely more complicated for the commercial traveler with his unusual baggage. That his problems are real ones is evidenced by the fact that many trade agreements attempt to minimize the customs formalities connected with the comings and goings of commercial travelers by provisions such as the following: "The stipulations of the present Agreement with regard to the mutual accord of most-favored-nation treatment shall apply unconditionally to the treatment of commercial travelers."

Often the article focuses not so much on the traveler as on the items which he usually carries. The following clause would cover the importation of such items by the itinerant salesman or to supply a local sales office or trade mission:

1. Each Party shall exempt from duties and charges of any kind samples of goods and advertising material of the other Party which are imported into its territory temporarily and taken out of it.

Following this general grant of duty-free entry, there may be found one or more conditions or limitations. It is not unusual to include a provision regarding the posting of security as a guarantee that a sample admitted duty-free is eventually taken out of the territory and is not, as sometimes happens, introduced into the stream of local commerce.

2. Duty-free admission of articles pursuant to the provisions of paragraph 1 shall be conditioned on compliance with the customs regulations and formalities established to ensure reexportation or the payment of the prescribed customs duties if not reexported within the period allowed by law.

The regulations referred to could include a requirement that an amount equal to the potential customs duty be deposited with the customs authorities or a bond for that amount be so deposited. The "regulations and formalities" would depend on the nature of the product, e.g. the ease with which it might be introduced into local commerce, its value, etc. Where an importing state is especially cautious about permitting the free entry of samples, its trade agreements sometimes provide that:

3. The privilege provided for in paragraph 1 shall not extend to articles which, owing to their quantity or their nature could not be identified upon reexportation.

Finally, some states exempt items from the broad grant of duty-free admission. Tanzania, for example, does not permit duty-free entry of "commercial advertising films." [1]

The importation of samples and advertising material has also been dealt with on a multilateral basis. Forty-eight countries are parties to the International Convention to Facilitate the Importation of Commercial Samples and Advertising Material, *done* at Geneva, November 7, 1952.[2] As an alternative to the clauses suggested, provisions of that agreement may be included in a trade agreement (excerpts from the Convention are reprinted in Appendix I to this chapter). Or the text of the Convention may be incorporated into the trade agreement by reference. A provision accomplishing the latter would read:

Each Party shall, with respect to exemptions from duties and charges of any kind on samples of goods and advertising material of the other Party which are imported into its territory temporarily and taken out of its territory, conform to the relevant provisions of the International Convention to Facilitate the Importation of Commercial Samples and Advertising Material, *done* at Geneva, November 7, 1952, or any convention amendatory or supplementary thereto.

In addition to samples and advertising materials, there are additional categories of goods whose temporary importation is also generally permitted on favorable terms. Agreements vary on whether they may be imported duty-free or on a most-favored-nation basis. The following provision incorporates these two alternatives in brackets:

Each Party shall [exempt from duties and charges] [accord most-favored-nation treatment with respect to the exemption from duties and charges on] the following articles of the other Party which are brought into temporarily and taken out of its territories:

---

[1] See art. 12, Trade Agreement between Poland and Tanganyika, *done* at Dar es Salaam, October 5, 1963.
[2] 221 U.N.T.S. 255 (1955).

(a) articles destined for exhibitions, contests and fairs,
(b) articles and material to be repaired and materials required for repairing,
(c) articles intended for use in tests and experiments,
(d) tools to be used in assembling and installing equipment,
(e) containers of imported goods.

The importation of some of these items is also the subject of multilateral agreement. Excerpts from the Customs Convention Concerning Facilities for the Importation of Goods for Display or Use at Exhibitions, Fairs, Meetings and Similar Events, *done* at Brussels, June 8, 1961,[3] and the Customs Convention on the Temporary Importation of Professional Equipment, *done* at Brussels, June 8, 1961,[4] are reprinted in Appendix II and III of this chapter.

ENTRY OF PERSONS

Aside from the goods they carry, trade is facilitated by rendering as easy as possible the entry of those persons who are involved in the trading process. To facilitate such movement back and forth, trade agreements may provide that:

Nationals of either Party shall be permitted to enter the territories of the other Party for the purpose of carrying on trade between the territories of the two Parties and for the purpose of engaging in related commercial activities, and to remain therein for such purposes, upon terms no less favorable than those accorded to nationals of any third country who are permitted entry for the purpose of carrying on trade between the territories of such other Party and the territories of such third country and of engaging in related commercial activities.

"Nationals" of a particular state are persons, whether citizens or not, who owe permanent allegiance to that state. For administrative convenience, "nationals" are usually defined as persons "in possession of a valid passport issued by the competent authorities of either Party, or a valid identifying document so issued."

[3] Gr. Brit. T.S. No. 61 (CMD. 2115) (1963).
[4] Gr. Brit. T.S. No. 62 (CMD. 2125) (1963).

When the volume of trade between two countries has reached the point where nationals of one party begin to reside for commercial purposes in the territory of the other it is advisable for their governments to consider entering into a Treaty of Establishment. Closely related to trade agreements, treaties of establishment deal with rights of nationals and companies of one party in the territory of the other and, in particular, cover such matters as taxes, rights to ownership of real and personal property, protection of patent rights, and access to the local courts.

Drawbacks of Customs Duty

To further facilitate the mutual exchange of goods between countries, especially in the case of the introduction into a market of goods of a new type or quality, an exporting country may seek to have inserted into a trade agreement a provision allowing it to obtain a return of the customs duty paid on goods shipped to a foreign market which remained unsold and are thereafter removed from that market. "The Parties shall refrain from levying export charges and shall refund the customs duty already paid on such goods of the other Party as shall be reexported."

Such a provision may not appeal to developing countries for whom customs duties are an important source of government revenue. In such a case they may seek to limit refunds of customs duties to cases where, for example, the goods prove to be defective, or are not the goods which were ordered, or were ordered by mistake.

Trade Fairs

The groundwork for an increasing amount of international trade is being laid at trade fairs and exhibitions. Trade fairs are not, of course, unique to the twentieth century. Many of the European trade fairs trace their origins back to the Middle Ages. For the developing countries, however, trade fairs are a relatively new phenomenon. It is not surprising, therefore, to find that developing countries, in an effort to insure the success of their trade fairs, have sought the assistance of international bodies such as GATT and the United Nations, as well as the help of their trade agreement partners. Insofar as the latter are concerned several developing countries have included in their trade agreements a provision such as the following. "Each Party shall encourage participation in Trade Fairs and Exhibitions organized in the territory of the other Party." [5]

In addition to organizing their own trade fairs, many developing countries seek to participate in the trade fairs of other countries. The value of such participation has been widely recognized in the developing world as a means of familiarizing foreign buyers with the products of the country and, more broadly, with the country itself.[6] Thus the trade agreements of developing countries frequently include provisions such as the following: "The two contracting Parties shall grant each other all possible facilities for participation in trade fairs and exhibitions held in their respective territories. . . . ." [7]

Where a developing country has available a wide range of products for export, it will sometimes wish to hold a trade fair or exhibition of its own in another country. In such a case, it will seek to incorporate in its trade agreements a clause reading: "Each Party shall permit the holding of temporary trade fairs and exhibi-

---

[5] Trade Agreement between Kenya and the U.S.S.R. *done* at Nairobi, April 29, 1964.

[6] See, e.g., MONTHLY BULL. OF THE ADDIS ABABA CHAMBER OF COMMERCE, Sept. & Oct. 1966, at 2 ("Such participation and tours play vital roles to help to reach the foreign buyers . . . paramount necessity of participation in foreign trade fairs. . . ."); Ahmad, *Export Promotion Measures in Pakistan*, INT'L TRADE F., Dec. 1966, at 28, 31. ("Participation in international trade fairs and exhibitions plays a vital role in the promotion and diversification of export trade."); Berlin, *Export Promotion Policy in Mexico, id.* at 14, 16, ("One very important objective of Mexico's trade policy is to *encourage domestic producers to participate in international trade fairs and exhibitions.* . . ."); Kolo, *Export Promotion in Nigeria, id.* at 24, 26, ("The export promotion value of trade fairs and exhibitions have long been recognized and since the attainment of independence in 1960, the Government of Nigeria has successfully utilized this medium.")

[7] Art. VIII, Trade Agreement between Turkey and Iraq, *done* at Baghdad, August 3, 1965.

tions on its territory and shall extend to the other Party all facilities necessary for holding such fairs and exhibitions."

The "facilities" referred to in such provisions would normally include most-favored-nation or preferential customs treatment for articles displayed at the trade fair. Parties wishing to spell out the details of such treatment could turn to the Customs Convention Concerning Facilities for the Importation of Goods for Display or Use at Exhibitions, Fairs, Meetings or Similar Events, *done* at Brussels June 8, 1961, portions of which are reprinted in Appendix B to this chapter.

Transit

A provision common to almost all trade agreements is one granting freedom of transit for the goods of one party across the territory of the other. In substance freedom of transit means the right to move goods across the territory of a party without those goods being subject to customs duties, or any other charges except the actual costs of transportation. The party granting freedom of transit benefits from the increased use of its ports, harbors, rail road, and other transit facilities.

The granting of the free transit privilege was not always the prevailing situation. Until the end of the nineteenth century, transit duties were a common instrument of commercial policy. These duties were levied on all goods passing through a particular nation. It was not until the Convention and Statute on Freedom of Transit, *done* at Barcelona, April 20, 1921,[8] that the major commercial powers agreed to do away with transit duties.[9]

Although the concept of freedom of transit seems, in essence, a simple one, interference in the past has been so widespread that

---

[8] 7 L.N.T.S. 11, 27, art. 3 (1921) (art. 3).

[9] Transit duties continue to exist, however, with regard to certain specialized commodities. For example, an oil pipeline from the oil fields in Northern Iraq to the Mediterranean runs across Syria. For the privilege of transporting the oil across Syria, the Iraq Petroleum Company pays Syria "transit dues" in quite substantial amounts.

the language used to incorporate the idea into trade agreements is lengthy and complex.

1. There shall be freedom of transit through the territory of each Party, via the route most convenient for international trade, for traffic in transit to or from the territory of the other Party. No distinction shall be made which is based on the flag of the vessels, the place of origin, departure, entry, exit or destination, or any circumstances relating to the ownership of goods, of vessels or of other means of transport.

2. Goods shall be deemed to be in transit across the territory of a Party when the passage across that territory, with or without transshipment, warehousing, breaking bulk, or change of mode of transport, is only a portion of a complete journey beginning and terminating beyond the frontier of the Party across whose territory the traffic passes. Traffic of this nature is termed in this Article 'traffic in transit.'

3. Either Party may require that goods in transit through its territory be entered at the proper custom house.

4. Traffic in transit through the territory of one Party to or from the territory of the other shall not, except in case of failure to comply with applicable customs laws and regulations, be subject to any delays or restrictions other than to the minimum extent that may be necessary to insure compliance with the applicable customs laws and regulations.

5. With respect to all charges, regulations and formalities in connection with transit, each Party shall accord to traffic in transit to or from the territory of the other treatment no less favorable than that accorded to traffic in transit to or from any other foreign country and in no case shall such traffic in transit be subject to customs duties, transit duties or other charges imposed in respect of transit except charges which are the equitable and reasonable costs of services pertaining to transit operations.

6. The provisions of this Article shall not apply to the operation of aircraft in transit.[10]

Paragraph 6 is necessary because the question of international air transit is dealt with in a multilateral international agreement,

---

[10] See, e.g., art. V, GATT, 55 U.N.T.S. 188, 208-12 (1950). The provisions are derived from the Barcelona Convention, *supra* note 8.

the Convention of International Civil Aviation, *done* at Chicago, December 7, 1944.[11]

A provision somewhat related to the usual transit provisions, but going well beyond their scope, is occasionally found in trade agreements.

Goods of any origin dispatched in the territory of one of the Parties to the territory of the other Party or through the latter territory to that of a third state shall not receive less favorable treatment as regards dispatch, transport rates and public charges on consignments, than goods of the home country or any other country, which has been dispatched to the territory of the other Party or a third country under the same conditions, to the same destination and by the same route.

The operation of this provision may be illustrated by assuming that it is contained in a trade agreement between Country A and Country C. Assume further that Country A holds a quantity of the goods of Country B. In providing facilities for shipping those goods to Country C, or through Country C to Country D, A will treat B's goods as favorably as A treats its own or the most-favored-nation's goods. It will thus be seen that the provision covers a number of situations not normally covered by the transit traffic clauses. First, it deals with goods of B located in A ("goods of any origin") but not necessarily in transit through A. Such goods, for example, could have been shipped to A for sale, but due to mistake, or any of a host of other factors, remained unsold. The exporter in B then resells the goods to an importer in C. By requiring that the dispatch of the goods from A to C be executed under conditions of national and/or most-favored-nation treatment, both B and C benefit. This is clear under the assumption that any discrimination by A with regard to "dispatch, transport rates and public charges on assignments" would tend to increase the landed cost of B's goods in C. Second, if B's goods are to be shipped through C to D, countries B, C, and D benefit from such a provision. In this case, C gains by preventing A from engaging in

[11] 15 U.N.T.S. 295 (1948).

any discriminatory practice which would deprive C of the benefits of transit traffic through C to D. Third, the provision covers the shipment of A's own goods through C to D. Here again C and D would benefit as indicated above. Finally, the suggested paragraph deals with consignments of A's goods to C. Here C is protected from the increased transport costs it might have to bear as a result of discrimination by A, a situation not encompassed by the usual transit provision. In this case it deals with the same matters discussed in Chapter V with regard to discriminatory freight rates.

Conclusion

These, then, are some of the kinds of minor problems which have been and are normally dealt with in trade agreements. Their relevance to any particular agreement will, of course, vary with the interests of the parties. Where the interest of the parties in one of the issues discussed in this chapter is significant they may wish, as mentioned above, to deal with the matter in a separate agreement. In any event, however, after the hard bargaining has taken place negotiators should devote some time to these matters, the resolution of which will serve to lubricate the mechanism of trade between the parties.

APPENDIX A

Excerpts from the International Convention to Facilitate the Importation of Commercial Samples and Advertising Material, *Done* at Geneva, 7 November 1952

ARTICLE I
Definitions

. . .

(a) The term "import duties" means Customs duties and all other duties and taxes payable on or in connexion with importation, and shall include all internal taxes and excise duties chargeable on imported goods, but shall not include fees and charges which are limited in amount to the approximate cost of services rendered and do not represent an indirect protection to domestic products or a taxation of imports for fiscal purposes. . . .

. . .

ARTICLE II

Exemption from Import Duties
for Samples of Negligible Value

1. Each Contracting Party shall exempt from import duties samples of goods of all kinds imported into its territory, provided such samples are of negligible value and are only to be used for soliciting orders for goods of the kind represented by the samples with a view to their importation.

. . .

2. The Customs authorities of the territory of importation may require that, as a condition of their being exempted from import duties in accordance with paragraph 1 of this article, samples shall be made useless as merchandise by marking, tearing, perforation or other treatment, but not, however, so as to destroy their usefulness as samples.

ARTICLE III

Temporary Duty-Free Admission
of Other Samples

1. For the purpose of this article, the term "samples" means articles which are representative of a particular category of goods already produced or are examples of goods the production of which is contemplated, on condition that they:

(a) are owned abroad and are imported solely for the purpose of being shown or demonstrated in the territory of importation for the soliciting of orders for goods to be supplied from abroad; and

(b) are not sold or put to normal use except for purposes of demonstration or used in any way for hire or reward while in the territory of importation; and

(c) are intended to be re-exported in due course; and

(d) are capable of identification on re-exportation;

but does not include identical articles brought in by the same individual or sent to a single consignee, in such quantity that, taken as a whole, they no longer constitute samples under ordinary commercial usage.

2. Samples which are chargeable with import duties shall . . . be temporarily admitted free of import duties, subject to the amount of the import duties and any other amount that may be payable being deposited or security being given for payment if necessary. Any deposits taken . . . shall not, however, exceed the amount of the import duties by more than 10 per cent.

. . .

5. The period allowed for re-exportation of samples . . . shall not be less than six months.

. . .

ARTICLE IV
Duty-free Admission of Advertising Material

1. Each . . . party shall exempt from import duties catalogues, pricelists and trade notices relating to
(a) goods offered for sale or hire, or
(b) transport or commercial insurance services offered. . .

. . .

APPENDIX B

Excerpts from the Customs Convention Concerning Facilities for the Importation of Goods for Display or Use at Exhibitions, Fairs, Meetings, or Similar Events, *Done* at Brussels, 8 June 1961

ARTICLE 1

For purposes of the present Convention:
(a) the term "event" means:
1. A trade, industrial, agricultural or crafts exhibition, fair, or similar show or display; or
2. an exhibition or meeting which is primarily organised for a charitable purpose; or
3. an exhibition or meeting which is primarily organised to promote any branch of learning, art, craft, sport or scientific, educational or cultural activity, to promote friendship between peoples, or to promote religious knowledge or worship; or
4. a meeting of representatives of any international organisation or international group of organisations, or

5. a representative meeting of an official or commemorative character; except exhibitions organized for private purposes in shops or business premises with a view to the sale of foreign goods;

(b) the term "import duties" means Customs duties, and all other duties and taxes payable on, or in connection with importation and shall include all internal taxes and excise duties chargeable on imported goods, but shall not include fees and charges which are limited in amount to the approximate cost of services rendered and do not represent an indirect protection to domestic products or a taxation of imports for fiscal purposes;

(c) the term "temporary admission" means temporary importation free of customs duties and free of import prohibitions and restrictions, subject to re-exportation;

. . .

ARTICLE 2

1. Temporary admission shall be granted to:
   (a) goods intended for display or demonstration at an event;
   (b) goods intended for use in connection with the display of foreign products at an event, including:
      (i) goods necessary for the purpose of demonstrating foreign machinery or apparatus to be displayed,
      (ii) construction and decoration material, including electrical fittings, for the temporary stands of foreign exhibitors,
      (iii) advertising and demonstration material which is demonstrably publicity material for foreign goods displayed; for example, sound recordings, films and lantern slides, as well as apparatus for use therewith;
   (c) equipment including interpretation apparatus, sound recording apparatus and films of an educational, scientific or cultural character intended for use at international meetings, conferences or congresses.

2. The facilities referred to in paragraph 1 of this Article shall be granted provided that:
   (a) the goods are capable of identification on re-exportation;
   (b) the number or quantity of identical articles is reasonable having regard to the purpose of importation;
   (c) the Customs authorities of the country of temporary importation are satisfied that the conditions of the present Convention shall be fulfilled.

ARTICLE 3

Unless the national laws and regulations of the country of temporary importation so permit, goods granted temporary admission shall not, whilst they are the subject of the facilities granted under the present Convention:

(a) be loaned, or used in any way for hire or reward; or

(b) be removed from the place of the event.

ARTICLE 4

1. Goods granted temporary admission shall be re-exported within six months from the date of importation. However, Customs authorities of the country of temporary importation may, with due regard to the circumstances and in particular the duration and nature of the event, require that the goods be re-exported within a shorter period which shall, nevertheless, extend at least one month after the termination of the event.

2. Notwithstanding the provision of paragraph 1 of this Article the Customs authorities shall allow such goods which are to be displayed or used at a subsequent event to remain within the country of temporary importation, subject to compliance with such conditions as may be required by the laws and regulations of that country and provided that the goods are re-exported within one year from the date of importation.

.   .   .

ARTICLE 6

1. . . . [I]mport duties shall not be levied and import prohibitions and restrictions shall be waived, and where temporary admission has been granted re-exportation shall not be required, in respect of the following goods:

(a) Small samples which are representative of foreign goods displayed at an event, including such samples of foods and beverages, either imported in the form of such samples or produced from imported bulk materials at that event, provided that:

    (i) they are supplied free of charge from abroad and are used solely for distribution free of charge to the visiting public at the event, for individual use or consumption by the persons to whom they are distributed,

(ii) they are identifiable as advertising samples and are individually of little value,

(iii) they are unsuitable for commercial purposes and are, where appropriate, packed in quantities appreciably smaller than than the smallest retail package,

(iv) samples of foods and beverages which are not distributed in packs as provided for in (iii) above are consumed at the event, and

(v) the aggregate value and quantity of the samples are, in the opinion of the Customs authorities of the country of importation, reasonable having regard to the nature of the event, the number of visitors to it and the extent of the exhibitor's participation therein;

(b) Goods imported solely for demonstration or for the purpose of demonstrating the operation of a foreign machine or apparatus displayed at an event and consumed or destroyed in the course of such demonstration, provided that the aggregate value and quantity of such goods are, in the opinion of the Customs authorities of the country of importation, reasonable having regard to the nature of the event, the number of visitors to it and the extent of the exhibitor's participation therein;

(c) Products of low value used up in constructing, furnishing or decorating the temporary stands of foreign exhibitors at an event, such as paint, varnish and wallpaper;

(d) Printed matter, catalogues, trade notices, price lists, advertising posters, calendars, whether or not illustrated, and unframed photographs, which are demonstrably publicity material for the foreign goods displayed at an event, provided that:

(i) they are supplied free of charge from abroad and are used solely for distribution free of charge to the visiting public at the event, and

(ii) the aggregate value and quantity of such goods are, in the opinion of the Customs authorities of the country of importation, reasonable having regard to the nature of the event, the number of visitors to it and the extent of the exhibitor's participation therein.

2. The provisions of paragraph 1 of this Article shall not be applicable to alcoholic beverages, tobacco goods and fuels.

· · ·

ARTICLE 10

1. Customs examination and clearance on the importation and re-exportation of goods which are to be, or have been, displayed or used at any event shall, whenever possible and appropriate, be effected at that event.

. . .

ARTICLE 11

Products obtained incidentally during the event from temporarily imported goods, as a result of the demonstration of displayed machinery or apparatus, shall be subject to the provisions of the present Convention.

APPENDIX C

EXCERPTS FROM THE CUSTOMS CONVENTION ON THE TEMPORARY IMPORTATION OF PROFESSIONAL EQUIPMENT, *Done* AT BRUSSELS, 8 JUNE 1961

ARTICLE 1

For the purposes of the present Convention:
  (a) the term "import dutites" means Customs duties and all other duties and taxes payable on or in connection with importation and shall include all internal taxes and excise duties chargeable on imported goods, but shall not include fees and charges which are limited in amount to the approximate cost of services rendered and do not represent an indirect protection to domestic products or a taxation of imports for fiscal purposes;
  (b) the term "temporary admission" means temporary importation free of import duties and free of import prohibitions and restrictions, subject to re-exportation;

. . .

ARTICLE 2

Each Contracting Party bound by any Annex to the present Convention shall grant temporary admission to the equipment referred to in that Annex . . . The term "equipment" shall be taken to include any relevant ancillary apparatus and accessories.

. . .

ARTICLE 4

Equipment granted temporary admission shall be re-exported within six months from the date of importation. For valid reasons the Customs authorities may, within the limits laid down by the laws and regulations of the country of temporary importation, either grant a longer period or extend the initial period.

. . .

ANNEX A
Equipment for the Press or for Sound or Television Broadcasting

. . .

ANNEX B
Cinematographic Equipment

. . .

ANNEX C
Other Professional Equipment

I. DEFINITION AND CONDITIONS

1. *Definition*

For purposes of the present Annex, the term "other professional equipment" means equipment, of a kind not referred to in the other Annexes to the present Convention, necessary for the exercise of the calling, trade or profession of a person visiting a country to perform a specified task. It does not include equipment which is to be used for internal transport or for the industrial manufacture or packaging of goods or (except in the case of hand-tools) for the exploitation of natural resources, for the construction, repair or maintenance of buildings or for earth moving and like projects.

2. *Conditions of grant of temporary admission.*

The equipment:

(a) shall be owned by a natural person resident abroad or by a legal person established abroad;

(b) shall be imported by a natural person resident abroad or by a legal person established abroad;

(c) shall be capable of identification on re-exportation;

(d) shall be used solely by or under the personal supervision of the visiting person.

II. ILLUSTRATIVE LIST

A. Equipment for erection, testing, commissioning, checking, control, maintenance or repair of machinery, plant, means of transport, etc., such as:

Tools:

Measuring, checking or testing equipment and instruments (temperature, pressure, distance, height, surface, speed, etc.) including electrical instruments (voltmeters, ammeters, measuring cables, comparators, transformers, recording instruments, etc.) and jigs;

Apparatus and equipment for taking photographs of machines and plant during or after erection;

Apparatus for survey of ships.

. . .

C. Equipment necessary for exports undertaking topographical surveys or geophysical prospecting work, such as:

Measuring instruments and apparatus;

Drilling equipment;

Transmission and communication equipment.

. . .

H. Vehicles designed or specially adapted for the purposes specified above, such as mobile inspection units, travelling workshops and travelling laboratories.

X. Exceptions to the Coverage of a Trade Agreement

Trade in Particular Commodities

General principles of international law establish that a state may always act to protect its security and the health, safety, and welfare of its nationals without regard to whether such rights are specifically reserved in a trade agreement. A state will thus retain virtually unrestricted freedom of action concerning those aspects of its commercial policy regulating the import and export of arms and implements of war. While the security exception will be read into a trade agreement if the parties have omitted it, the usual pratice is to include such a provision in the agreement. For example, Article VII of the Agreement on Commerce between Japan and the Republic of Peru, *done* at Tokyo, May 15, 1961,[1] provides that:

> This Agreement shall not preclude the application of measures
> . . .
> (b) relating to fissionable materials, to radioactive by-products or the utilization or processing thereof, or to materials that are the source of fissionable materials;
> (c) regulating the production of or traffic in arms, ammunition, or implements of war, or traffic in other materials carried on directly or indirectly for the purposes of supplying a military establishment;
> (d) necessary to fulfill the obligations of a Party in the maintenance or restoration of international peace and security, or necessary to protect its essential security interests.
> . . .

[1] 451 U.N.T.S. 3, 36 (1963).

Needless to say, such a provision leaves a wide area of discretion in the hands of each of the parties. In this context it has been recognized, however, that a party must be given wider latitude to determine its legitimate security interests than it would have to determine its commercial interests. Instances where a party has been accused of regulating beyond the bounds of its security interests are thus rare, despite the fact that the world abounds with restrictions on trade in "strategic" goods.

This absence of controversy has not been the case where sanitary regulations have been concerned. Sanitary regulations purport to protect the health of the residents of a state by barring the importation of diseased food and related products. "Nothing in the present Agreement shall preclude the application of measures relating to the protection of public health and the protection of animals and plants against disease, harmful insects and parasites." [2]

While innocent on their face, such sanitary regulations have often been used as a subterfuge to discriminate against the products of certain countries, when to do so directly would have been a violation of a most-favored-nation commitment. For many years European governments prohibited the importation of pork from America, on the ground that there was a danger that such pork was infected with trichinosis, even though it could be clearly shown that this danger was nonexistent. Such embargoes were designed to protect local pork producers against American competition. And Britain has, in the past, barred the importation of American apples because of fear that they were infected with fruit flies, while at the same time permitting imports of Canadian apples, which were just as likely to be infected. The United States Government, on the other hand, once sought to protect its livestock industry by barring all imports of meat products from countries where rinderpest or foot- and mouth disease existed. While this aim is a legitimate one, the two diseases in question can be,

[2] This formulation is based on art. 4 (4) of the Convention on the Abolition of Import and Export Prohibitions and Restrictions, *done* at Geneva, November 8, 1927, LEAGUE OF NATIONS, II.A. ECONOMIC AND FINANCIAL 7, at 9 (1928).

and usually are, confined to particular local areas in a producing country. To prohibit all imports from that country seems a fairly heavy-handed means of dealing with the issue. At the time this action was taken, one scholar noted that "there can be no other explanation of the new legislation except that Congress designed it to afford economic protection to the American livestock industry." [3]

To deal with such potential abuses, the parties to a trade agreement would provide first that all sanitary regulations be published and thus made accessible to the other party. In addition they might agree that no such regulation shall come into effect until X days after it has been published, so as to give all affected parties time to study its impact. An alternative approach would be to agree that: "Each Party, before applying a new measure of a sanitary character, will consult with the other Party with a view to insuring that there will be as little injury to the commerce of the latter as may be consistent with the purpose of the proposed measure."

For countries which export large quantities of unprocessed or semiprocessed foodstuffs or other goods of a type normally subject to sanitary regulations, the best course would be to deal with the matter in a separate agreement.[4] As an alternative, the parties could incorporate by reference into the trade agreement the relevant provisions of the International Sanitary Convention, *done* at Paris, June 21, 1926, *modified* at Washington, December 15, 1944.[5]

Somewhat related to sanitary regulations are prohibitions on the importation of goods which are the products of prison labor. These limitations are designed to express a government's distaste for such a system. They are also a means of protecting local industries from what a government may consider the unfair competition of products produced by the use of such low-cost labor. "Nothing in this Agreement shall be construed to prevent the adoption or

---

[3] P. BIDWELL, THE INVISIBLE TARIFF 213 (1939).
[4] See e.g., the Sanitary and Veterinary Convention between Roumania and Yugoslavia, *done* at Belgrade, May 13, 1937, 197 L.N.T.S. 161 (1939).
[5] 17 U.N.T.S. 305 (1948).

enforcement by either Party of measures relating to the products of prison labor."

To some extent this exception is in conflict with concepts of modern penology which seek to rehabilitate offenders by providing work opportunities in prisons. This process would be aided if the products which result from the rehabilitation process could be widely marketed. It is, however, difficult to generalize since "prison labor" may represent convicts used to harvest agricultural products or mine coal under inhuman conditions at little or no wages, or the term may cover prisoners working in prison-owned factories under conditions almost identical with those of the average industrial worker. Because of the disparities in such conditions, most countries prefer to retain for themselves the legal right to discriminate against goods which, in their view, were produced under intolerable conditions. [6]

Some trade agreements reserve to the parties the power to take any action directed toward conserving scarce and depletable natural assets. The United States, for example, has barred the importation of the skins of fur seals and sea otters taken in the Pacific Ocean north of 30° north latitude in an effort to preserve the rapidly diminishing supply of such animals. To the same end several African states have barred or limited the export of certain animal skins and skin products. Countries interested in retaining freedom of action with regard to such matters should include in their trade agreements a provision reading: "Nothing in the present agreement shall be construed to prevent the adoption or enforcement by either Party of measures designed to conserve its exhaustible natural resources."

Note that, in addition to wildlife, this provision would apply to mineral resources such as copper and oil, which are of far greater significance in international trade. States which import these commodities may object to such a provision on the ground

---

[6] In some cases countries have gone further and prohibited the importation of goods produced by "forced labor" and "indentured labor." See BIDWELL, *supra* note 3, at 105.

that it would deprive them of most-favored-nation treatment and thus lay them open to discrimination. The importing states would seek to insure that such measures as the other party takes are really aimed at conserving its natural resources by adding to the above provision the following clause: "Provided that such measures are made effective in conjunction with restrictions on domestic production or consumption." In addition, importing states may wish to make any such measures subject to most-favored-nation treatment.

States bordering the sea usually reserve some portion of their fishing grounds and facilities for the exclusive use of their own fishermen and/or fishermen of certain friendly countries. Although justified as a conservation measure, these regulations more probably represent an effort to protect local fishing industries. A typical reservation reads:

The present Agreement shall not preclude the application by either Party of measures reserving rights and privileges with respect to its national fisheries and marine hunting, and the landing in its ports of fish or fish products or the catch or products of marine hunting taken on board the transporting vessel at sea.[7]

Finally, history is replete with cases of the removal of the national treasures of various subject people from colonial territories and their transportation to museums of the metropolitan power. It is only natural then that newly independent states should seek to conserve the remainder of these relics of their past by strictly controlling trade in such commodities. They have therefore sought to include in their trade agreements provisions exempting from their scope "regulations imposed for the protection of national treasures of artistic, historic or archeological value." [8]

---

[7] See Treaty of Friendship, Commerce and Navigation between the United States and Germany, *done* at Washington, October 29, 1954. art. XXIV, 273 U.N.T.S. 3, 30, 32 (1957).

[8] This language is based on that of the Convention on the Abolition of Import and Export Prohibitions and Restrictions, art 4 (5), LEAGUE OF NATIONS II.A. ECONOMIC AND FINANCIAL 7, at 9 (1928).

Trade With Particular Countries

The geographical proximity of countries has always been a reason for exceptions to the "equal treatment" provisions of a trade agreement. The most widely utilized of those exceptions is that which excludes "frontier traffic." Frontier traffic is local, over the border, traffic among inhabitants of adjoining countries. The character of frontier traffic may be illustrated as follows. Assume that Country *A* and Country *B* adjoin each other. In Country *A* there is a village approximately three miles from the common border. The nearest market to this village in Country *A* is forty miles to the interior. On the other hand, there is a market five miles on the other side of the border in Country *B*. Clearly it would be natural for the villagers in Country *A* to go the eight miles to the market in Country *B* rather than the forty miles involved in going to the market place in their own country. And this is what in fact occurs throughout the world. Such border crossings are particularly widespread in the developing world where boundaries were artificially drawn so that traditional market areas frequently were separated from the homes of consumers. To apply the full regime of import and export regulations to such local traffic would be inconvenient and foolish. Instead such trade is carried on virtually free of restriction, and the governments of the countries in which such traffic takes place include in their trade agreements a provision reading: "It is understood that the provisions of the present Agreement shall not apply to advantages which are or may be hereafter accorded by either Party to adjacent countries with a view to facilitating frontier traffic." [9]

[9] The phraseology which is sometimes employed to introduce this exception—". . . understood that whenever most-favored-nation treatment is prescribed by the present Agreement . . ."—has been modified here. Since it has been suggested that the most-favored-nation clause may not be the optimal way of dealing with import licensing, see pp. 70-71 *supra*, and exchange controls, see pp. 88-90 *supra*, limiting the exception to those instances where most-favored-nation treatment has been provided for might give rise to a claim that insofar as the allocation of licenses and exchange are concerned, the exception is inoperative.

Note that "frontier traffic" does not include all trade which takes place near the border. Thus if Country *A* imposed an import duty of 100 per cent ad valorem on the importation of cigarettes into its territory, but provided that the duty would not apply to frontier traffic, this would not mean that all residents in Country *A* could flock across the border to *B* and bring in unlimited quantities of cigarettes free of duty. Recalling the ilustration of frontier traffic given earlier, it becomes clear that frontier traffic is solely for the benefit of *residents* of the frontier area. This is occasionally made explicit in a trade agreement:

> It is understood that the provisions of the present agreement shall not apply to any advantages which have been or may be granted by one of the Parties to neighboring countries for the object of facilitating frontier traffic within a zone which, as a general rule, may not exceed fifteen Kilometers breadth on either side of the common frontier.[10]

PREFERENCES, FREE-TRADE AREAS, AND CUSTOMS UNIONS

As noted in Chapter I the search for wider markets, a prime requisite for economic growth, has led many countries to enter into special preferential arrangements with neighboring or nearby states. To prevent such arrangements from being undermined, each state which is a party to them must agree not to extend the preferences to outside third countries. Thus if Country *A* and Country *B* grant each other preferences in the exchange of certain commodities, neither can enter into an agreement extending those preferences to Country *C* without destroying the whole scheme. *A* and *B* will, therefore, exclude from the scope of their trade agreements with *C* those "special privileges" which *A* and *B* extend to each other. To make matters more concrete, assume that *A* has a three-line tariff with a 10, 20, and 30 per cent ad valorem

---

[10] See Commercial Convention between Estonia and France, *done* at Paris, October 16, 1937, art. 33, 183 L.N.T.S. 41, 63 (1937). See also *Report of the Subcommittee on the Most-Favored-Nation Clause,* adopted by the Committee of Experts for the Progressive Codification of International Law, reprinted in 22 AM. J. INT'L L., 134, 152 (1928).

import duty on shoes. 10 per cent is the preferential rate, 20 per cent the most-favored-nation rate and 30 per cent the general rate. A now enters into a trade agreement with C, promising C most-favored-nation treatment. C claims it is entitled to export shoes to A subject to the 10 per cent duty. For if shoes exported from B to A only pay 10 per cent, then B is the most-favored-nation and C is entitled to be treated on a par with B, i.e., C is entitled to most-favored-nation treatment. Such treatment extended to C would, however, upset the preferential arrangement between A and B. In order to protect that arrangement A, in its trade agreement with C, must explicitly exclude from the scope of the most-favored-nation clause any special concessions A has granted to B.[11]

It is understood that the provisions of the present Agreement shall not apply to
". . . advantages which Peru accords to Chile and to the Argentine Republic or which it may accord to such countries . . .[12]
[or]
Advantages accorded by either Party to members of a free trade area or customs union of which that Party is or may become a member.
[or]
advantages accorded by _____ to members of the [East African Common Market] [Latin American Free Trade Area]

Subject to Separate Agreement

A third broad category of exceptions to a trade agreement excludes from coverage those matters which are the subject of general

[11] In the absence of such an explicit exception, a party to a trade agreement is entitled to concessions made by the other party to all third countries. See A. McNair, The Law of Treaties 282 (1961). The inclusion of such an exception clause may be specifically required by the preferential arrangement. See, e.g., art. XXV of the General Treaty on Central American Economic Integration, *done* at Managua, December 13, 1960, 1 United Nations, Multilateral Economic Cooperation in Latin America, U.N. Doc. E/CN 12/621, at 9 (1962). ("[The Signatory States] further agree to maintain the 'Central American exception clause' in any trade agreements they may conclude on the basis of most-favoured-nation treatment with any countries other than the Contracting States.")

[12] Agreement on Commerce between Japan and Peru, *done* at Tokyo, May 15, 1961, art. VI, 451 U.N.T.S. 3, 34, 36 (1963).

international conventions. States will, in the ordinary course of events, seek to protect their multilateral commitments from encroachment by any bilateral obligations they may undertake. This preference reflects a judgment that those agreements which are in the interest of the international community as a whole are to be preferred to those which reflect the interest of one or two nations. This judgment should not, however, be given undue weight, since it is usually not articulated with regard to any particular bilateral or multilateral commitment. It is, instead, a decision that in the event of a minor, presently unconsidered, conflict, the matter should be resolved in favor of the multilateral obligation. Such a catchall would not be required in the best of all possible worlds where the negotiators were aware of the full range of their client states' multilateral treaty obligations. Frequently, however, this is not the case. Futhermore, multilateral commitments change, new ones arise, and states generally prefer to retain a free hand in entering into such new obligations.[13] For these reasons, trade agreements may provide that: "This agreement shall not be deemed to confer any right or to impose any obligation in contravention of any general international convention to which either of the two Parties are, or hereafter may become, parties."

The term "general international convention" is intended to cover any multilateral agreement to which all or most nations are eligible to accede. Note that this provision covers the situation in which only one of the parties to the trade agreement is a party to a particular international convention. This is not the usual practice. Yet an exception is unsatisfactory when it provides that

---

[13] This preference must, however, be weighted against the possibility of one of the parties entering into a commitment which would override the trade agreement. If this prospect should weigh more heavily than the desire for flexibility, the parties may agree that: Nothing in the present Agreement shall prejudice the rights and obligations which the Parties may derive from general international conventions in force to which they *are* parties. See Convention on the Abolition of Import and Export Restrictions and Prohibitions, *done* at Geneva November 8, 1927, art. 11, LEAGUE OF NATIONS, II.A. ECONOMIC AND FINANCIAL 7, at 11 (1928).

See also the Treaty Establishing the European Economic Community, art. 234, 298 U.N.T.S. 3, 91 (1958). Bilateral and multilateral agreements concluded prior to entry into force of the Treaty "shall not be affected by the provisions of this Treaty."

obligations which countries have undertaken as parties to a multi-lateral convention shall only take precedence over the provisions of a trade agreement where *both* countries are parties to the convention. It leaves open the situation where a provision of a multilateral convention to which only one of the trade agreement countries is a party is in conflict with the trade agreement. Here again, the interests of the international community militate in favor of a decision that the multilateral convention obligation takes precedence. And in the abstract most countries would probably agree with this. The reasons why this preference is not, however, stated explicitly in most trade agreements are twofold. First, as a practical matter, if a country agrees that multilateral obligations will override bilateral ones only where both parties to the bilateral agreement are also parties to the multilateral one, that country need know nothing of the multilateral agreements to which the other country is a party. A country knows that if it examines its own multilateral commitments and finds no conflict with a bilateral agreement, the overriding clause will never come into operation.[14] Where, however, a conflict between the bilateral agreement and a multilateral obligation of only one of the parties will give precedence to the multilateral obligation, the other party must be aware of the first party's multilateral commitments. This entails the parties exchanging information concerning their multilateral commitments and careful scrutiny by each side of the other's obligations. To avoid this administrative burden, the overriding clause has usually been limited to cases where both countries are parties to the conflicting multilateral convention. The second reason for this limitation is more in the realm of politics. Some countries desire, for policy reasons of their own, to undermine the multilateral commitments of others. This is especially true where such countries are in fundamental disagreement with the structure, aims, and purposes of a multilateral organization. In their "war" on such organizations, countries may attempt to

---

[14] Assuming, of course, both parties agree on the interpretation of their bilateral and multilateral obligations, which may be a rather sweeping assumption.

lead others into making commitments which they know conflict with an obligation owed to such multilateral organization. Disheartening as this may be, it is nevertheless a fact which must be recognized in negotiating a trade agreement.

While, as noted above, this effort to avoid inconsistency between bilateral and multilateral obligations is directed, in the main, to *unforeseen* conflicts, there are multilateral conventions which deal with subject matter that is of immediate concern to the trade agreement partners, and must be specifically considered by them in any trade negotiation. The most important of these are the international commodity agreements designed to control the supply and thereby stabilize the price of certain primary products. As these products, and the agreements concerning them, are of vital interest to the international trade of developing countries, it is of the utmost importance when incurring bilateral trade obligations that they reserve the right to take such action as may be required of parties to the commodity agreements.

The possible conflict between bilateral and multilateral obligations may be illustrated by reference to the International Wheat Agreement, *done* at Washington, April 19, 1962.[15] By the terms of the Agreement, importing members are obligated to take a specified portion of their requirements from exporting members at a given price.[16] To illustrate how this duty may conflict with the provisions of a trade agreement, assume that Country *A* is an importing member of the Wheat Agreement and that *A* has a trade agreement with Country *B* providing for most-favored-nation treatment. *B* is a wheat exporter, but not a member of the Wheat Agreement. If *B* offers to supply all the wheat *A* needs at a price lower than that provided for the International Wheat Agreement, Country *A* is not free to satisfy its total wheat requirements by purchasing solely from Country *B*. By virtue of its obligations under the Wheat Agreement, *A* must continue to purchase a stated amount of wheat from one or more of the export-

---

[15] 444 U.N.T.S. 3 (1960).
[16] Article 4 (a), *id.* at 14.

ing members of the Agreement, even though Country B's price is lower. To this extent Country B is discriminated against as a result of governmental action on the part of Country A, which action would violate the most-favored-nation provision in the trade agreement between A and B, absent an exception.

The converse of this situation would also violate a requirement of most-favored-nation treatment. Under the terms of the International Coffee Agreement, for example, coffee-exporting countries have a quota on the amount of coffee they may export. Should an importing country wish to buy more coffee from a particular country than its quota allows to be exported, the exporting country could not supply it because of its obligations under the Coffee Agreement. The Agreement, however, establishes a category of "non-quota" countries to which exports may be made outside the quota limit. An importing country, subject to the quota, seeing exports going to non-quota countries may, with good reason, feel that it is being discriminated against by the exporting country. The discrimination, however, is required by the terms of the Coffee Agreement. To insure that such multilateral obligations can be met without running into accusations of discrimination from trade agreement partners, countries which are parties to international commodity agreements usually provide in their trade agreements that: "Nothing in the present Agreement shall be construed to prevent the adoption or enforcement by either Party of measures undertaken in pursuance of obligations under any intergovernmental commodity agreement." [17]

---

[17] The General Agreement on Tariffs and Trade provides for a somewhat narrower exception in regard to commodity agreements. The exception is limited to commodity agreements: "which conforms to criteria submitted to the CONTRACTING PARTIES and not disapproved by them or which is itself so submitted and not so disapproved." Article XX(h), GATT, III BASIC INSTRUMENTS AND SELECTED DOCUMENTS 43 (1958). The "criteria" referred to are those "approved by the Economic and Social Council in its Resolution 30 (iv) of 28 March 1947." Ad Article XX, GATT, III BASIC INSTRUMENTS AND SELECTED DOCUMENTS 76 (1958). The pertinent part of that resolution reads: ". . . pending the establishment of the International Trade Organization, Members of the United Nations [are advised to] adopt as a general guide in inter-governmental consultation or action with respect to commodity problems the principles laid down in Chapter VII as a whole, i.e. the

The possibilities of conflict between trade agreements and multilateral obligations are even more immediate where one or both of the parties to the trade agreement are Contracting Parties to the General Agreement on Tariffs and Trade and/or the Articles of Agreement of the International Monetary Fund. Both of these conventions put limits on the freedom in commercial policy matters which their member states would otherwise possess. And here the issue is not only a general preference for multilateral obligations in the interest of the world community, an interest that may or may not carry weight in the councils of a particular state. Because of the recurrent balance of payments crises which afflict them, membership in the IMF and access to its resources are of crucial concern to developing countries. Moreover, to be cut off from the Fund's resources is also to minimize the chances of receiving financial assistance from virtually any other source. Thus adherence to commitments in the Articles of Agreement of the Fund, and the "rules of the game" laid down by the Fund's executive directors, is a matter of immediate importance to most developing countries. This is also true with regard to GATT obligations. For the developing countries, even collectively, do not wield sufficient economic power to unilaterally bring about the changes they desire to see made in the rules and practices of international trade. To a large extent their ability in this direction is dependent on the goodwill of the industrially developed countries, a fact clearly brought home at the first UNCTAD meeting. And the goodwill is generated not by openly flaunting the provisions of the GATT, but by working within its framework. Moreover, even where a developing country embarks on a course of commercial policy in conflict with certain of its GATT obligations, other Contracting Parties have been known to wink at

---

chapter on inter-governmental commodity arrangements of the draft charter appended to the report of the first session of the Preparatory Committee of the United Nations Conference on Trade and Employment . . ." The report referred to in the resolution is printed in U.N. Doc. E/PC/T/34 (1947). The relevant provisions of Chapter VII of the Charter are reprinted in Appendix I to this chapter.

such violations where this is possible. It has thus proven a good and useful strategy to, at the least, pay lip service to a state's GATT obligations. For these reasons, developing countries will seek to include in their trade agreements a provision such as the following: "Nothing in this agreement shall affect the rights and obligations that either Party has or may have as a Contracting Party to the General Agreement on Tariffs and Trade or to the Articles of Agreement of the International Monetary Fund or to any multilateral agreement amending or supplementing the same."

Finally, provision is normally made for the possible conflict between the provisions of a trade agreement and those international agreements which deal with a subject whose problems are so particular and specialized that they may be considered *sui generis.* The most common examples are those agreements concerning patents and copyrights.[18] These questions are dealt with in the Berne Convention for the Protection of Literary and Artistic Works, *done* at Paris, September 9, 1886, *revised* at Brussels, June 26, 1948,[19] the Universal Copyright Convention, *done* at Geneva, September 6, 1952,[20] and the International Convention for the Protection of Industrial Property, *done* at Paris, March 20, 1883, *revised* at Lisbon, October 31, 1958.[21] To exclude patent and copyright questions from the ambit of a trade agreement, the parties would provide that: "Nothing in the present Agreement shall be construed so as to grant any right or impose any obligation in respect of copyrights or industrial property rights."

Conclusion

After reading this chapter, it may appear that so many exceptions have been provided to the obligations of the parties to a trade

[18] Nonetheless, "[n]ational patent and trade-mark systems are employed to bar goods which originate in other countries." Massel, *Non-Tariff Barriers as an Obstacle to World Trade,* THOMPSON, THE EXPANSION OF WORLD TRADE: LEGAL PROBLEMS AND TECHNIQUES 63 (1965).

[19] 331 U.N.T.S. 217 (1959).

[20] 216 U.N.T.S. 132 (1955).

[21] [1962] Gr. Brit. T.S. No. 38 (CMD. 1715).

agreement that the agreement has lost all significance. This is not, of course, true. As indicated at the outset, a group of exceptions will be read into an agreement whether or not expressly incorporated. More importantly, no state enters a negotiation with a "clean slate." In each negotiation, account must be taken of existing international commitments. Within this framework however, there remains a large range of possible lines of commercial policy which are, legally at least, negotiable.

APPENDIX

EXCERPTS FROM THE HAVANA CHARTER
INTERGOVERNMENTAL COMMODITY ARRANGEMENTS

ARTICLE 46
*General Statement on Difficulties
Relating to Primary Commodities*

Members recognize that the relationship between production and consumption of some primary commodities may present special difficulties. These special difficulties are different in character from those which manufactured goods present generally. They arise out of such conditions as the disequilibrium between production and consumption, the accumulation of burdensome stocks and pronounced fluctuations in prices. They may have a seriously adverse effect on the interests of both producers and consumers. Moreover, they may have widespread repercussions which would jeopardize the general policy of economic expansion.

ARTICLE 47
*Objectives of Inter-governmental
Commodity Arrangements*

Members agree that inter-governmental commodity arrangements may be employed to achieve the following objectives:

(1) To enable countries to find solutions to the special commodity difficulties referred to in Article 46 without resorting to action inconsistent with the purpose of the Charter.

(2) To prevent or alleviate the serious economic problems which

may arise when production adjustments cannot be effected by the free play of market forces as rapidly as the circumstances require.

(3) To provide, during the period which may be necessary, a framework for the consideration and development of measures which will have as their purpose economic adjustments designed to promote the expansion of consumption or a shift of resources and manpower out of over-expanded industries into new and productive occupations.

(4) To moderate pronounced fluctuations in the price of a primary commodity above and below the level which expresses the long term equilibrium between the forces of supply and demand.

(5) To maintain and develop the natural resources of the world and protect them from unnecessary exhaustion.

(6) To provide for expansion in the production of a primary commodity which is in such short supply as seriously to prejudice the interests of consumers.

· · ·

ARTICLE 51
*General Principles of Inter-governmental
Commodity Arrangements*

Members undertake to adhere to the following principles governing the operation of all types of inter-governmental commodity arrangements:

· · ·

(3) Such arrangements shall include provision for adequate participation of countries substantially interested in the importation or consumption of the commodity as well as those substantially interested in its exportation or production.

(4) In such arrangements participating countries, which are largely dependent for consumption on imports of the commodity involved shall, in determinations made relating to substantive matters, have together a voice equal to that of those largely interested in obtaining export markets for the commodity, provided that those countries, which are largely interested in the commodity but which do not fall precisely under either of the above classes, shall have an appropriate voice.

· · ·

ARTICLE 52
*Circumstances Governing the Use
of Regulatory Agreements*

Members agree that regulatory agreements may be employed only when

(1) A burdensome surplus of a primary commodity has developed or is expected to develop which, because a substantial reduction in price does not readily lead to a significant increase in consumption nor to a significant decrease in the production of that commodity, would not, in the absence of specific governmental action, be corrected by normal marketing forces alone in time to prevent serious hardship to producers among whom are small producers who account for a substantial portion of the total output; or

(2) Widespread unemployment in connection with a particular primary commodity, arising out of difficulties of the kind referred to in Article 46, has developed or is expected to develop, which, in the absence of specific governmental action, would not be corrected by normal marketing forces alone in time to prevent widespread and undue hardship to workers because, in the case of the industry concerned, a substantial reduction of price does not lead to a significant increase in consumption but to the reduction of employment, and because areas in which the commodity is produced in substantial quantity do not afford alternative employment opportunities for the workers involved; or . . .

. . .

ARTICLE 53
Additional Principles Governing Regulatory Agreements

. . .

(5) Such agreements shall, with due regard to the need during a period of change for preventing serious economic and social dislocation and to the position of producing areas which may be suffering from abnormal and temporary disabilities, make appropriate provision to afford increasing opportunities for satisfying world requirements from sources from which such requirements can be supplied most effectively and economically.

(6) Participating countries shall formulate and adopt a programme
of economic adjustment believed to be adequate to ensure substantial progress toward solution of the problem within the time
limits of the agreement.

. . .

ARTICLE 60

Definitions

. . .

(4) A regulatory agreement is an inter-governmental commodity
arrangement involving regulation of the production, export or
import of a commodity or regulation of prices.

XI. Conclusion

A Trade Policy

Most developing countries lack a comprehensive trade policy. Unlike the situation which obtains with respect to internal development, where elaborate plans abound, planning for foreign trade is at best an afterthought. In part this is due to a conception of the development process which emphasizes visible progress at the local level in terms of new factories, new jobs in industry, and new goods for home consumption. More probably this situation prevails because most of the exports of the developing countries are primary products which are sold on commodity exchanges at world market prices or, in the case of petroleum, under long-term agreements. Primary product exporters are concerned with the production (or overproduction) of their goods. The marketing generally takes care of itself. Whatever is produced is sold through a commodity exchange at a price set by some mysterious market forces over which the primary product exporter has little control.

This view is changing, and the developing countries now know that they can affect the price at which their primary products are sold by joining together to restrict production and/or marketing of their crops. The International Coffee Agreement is the outstanding example of such a combination of producers (and consumers). By incorporating the concepts of the selective price system and the nonquota country, the Coffee Agreement has placed a new emphasis on aggressive marketing of primary products. In addition, and of even more significance, is the fact that many developing countries are now producing manufactures and semi-manufactures for export. Here there are no commodity exchanges and world market prices. Manufactures must be sold, not simply produced. There is no central commodity exchange through which textiles, radios, or bicycles will be purchased by interested buyers. Producers must go out and establish contact with buyers, many in new and unfamiliar markets. This shift in emphasis from production to marketing gives rise to the need for a trade policy which will attempt to identify prospective markets for the products of local enterprise.

A Trade Agreement?

If a particular country appears to trade planners to offer a prospective market for exports, should an approach be made to that country to enter into a trade agreement? The writer's experience is that the answer in the trade ministries of most developing countries would be an immediate "yes." For there is current in the developing world the idea that a trade agreement in some way insures trade between the parties. But this is not necessarily so. A trade agreement provides a framework within which trade may be conducted, it does not in and of itself insure trade. For trade depends on wants of buyer and seller and availability of the means of supplying these wants.

A trade agreement, in addition, can be a benefit *or* a burden. For without such an agreement a country can, in theory, pursue any trade policy it pleases. It can limit imports from another country, discriminate between sources of supply and customers, and pursue other policies normally restricted or prohibited by a trade agreement. By entering into a trade agreement a country will normally give up this right of absolute discretion in trade policy. Moreover, a party may make valuable concessions in a trade agreement without receiving a *quid pro quo*. A developing country which enters into a trade agreement promising most-favored-nation treatment to a centrally planned country and receives a similar promise in return has made a bad bargain. For a most-favored-nation commitment made by a country which practices state trading is of little value. In exchange for giving up its "right" to discriminate, the developing country should obtain a commitment that the centrally planned country will purchase a specified amount of goods, or that trade will be "balanced," or, at least, that the state-trading organizations of the centrally planned country will make their purchases in accordance with "commercial considerations."

WHAT KIND OF TRADE AGREEMENT?

GATT MEMBERS

Should a developing country wish to enter into an agreement establishing the ground rules on which its trade with another country will be conducted, what kind of trade agreement should it be? For many developing countries the question has already been answered. If they are members of GATT, and the prospective trading partner is also a member of GATT, there is already a trade agreement in force between them. This is a fact often overlooked by trade planners in developing countries. Even if the planners are aware of the mutual GATT membership, they may believe a new agreement is worthwhile, either under the mistaken belief noted earlier—that trade agreements mean trade—or because of the view that a new trade agreement will add to the friendly relations existing between the two states. In such a situation, the new trade agreement may simply restate each party's GATT commitments. If, however, both parties are developing countries they may desire to "supplement" the GATT rules. Where it seems unlikely that either party will find a market for its new manufactures in the territory of the other party if each continues to grant nondiscriminatory treatment to third countries, the parties may wish to grant each other preferences on their prospective exports. Although a trade agreement granting preferences on a limited number of products would conflict with GATT obligations, developing countries which are GATT members have been known to enter into such agreements. To forestall objections from other Contracting Parties, however, it is more likely that developing countries wishing to grant each other preferences will either request a waiver of their GATT obligations or will do so within the context of an agreement creating a customs union or free-trade area.

The precedents established by GATT treatment of existing customs unions and free-trade areas indicate that developing countries wishing to merge their markets may do so with considerable flexibility. The association agreement between Greece and the EEC indicates that the parties may have up to twenty-two years to bring their customs union or free-trade area to fruition. And the association agreement between Turkey and the EEC is precedent for a plan conditioning the completion of a customs union on the occurrence of a condition precedent, future agreement by the parties that they will continue with the arrangement. In the interim before the occurrence of this condition, the transition period, the parties may apparently put into effect a limited preferential arrangement of their own choosing. Furthermore the GATT requires that the plan for a customs union or free-trade area shall result (after twenty-two years, or the occurence of a condition precedent) in freeing "substantially all of the trade" between the parties. But "substantially" has been whittled down to 75 per cent by the LAFTA countries. And "trade" need not include trade in agricultural products according to the Stockholm Convention establishing the EFTA. Finally, the Contracting Parties have taken a very lenient attitude towards regional trading arrangements among developing countries. With this in mind developing countries should be able to fashion agreements among themselves to facilitate mutual exchanges of manufactures and semimanufactures.

In implementing a trade strategy towards the centrally planned countries, a developing country must recognize at the outset that there are unique questions involved which do not generally arise when an agreement is made with a free-market country. The state-trading system must be dealt with in the agreement—either by a commitment to purchase a specific volume of goods, or to balance trade, or through the use of a "commercial considerations clause." Where the latter course is selected, the developing country must seek to ensure that it will have available the means for determining whether the clause is being adhered to. In addition, the currencies of the centrally planned countries are not convertible. The trade agreement should provide, therefore, that all trade settlements are to be made in convertible currencies. Alternatively, the agreement may contain a clearing or payments provision. If this facility is established, however, the developing country would be wise to examine closely the provisions for swing credits and the time at which and the manner in which the credit balances are to be settled. A third question which should be dealt with in the agreement is "dumping," for the usual provision (based as it is on internal sales in the exporting country) will not be relevant where the exporter is a centrally planned country. Some other criterion for determining the existance of dumping must be written into the provision. Finally, the reexport of primary commodities has occasionally characterized the trade policy of centrally planned countries. To forestall such practices, a "no reexport" clause should be included in the trade agreement. This is particularly important in trade agreements between centrally planned countries and developing countries which export coffee. Under the terms of the International Coffee Agreement most centrally planned countries are nonquota markets. There is thus a great incentive for a developing country to market its surplus coffee in a centrally planned country at virtually any price. But the prospect of highly profitable trade must not blind a developing country to the fact that coffee shipments to centrally planned countries have, from time to time, been reexported into quota markets.

MULTILATERAL AGREEMENTS

In addition to the regional trade arrangements already referred to, several other types of multilateral trade agreements will form an important part of the future trade framework of the developing countries. Of primary importance will be a new multilateral agreement concerning preferences from the industrial countries to the developing countries, should such a system gain acceptance among the industrial countries. A new agreement would incorporate a revision of the traditional principle of most-favored-nation treatment creating two classes of countries—the developing and the developed. The latter would be granted most-favored-nation treatment on the basis that presently obtains, while the former would be granted most-favored-nation treatment with regard to the elimination of tariff barriers on their exports of manufactures and semimanufactures. At first, because the effect of the granting of preferences cannot be accurately predicted, the developed countries may retain or establish quota restrictions on the total volume of goods permitted to end their markets under the preferential arrangements. And these quotas may be allocated if it appears that preferences would otherwise benefit only a handful of developing countries. To prevent the freezing of market shares, developing countries not able to utilize their full quotas may be permitted to transfer the unused portion to other developing countries.

There is no clear indication at the time of this writing if a multilateral preferential arrangement will come into being. The principal opponents of such a system at the first UNCTAD, however, seem to be softening their positions. The United States Government, traditional champion of nondiscrimination, has gone on record as willing to consider a system of generalized preferences as one means of assisting the developing countries. And the EEC Commission has begun a study of the likely effects of implementing such a system. On the other hand, action under the Long-Term Cotton Textile Arrangement leaves considerable doubt about the willingness of the industrial states to open their borders to imports from the developing world. Moreover, a multi-lateral preferential arrangement would involve some measure of agreement between the industrial states as to how the burdens involved would be shared. Whether the developed countries can come together to agree on this question is also open to doubt. In the absence of such agreement, future developments may take a somewhat different path.

One of the most interesting aspects of the association agreements between the developing countries and the EEC is the fact that they incorporate trade and aid questions within the four corners of one document. The agreements recognize the intimate relation between trade and aid in that both aim at providing the develop-ing countries with the external resources necessary to promote their economic development. And in the course of negotiating the agreement various trade concessions have been exchanged for in-creased aid commitments. This practice is one that should be emulated by other developing countries. In the negotiation of a trade agreement with an industrial country or a centrally planned country, the starting point might well be an agreed upon figure representing the total external resources necessary to achieve a given rate of growth. The total could then be divided pro rata among the trading partners and aid donors. Thereafter, individual trade negotiations should aim at either generating a volume of trade to provide the needed resources or guaranteeing aid sufficient to make up the shortfall. The essential point of this strategy is for the developing country to bring home to its trading partner the cost of various trade restrictions which must be borne by a developing country. As Professor Kaldor has noted, "[there] is a glaring inconsistency between a professed aim of the developed countries to assist in the development of the nations through large-scale economic aid, and their commercial policies which prevent such aid from bearing fruit."

Trade negotiations may, alternatively, take place in the context of discussions concerning aid. In fact they seem more likely to do so since most of the principal aid donors are members of GATT and thus do not see the need for trade negotiations outside GATT. These countries do, however, periodically discuss aid commitments with developing countries. This dichotomy should be brought to an end. In particular, where there are aid consortia, organized under the auspices of OECD, the IMF, or IBRD, discussions between aid donors and aid recipients should be extended to the subject of trade restrictions. And the results of these discussions should be incorporated in a trade agreement.

The Future of GATT

The General Agreement on Tariffs and Trade will continue to exist and play a leading role in trade policies of the developing countries. GATT's continued existence seems assured because of the valuable role it has played from the point of view of the developed countries in preventing a return to the chaotic trade policies of the 1930s. Moreover, the GATT Secretariat is the repository of much of the world's expertise concerning trade problems in general and those of the developing countries in particular. The International Trade Center, sponsored and staffed by the GATT, seems likely to continue in its role of the leading agency where developing countries can turn for assistance in solving the day-to-day practical problems of international trade.

The Agreement itself, however, might well be reexamined with a view to a *de jure* revision in line with current practice and the needs of the developing countries. The present ban on export subsidies for manufactures contained in Article XVI should be amended to make it conform to the Declaration of November 19, 1960, so as to make it evident that the prohibition does not apply to developing countries. As a corollary, and of more importance, Article VI should be changed to prohibit the imposition of countervailing duties on the subsidized exports of developing countries. Both articles might be revised in such a way as to limit the subsidy which a developing country can grant to its infant export industries. Professor Kaldor, for example, has suggested limiting the subsidy to the same percentage of the cost of producing the goods that one-half a developing country's primary product exports bear to its total exports. Thus a country whose manufactures amounted to 10 per cent of its total exports would be permitted to subsidize manufactured exports to up to 45 per cent of the cost of production. As the manufactured percentage of its export mix increased, the permissible limit of subsidization would decline.

Article XXIV dealing with customs unions and free-trade areas is in need of revision. The various attempts to apply it to proposed economic unions have been occasions for disagreement on virtually every criterion proposed in that article. The *de facto* position amounts to a "wait and see" attitude, and this should be incorporated in the GATT. A new Article XXIV providing for notification of the Contracting Parties of any new multilateral trade arrangement and a procedure for hearing objections to the proposal would conform to current practice. Moreover, general criteria such as the effect on world trade and on the welfare of the participating states would seem more relevant to an examination of an arrangement than the present formal requirements concerning tariff levels and the freeing of intra-area trade.

A better means must be found to deal with the infant industry question than is presently incorporated in Article XVIII. Sections A and C are so cumbersome that they are rarely used. And Section B, the great loophole, focuses on balance of payments problems as opposed to the infant industry question. Moreover, Section B sanctions the use of quantitative restrictions where an import surcharge might be the preferred course of action. Since Contracting Parties already permit import surcharges under the waiver procedure, the position should be regularized to permit tariff increases for infant industry protection. Moreover, developing countries should be given discretion to choose the industries they are willing to protect since it is their own populace who bear the costs of ill-conceived high cost infant industries. If the people are willing to pay these costs in the effort to industrialize, the loss of markets by exporting industrial states seems a tolerable burden. A compromise might be reached by allowing a developed country to take retaliatory action where a particular restriction led to an agreed upon percentage of decline in its gross national product. The alternative of subjecting the infant industry proposals of developing countries to international examination and discussion smacks of a double standard, since the infant industries of the industrial powers were never subjected to such international scrutiny.

These, then, are the likely areas of growth in the trade agreement activities of the developing countries. These efforts will entail considerably more attention being devoted to trade matters and trade policy than has heretofore been the case. They will, in addition, require a much greater familiarity with the substantive provisions usually found in trade agreements than has hitherto obtained. The contribution which this volume is intended to make is to further the knowledge of and familiarity with such provisions in the developing world.

INDEX